MW01012600

THE BURDEN OF GUILT

Also by Daniel Allen Butler

"Unsinkable"—The Full Story
of RMS Titanic

The Lusitania: *The Life, Loss, and Legacy*
of an Ocean Legend

Warrior Queens—the Queen Mary *and*
Queen Elizabeth *in World War Two*

The Age of Cunard—A Transatlantic History, 1939–2003

Distant Victory: The Battle of Jutland
and the Allied Triumph in the First World War

The First Jihad: The Battle for Khartoum
and the Dawn of Militant Islam

The Other Side of the Night:
The Carpathia, *the* Californian, *and*
the Night the Titanic *was Lost*

THE
BURDEN
OF
GUILT

*How Germany Shattered
the Last Days of Peace,
August 1914*

by

DANIEL ALLEN BUTLER

CASEMATE
Philadelphia & Newbury

Published in the United States of America in 2010 by
Casemate Publishers
908 Darby Road, Havertown, PA 19083

and in the United Kingdom by
Casemate Publishers
17 Cheap Street, Newbury, RG14 5DD

Excerpt from Eric Bogle's "No Man's Land (The Green Fields of France)"
© 1976 by Larrikin Music Ltd. Used with permission.

ISBN 978-1-935149-27-9

Cataloging-in-publication data for this book is available from the
British Library and the Library of Congress (LCCN: 2010921923).

Printed and bound in the United States of America.

10 9 8 7 6 5 4 3 2 1

For a complete list of Casemate titles, please contact:

United States of America
Casemate Publishers
Telephone (610) 853-9131, Fax (610) 853-9146
E-mail casemate@casematepublishing.com
Website www.casematepublishing.com

United Kingdom
Casemate Publishers
Telephone (01635) 231091, Fax (01635) 41619
E-mail casemate-uk@casematepublishing.co.uk
Website www.casematepublishing.co.uk

Mixed Sources
Product group from well-managed
forests and other controlled sources
www.fsc.org Cert no. SW-COC-002283
© 1996 Forest Stewardship Council
FSC

CONTENTS

To
Dotie and Stuart Carothers

Lady and Gentleman,
good friends and good people.

INTRODUCTION

Though it will not be immediately obvious to anyone who only knows me through my previous works, *The Burden of Guilt* is, apart from *"Unsinkable,"* the most personal of the eight books I have published thus far. It is personal in that it recounts the execution of a time, an era, a world of which I grew particularly fond in the early days of my development as an historian and author.

Growing up in the 1960s and 1970s, I came into self-awareness and adulthood in a time of tremendous social, political and economic upheaval and displacement. While still in grade school, the assassinations of President John Kennedy, his brother Robert, and Dr. Martin Luther King were stunning breaking news stories; the first disturbing specters raised by the environmentalist movement appeared; the first lunar landings and the subsequent abandonment of all the hopes and dreams they raised were current events; the Vietnam War was a nightly occurrence on the evening news. My years in high school were marked by the Watergate debacle, the Yom Kippur War and the first energy crisis. I graduated from college when the United States was in the worst social and economic depression—then-President Jimmy Carter described it as a "national malaise"—since the Great Depression. I came to manhood, married, and fathered a child before the nuclear wraith of Mutual Assured Destruction—at once bad grammar and bad strategy—was laid to rest. A popular song in my childhood urged me to "Cheer up—things are gonna get worse!" The

1

tenor of my formative years then was that the world was at best a melancholy place.

So it should come as little wonder that as I turned to the study of history as a vocation I should have been drawn to a time when hope was underlying almost every human endeavor, when "the future" was not simultaneously foreboding and attractive, and when "Progress" was written with an upper case "P" to symbolize that it was inherently a good thing. In other words, I found myself flying back to the late Victorian world and the Edwardian Era. I knew that they were in truth not the "paradise lost", which some historians would portray them to be, where everyone knew their place in the scheme of things and diligently kept to it, a time filled with happy, hard-working laborers, conscientious businessmen, and beautiful aristocrats. It was, I knew, a world that had as many troubles as my own. However, the essential difference was that it was a world that believed in itself and its ability to somehow, someday, discover solutions to every problem that might beset it. It was a world of what the last half of the 20th century and the first decade of the 21st was lacking—it was a world of confidence.

However, it was also a world that eventually turned upon itself and destroyed itself in the full knowledge of its own destruction. Yet even in that destruction there was a painful nobility, for it was a self-immolation undertaken in the hope that it would stop the spread of a systematic and self-perpetuating oppression that was the antithesis of Progress. It was a self-immolation embraced by the hope that, phoenix-like, a new and better world would rise out of its ashes. If I over-romanticized the pre-war world, so be it. It deserves to be remembered well, for if it failed, it failed striving magnificently.

I chose to write *The Burden of Guilt* in order to set the record straight for a generation for whom the Iraq War is a current event, Vietnam is their father's war, the Second World War "the one they fought in black and white," and the Great War is too often a moldering, distant conflict with no real relevance to the 21st century. However, the fearsome truth is that the modern world is, by far, more the product of the First World War than of any conflict that followed. Indeed, it can be easily and clearly demonstrated that each of the aforementioned wars had its roots in the dreadful years between 1914 and 1918—right down to the present day American occupation of Iraq. The message—and there truly is one here—which needs be stressed is that like almost every war in history, the First World War was not an accident. It did not begin because of a failure of diplomacy or statesmanship. It did not come about as a consequence of a tangle of interlocking alliances which no one really understood or appreciated. It was not a "world-historical" event made inevitable by social-economic-political forces beyond human control. The First World War—the Great War—was the bastard child of one nation's ambition, a Central European monarchy hell-bent on maintaining its position of political, economic, and military dominance over all of its neighbors—at any cost. The Great War exploded across Europe because Germany wished it to do so, and the German government and military leaders made it happen. How that came about is the story told in these pages. If there is a moral here, it is that when one nation, placed in a position of superiority, confuses its responsibility to lead by example with permission to dominate through coercion, tragedy will inescapably follow.

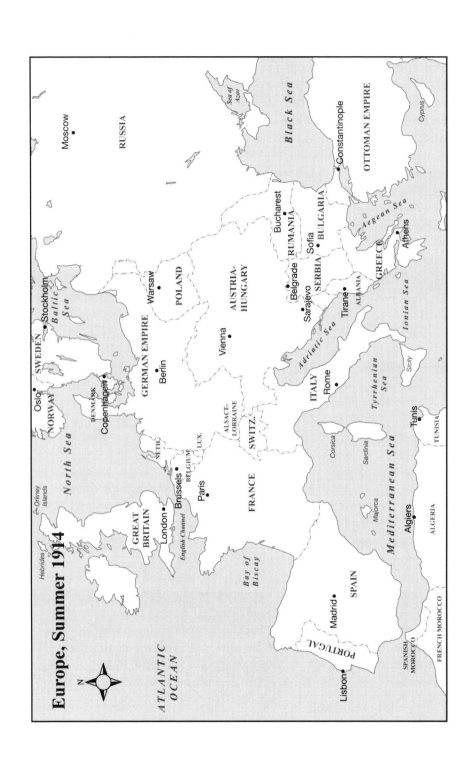

Europe, Summer 1914

N

ATLANTIC OCEAN

GREAT BRITAIN

London

English Channel

Hebrides

Orkney Islands

North Sea

Bay of Biscay

FRANCE

Paris

Brussels

BELGIUM

NETH.

LUX.

ALSACE-LORRAINE

SWITZ.

SPAIN

Madrid

PORTUGAL

Lisbon

Corsica

Sardinia

Majorca

Mediterranean Sea

Algiers

ALGERIA

Tunis

TUNISIA

SPANISH MOROCCO

FRENCH MOROCCO

NORWAY

Oslo

SWEDEN

Stockholm

Baltic Sea

DENMARK

Copenhagen

GERMAN EMPIRE

Berlin

POLAND

Warsaw

Vienna

AUSTRIA-HUNGARY

ITALY

Rome

Tyrrhenian Sea

Sicily

Adriatic Sea

RUSSIA

Moscow

Sea of Azov

Black Sea

Bucharest

RUMANIA

Belgrade

SERBIA

Sarajevo

Sofia

BULGARIA

Tirane

ALBANIA

GREECE

Athens

Aegean Sea

Ionian Sea

Constantinople

OTTOMAN EMPIRE

Cyprus

Chapter I

TWO BULLETS IN SARAJEVO

The first shots of the Great War were a quintet of bullets fired at a happily married couple on holiday in an obscure city in the Balkans. Archduke Franz Ferdinand, heir to the throne of the Dual Monarchy, the Austro-Hungarian Empire, had consented as a gesture of goodwill to the often-restive people of the province of Bosnia to visit their capital, Sarajevo, accompanied by his wife, Sophie. Arriving there in mid-morning on June 28, 1914, the Archduke gave orders for what he believed would be a demonstration of his confidence in the loyalty of the Bosnian people, requesting that the troops who would normally have lined the streets for his protection during the Imperial visit be dispersed. It was the worst mistake he ever made—it was also the last.

As the Archduke's motorcade made its way from Sarajevo's train station to the town hall where Franz Ferdinand was scheduled to meet with city and provincial officials, a terrorist's bomb was thrown at the passing cars, missing the Imperial couple but wounding an officer in one of the following vehicles. Furious, Franz Ferdinand stormed into the City Hall, shouting, "One comes here for a visit and is welcomed by bombs!" The meeting was cut short, and the Archduke, outraged and concerned as much for the safety of his wife as for his own well-being, climbed back into the waiting automobile to return to the train station. Confusion over the route to be taken caused the driver of the Archduke's car to stop suddenly, by the most evil mischance, directly in front of 19-year-old Gavrillo Prinzip, a Bosnian Serb who had come to Sarajevo that day armed with a pistol, intent on shooting Franz Ferdinand. Five shots rang out in as many seconds; two bullets found their mark, one in Franz Ferdinand's neck, the other in Sophie's chest. Muttering "Sophie! Sophie! Don't die! Live for our children!" the Archduke expired almost immediately; within minutes his wife was dead as well.

With those two bullets in Sarajevo, the First World War began.

Franz Ferdinand has been something of an enigma to history: while much is known about his life, the true character of the man himself remains obscured, often overdrawn by the dictates of nationalistic or ethnic bias. He was born in Graz, Austria, in 1863, third in line to the Hapsburg throne, occupied at that time by the Emperor Franz Josef I. After the Emperor's son, Crown Prince Rudolf, committed suicide in 1889, and his own father Archduke Charles Louis, Franz Josef's brother, died in 1896, Franz Ferdinand unexpectedly became the heir apparent. He projected an aura of arrogant pride and mistrust, was notably short-tempered and was regarded as not particularly cultured by Viennese standards. Unlike Franz Josef, Rudolf, or even his own father, Franz Ferdinand lacked the classic Hapsburg charisma, which together with his outwardly abrasive nature assured that he would never be personally popular with the people who would one day be his subjects.

However, there remains the very real possibility that at least some of Franz Ferdinand's harsh nature was something of a sham, the facade of a rather shy man thrust into a position of responsibility for which he was emotionally and circumstantially unprepared. In his private life he demonstrated an emotional depth and filial devotion which was entirely at odds with the cold and abrasive persona he presented to the world. His marriage was an extraordinarily happy one: unusual among Hapsburgs, Franz Ferdinand married for love rather than dynastic reasons. He met a young, pretty Hungarian countess, Sophie Chotek von Chotkova, and married her in 1900—they eventually had three children, whom Ferdinand adored and on whom he endlessly doted.

The marriage provoked a crisis with the Emperor, Franz Josef, who did not approve of the Countess Chotek, believing her social rank to be beneath the station of a Hapsburg archduke. Franz Ferdinand, determined to wed Sophie, dug in his heels, going so far as to threaten to abdicate his position as heir apparent. The Emperor finally relented, but only after Ferdinand agreed to renounce all rights of succession to the Hapsburg throne for his children. Even more than affirming beyond all doubt Ferdinand's devotion to his wife, the incident established that the Archduke was very much his own man, willing to break with tradition to accomplish his ends.

That willingness began to assume tremendous importance as Franz Josef grew older and the day when Franz Ferdinand would ascend to the Austro-Hungarian throne began to loom as a reality. Knowing that the Dual Monarchy could not long continue in its present form, as Slav unrest and Hungarian intransigence combined to bring the workings of the Imperial government to a near-standstill, he proposed to replace Austro-Hungarian dualism with what was commonly called "Trialism," a triple monarchy in which the empire's Slavs would have an equal voice in their governance with the Germans and Magyars. It was a solution which, he knew, would find little popular support, especially among the Hungarians, who suspected, with some justification, that they would be giving up a greater share of their authority than would the Austrians of theirs. At some point he even went so far as to consider abolishing the traditional "royal and imperial" monarchy for a form of federalism where the Hapsburg empire would take the form of sixteen states sharing power equally, all owing ultimate allegiance to the Emperor. Above all, Franz Ferdinand was determined to keep the Austro-Hungarian empire from collapsing altogether.

The Hungarian nobility, with all of the possessiveness of the *arriviste* (the Magyars had only been granted equal status and authority within the Empire in 1867), were virulently opposed to any reformation of the imperial structure which would dilute their power and prerogatives in the slightest. At the same time, much of the Empire's Slavic population felt that such reforms did not go far enough—many of the Empire's Slavic subjects had little interest in sharing power: what they sought was outright autonomy and independence.

The two provinces of Bosnia and Herzegovina in particular were centers of Slavic separatist movements which threatened to fragment Austria-Hungary. Administered by the Empire since 1878, when they broke away from the Ottoman Empire, the two provinces were annexed outright by Austria in 1908, a move which outraged Serbian nationalists, who wanted the provinces to be absorbed by the kingdom of Serbia instead. It was to placate Serb anger in the two provinces and demonstrate his sensibility to their grievances that the Archduke, in his role as Inspector General of the Royal and Imperial Army, accepted an invitation from General Oskar Potiorek to visit the capital of Bosnia, Sarajevo, after observing army maneuvers in the nearby countryside.

Gavrillo Prinzip, Franz Ferdinand's assassin, who as a native Bosnian was a citizen of the Austro-Hungarian Empire, was a passionate separatist who wanted to see Bosnia break away from Imperial control and join the Kingdom of Serbia. He was one of six compatriots, each armed with a handgun and a bomb, who had come to Sarajevo, as he testified at his trial, hoping to "kill an enemy of the South Slavs." To them, Franz Ferdinand was "an energetic man who as a ruler would have carried through ideas and reforms which stood in our way." They were sponsored by a shadowy Serbian organization known as "The Black Hand," which though not openly recognized or encouraged by the Serbian government, had strong ties to several high-level Serbian officials. Bluntly, the Black Hand was a terrorist organization, dedicated to the use of the knife, the gun, and the bomb to coerce Austria-Hungary to release its hold on the Empire's Slavic provinces, most particularly Bosnia and Herzegovina. The six young would-be assassins were all arrested within a matter of hours following the murders, and Austrian officials almost immediately were able to determine that the handguns and explosives they carried had been supplied by the Black Hand, and had come from Serbian state arsenals. They had been smuggled across the border between Serbia and Austria with the help of Serbian customs officials, and the trail of evidence led back straight into Belgrade.

Regicide was nothing new to Serbian politics—Serbia's 1903 revolution had climaxed with King Alexander and Queen Draga being literally hacked to death by saber-wielding army officers in the royal palace in Belgrade, their bloody bodies thrown out of upper-storey windows to lie on the sidewalks below. Europe certainly had reason to believe that where the Serbs were concerned the veneer of civility that sheathed the barbarian beneath was indeed very thin in places. However, while Serbia's internal politics may have been of only marginal concern to the rest of Europe, what shocked the Continent was that all the evidence pointed to the Serbian government willingly exporting its own peculiar brand of political "dialogue" outside its own borders. From the moment the news broke in the European capitals, there was much sympathy for Austria-Hungary in general, Franz Josef in particular, and almost none for Serbia. Punishment for Serbia was inevitable, and there was no doubt in any of the chancelleries of Europe that the punishment would take the form of military action. Sir Edward Grey, then Great Britain's Foreign Minister, would later remember that:

> No crime has ever aroused deeper or more general horror throughout Europe. . . . Sympathy for Austria was universal. Both governments and public opinion were ready to support her in any measures, however severe, which she might think it necessary to take for the punishment of the murderer and his accomplices.

Predictably—and understandably—the Serbian government was quick to protest its innocence, which may have been true in the narrowest sense as there was no official sponsorship or knowledge of the plot on the part of the Serbian government as a whole. The protests fell on deaf ears, however, as it became clear that high-ranking members of the Serbian government, however unofficially, had known of the assassins' plans in advance, had made no effort to warn the Austrians or thwart the assassins' efforts, and had in some cases even aided them. It was already something of an open secret that the head of the Serbian intelligence service, Colonel Dragutin Dimitrijevic, known by the code name Apis, was the leader of the Black Hand, and it was widely believed that the Serbian government had actually turned a blind eye to preparations for the assassination that were being made on Serbian territory. The exact extent of Serbian complicity would never be determined, as several key figures perished in the coming war, some under very questionable circumstances, but in the end it mattered little. The perception of Serbian guilt was overwhelming, and it presented Austria with an opportunity that she was determined not to squander.

The news of the deaths of the Archduke and his wife was broken almost simultaneously to the three most powerful men in the Empire: the Emperor himself, Franz Josef; Count Istvan Tisza de Boros-Jeno, the Emperor's Prime Minister; and Count Leopold von Berchtold, the Foreign Minister. The week that followed the assassinations was filled with ever-growing tensions in Vienna, as a battle of wills was fought between the three men over the nature of how Austria-Hungary would react. Berchtold immediately, and openly, advocated military action to punish Serbia for her part—assumed as well as perceived—in the Sarajevo murders. Tisza was adamant in insisting that every possible diplomatic solution be explored before resorting to war. Franz Josef, who had seen enough of war and its consequences during his lifetime, wanted no part of yet another; at the same time he understood that Austria-Hungary had to punish Serbia in some way. Any reaction which appeared to be less than forceful and decisive would be perceived as an admission of Austro-Hungarian weakness, and would serve only to incite radical Serbs both within and without the Empire's borders to further acts of violence, while at the same time signaling to the Kingdom of Serbia that it could encourage such terrorists with impunity. It was not until July 4 that the arguments between the three men were resolved, the resolution taking the form of a note sent to Berlin, asking for a firm answer as to whether or not the German Empire would stand beside the Austro-Hungarian Empire should Franz Josef choose to go to war with Serbia. It was an outcome that wholly pleased only Count Berchtold.

Franz Josef was a majestic figure of tragic grandeur: few crowned heads have been held in such affection and respect both at home and abroad, or reigned through so many years of sadness. His reign lasted for so long that most of his subjects could remember no other monarch but him: in 1914 he had ruled the Dual Monarchy for sixty-six years. Much as Victoria in England, in the last decades of her reign, had been revered as almost more of an institution than as a mere person, so Franz Josef had come to be regarded on the Continent. Born on August 18, 1830, he had unexpectedly succeeded to the throne of Austria at the age of 18, amidst extraordinarily difficult circumstances. The year was 1848, revolution was sweeping across France, Prussia, and Austria, and in quick succession the Emperor Ferdinand, Franz Josef's uncle, abdicated his throne, while the heir-apparent, Archduke Franz Karl, Franz-Josef's father, renounced his rights to succession. Their acts were gestures of appeasement made in the futile hope of stemming the revolutionary tide which was flowing over Hungary and threatened to dissolve the Hapsburg monarchy. Instead that task was left to a handsome, melancholy young man barely into his majority. Franz Josef's sixty-eight-year reign would begin and end in turmoil and tumult—there would be few times of happiness and tranquility in between.

The Austria Franz Josef inherited had already passed its peak as a world power, although even in her decline Austria was strong. Still, the new Emperor found himself losing a war with France which had been forced upon him almost as soon as he had taken the crown, and a few years later, when Austria refused to support Imperial Russia during the Crimean War, her relationship with Russia suffered irreparable damage. Simultaneously, the wars of Italian unification led to Austria surrendering almost all of her possessions in Italy, including the provinces of Lombardy and Venetia. Franz Josef was prepared to accept the decline in Austria's international prestige caused by these losses. It was not that Austrian troops could not fight—their performance in the Seven Years' War and the Napoleonic Wars had proven that Austrian soldiers could show as much tenacity and courage as any in Europe—rather it was that at heart Franz Josef was not a violent man, and in the case of the Italian provinces, the thought of waging war against people who had once been his subjects caused him tremendous grief.

The single most important factor in Austria's decline, however, was the rise of Prussia. Following the north German kingdom's successful war with Austria in 1866 and her unification of the independent German states into the German Empire under the guidance of Chancellor Otto von Bismarck in 1871, Prussia replaced Austria as the dominant Germanic power on the Continent. While an alliance was quickly concluded between the two Teutonic empires, it was clear to everyone that it was not an alliance of equals; rather Austria was the junior partner in the arrangement.

While all of this was happening on the international stage, at home Franz Josef had to deal with growing demands for Hungarian autonomy. In 1867, after years of sometimes acrimonious negotiation, the Empire's German and Hungarian peoples agreed to the formation of a "dual monarchy," in which both were equal partners, establishing the empire of Austria-Hungary. Franz Josef retained his title as Emperor of Austria, and was now simultaneously styled King of Hungary. The two nations, which is what the new empire had essentially created, retained control of their own internal affairs, while foreign and military policies were the responsibility of the Emperor and his officials, in what was styled the "*königische und kaiserlich*" ("royal and imperial") government. It was an unwieldy system, but it worked after a fashion, and for nearly half a century Austria-Hungary muddled along, no longer powerful enough alone to determine the great issues of her day, but still capable of exerting enough force to be an influence on the European stage.

However, Franz Josef came to realize that simple "dualism" did not go far enough, and began to articulate the idea of granting some form of self-government to Austria's Slavs, who had in effect been marginalized by the structure of the Dual Monarchy. His efforts at introducing any form of power sharing, however short of full "Trialism" they might have been, met with frustration at the hand of the German and Magyar politicians and aristocrats who had little interest in seeing a further dilution of their power and prerogatives and so had no sympathy for any sharing of power with the Slavs. Frustrated at their continued relegation to second-class status the Empire's Slavic subjects, particularly the Czechs and Serbs, mistakenly directed their anger at the Imperial government itself rather than toward the politicians who were thwarting the Emperor's plans, leading to an atmosphere of on-going tension in the predominantly Slavic parts of the Empire. How and when that tension would find a release was anybody's guess, and the predominant question for every senior official serving the Emperor.

Franz Josef's misfortunes as sovereign were mirrored in his private life as well. His only son, and the heir apparent, Archduke Rudolf committed suicide in 1889 in the bizarre *denouement* of a love affair with a young woman less than half his age. Franz Josef's younger brother, Maximilian, was executed by a Mexican firing squad in 1867 following an unsuccessful three-year reign as Emperor of Mexico. The Emperor's other brother, Karl Ludwig, died in strange circumstances as well: in 1896 he contracted a fever from drinking contaminated water during a pilgrimage to the Holy Lands and died after weeks in a delirium. Finally, Franz Josef had become estranged from his wife, the Empress Elisabeth, who suffered from some form of undiagnosed mental instability, and spent more than three decades wandering across the Continent, a royal vagabond. In her twenties Elisabeth was known as the most beautiful woman in all of Europe, and as she entered her middle age, little of her legendary beauty had faded. However, it was no protection against a knife wielded by an Italian anarchist, who fatally stabbed the Empress as she stood on a train platform in Geneva in 1898.

The succession to the throne had, literally by a process of elimination, devolved on the Archduke Franz Ferdinand, the only male child of Karl Ludwig. Little affection was lost between the Emperor and the Archduke, although both appeared to have respected the other. The imbroglio of Franz Ferdinand's marriage to Sophie Chotek von Chotkova was never really resolved, having only come about because both the German Kaiser, Wilhelm II, and the Russian Tsar, Nicholas II, intervened on behalf of Franz Ferdinand. Franz Josef's opposition to marriage stemmed from his conviction that it was a violation of royal and imperial protocol, which the aging Emperor felt was an essential part of the fabric of the Empire. So offended was he, and so strong ran his disapproval of Sophie Chotek, that he refused to attend Franz Ferdinand's wedding. Nor, as events would have it, would he attend the Archduke's funeral.

The first of Franz Josef's ministers to receive the news of the Sarajevo tragedy and formulate a response was his Foreign Minister, Count Leopold von Berchtold. Berchtold was one of those rare historical figures so authentic in who and what he was that he appeared to approach caricature: he was the quintessential Viennese aristocrat. When once queried as to which part of the Empire to which he felt the most loyalty, he responded, "The side of the Emperor." On another occasion a French reporter, who had commented on the Count's multi-ethnic heritage, asked if he felt himself to be German, Hungarian, or Czech: Berchtold simply replied, "I am Viennese." Berchtold was a man of immense wealth, owning vast tracts of land in Austria, Hungary and Moldavia; reputedly he was the richest man in the Austro-Hungarian empire. Certainly he possessed some of the most impressive aristocratic credentials of any official in the Austrian government: the blood of nearly eight centuries of German, Czech and Hungarian nobility ran in his veins, and in that he could be rightly said to have been the physical embodiment of the Hapsburg Empire. Born on April 18, 1863, in Vienna, a career in government service was almost inevitable for Berchtold. That he should rise as high as he did in the Foreign Ministry was not due to any overabundance of talent or any display of great brilliance, although he was possessed of a first-class mind, but rather was mainly attributed to his courtly demeanor, cultivated yet unostentatious manners, and aristocratic connections. His fondness for, and appreciation of, fine art, beautiful women, and prize horses lent him the air of a dilettante rather than a dedicated foreign service officer, an impression that followed him into the office of Foreign Minister. His first overseas appointments were to London and Paris, where his social graces served him well; he was named ambassador to Russia in 1907, serving at St. Petersburg until 1912, at which time he returned to Vienna to take office as the Emperor's Foreign Minister.

Those who believed that Berchtold's responsibilities exceeded his abilities were wrong: he worked hard and, mindful of the limitations of Austro-Hungarian power, pursued a single-minded policy from his first days in office. An aristocrat to the core, Berchtold believed that the three great monarchies of Europe—Austria-Hungary, Germany, and Russia—should stand together as a bulwark against liberalism run rampant, as characterized by France and Great Britain. This would be best accomplished, as Berchtold saw it, by maintaining the status quo in the Balkans, primarily through suppressing and eliminating nationalistic aspirations, especially those of the Slavs, which he believed threatened the fabric of the Empire.

As long as Wilhelm II sat on the German throne, Berchtold was assured of Germany's cooperation in his policy: gaining Russia's acquiescence was not as easily accomplished. The Kingdom of Serbia was a particular source of irritation and frustration: a client state of Imperial Russia, Serbia counted on Russia's protection while it served as a safe haven for Serbian separatists who were agitating, often violently, within the Austro-Hungarian Empire for the "liberation" of the Empire's Serbian population. During the Balkan Wars of 1912–13 Berchtold had actually considered going to war with Serbia to settle the issue once and for all; he was over-ruled by Franz Josef, who would have no part of any war which could be legitimately avoided. Berchtold's position regarding Serbia hardened during this period into something resembling intransigence. Upon hearing the news of the assassination of Archduke Franz Ferdinand, Berchtold immediately saw an opportunity to humiliate and possibly even crush Serbia, suggesting almost at once that Austria-Hungary launch an immediate invasion of the Serbian kingdom without a prior declaration of war. At this point he ran headlong into the determined will of Austria-Hungary's Prime Minister, Count Tisza.

It would be difficult to find two political colleagues who were such complete opposites in temperament and character than were Counts Berchtold and Tisza. The differences ran far deeper than their ethnicity: Berchtold, of course, was German while Tisza was a Magyar—a Hungarian. While the Foreign Minister was a practicing Catholic with practiced tastes in good food, excellent wine, and beautiful women, the Prime Minister was a rather austere Calvinist Protestant. Berchtold was charming and accommodating, Tisza was aloof and sometimes abrasive. While Berchtold was genuinely concerned about what other people thought and believed, Tisza cared for no one's opinions but his own.

Berchtold's loyalty to the House of Hapsburg was absolute and incorruptible; Tisza was known to put his loyalty to the Hungarian people before his loyalty to the throne. Berchtold regarded the sharing of power between the Germans and the Magyars in the Dual Monarchy as a typical example of the sort of institutionalized improvisation which the House of Hapsburg had been making—and making work—for centuries; the question of how to eventually accommodate the Empire's Slavic population would ultimately resolve itself in similar fashion. Tisza, noting that in an empire composed entirely of minorities the Slavs already outnumbered the Magyars, was inimically opposed to any further restructuring of the Imperial government which might diminish Hungarian power. Most of all he feared the Empire becoming entangled in a war in the Balkans which the Empire's Slavs might use as a pretext for breaking away from Austria-Hungary entirely.

Istvan Tisza first served as Prime Minister at the age of forty-two (he was born in 1861) when he was the leader of Hungary's Liberal Party, a position he held from 1903 to 1905. Re-appointed for a second time in 1913, Tisza endlessly championed Hungarian rights within the Dual Monarchy; indeed, the case could be made that his advocacy of Hungarian interests was at times contrary to the best interests of the Empire. Unlike Berchtold, Tisza was convinced that a war—any war, no matter what the cause or pretext—which pitted Austria-Hungary against Serbia posed mortal danger to the Empire. While Berchtold believed that a war would create a spirit of unity among the peoples of the Empire, their loyalty centered on the father-figure of the old Emperor, Tisza feared that any setback Austria-Hungary might suffer would unleash an overwhelming flood of ethnic and nationalist feelings among the empire's perpetually discontented Slavs. Even a victorious war could be perilous, at least as far as Magyar interests were concerned: should a defeated Serbia be annexed by a victorious Empire, the much-dreaded "Triple Monarchy" would likely become a reality with the inclusion of so many new Slavic subjects, curtailing Hungarian power.

Tisza knew that Berchtold had as little desire as himself to see "Trialism" enacted, as it would diminish German power as much as Hungarian, nor had the Foreign Minister ever advocated military action against Serbia as a means of relieving or eliminating the tensions between the two nations. So it was something of a shock for Tisza to learn that Berchtold, supported by the Chief of Staff of the Austro-Hungarian Army, Field Marshal Conrad von Hötzendorf, had been urging the Emperor to use the Sarajevo murders as justification for "settling" matters with Serbia. Both men were pressing Franz Josef to authorize a full-scale surprise attack against the Serbs, even foregoing the formality of a declaration of war.

Part of Berchtold's sudden advocacy of a punitive war against Serbia was personal: Franz Ferdinand had been a close friend, and the Foreign Minister mourned him deeply. (Predictably, Tisza had never liked the Archduke, regarding him as an overbearing bore.) While Berchtold and Conrad refused to moderate their demand for immediate military action, they did agree to give Tisza time to go to Franz Josef with his arguments against such precipitate action. Since the ultimate authority rested with the Emperor, he would have the last word.

Conrad had been a loud and persistent proponent of a pre-emptive war against Serbia, first having proposed such a solution to Austria's Serbian problem as far back as 1908. Time and again Franz Josef refused to resort to force, gently but firmly informing the Field Marshal that, "A ruler's first duty is to preserve the peace." This time, however, was different: while Franz Josef stoically grieved for his nephew (at one point he was heard to murmur, "For me it is one great worry less," as he realized that the showdown between himself and Franz Ferdinand over the future of the Empire had been eternally postponed), at the same time he realized that the long-deferred confrontation with Serbia had arrived. Field Marshal Conrad began the preparations for a military campaign that would crush Serbia and, together with Foreign Minister Berchtold, pressed the Emperor for permission to launch his attack. Berchtold, for his part, was adamant, declaring it necessary that "the Monarchy with unflinching hand . . . tear asunder the threads which its foes are endeavoring to weave into a net above its head."

The only possible check to Austria's determination to settle accounts with Serbia was Russia: the Tsar might protest, or even threaten to mobilize his army, should the Austrians march on Belgrade, the Serbian capital. Yet there seemed to be no reason to believe that the Russians would come to Serbia's rescue: this was not a case of Austria-Hungary attempting to expand her power at Serbia's expense, as had happened in 1908, but rather a justifiable act of punishment for Serbia's tacit complicity in the assassinations. Certainly the Tsar, whose own grandfather was murdered by a revolutionary's bomb, had no love for regicides—he would hardly be expected to go to war in the defense of a Serbia that had royal blood on its hands. An even more formidable check on Russia's response, though, would be the certain knowledge that should Russia go to war with Austria-Hungary, she would in turn face war with Austria's ally, Imperial Germany.

It was this question that Franz Josef put to Conrad when the Field Marshal began pressing him to allow the Austrian Army to strike. "How," he asked, imagining the worst consequences should Austria-Hungary attack Serbia, "will you fight the war when everyone falls upon us, especially the Russians?"

"But we are covered by the Germans," was Conrad's reply.

"Are you sure of the Germans?"

"Your Majesty, we have to know where we stand."

Franz Josef's response was to inform Conrad of the contents of a diplomatic note that had just been sent to Berlin, requesting just such a clarification. Conrad was blunt in return: "And if the answer is that Germany will stand by us, will we make war on Serbia?"

With obvious anguish, but clearly determined, the aging Emperor replied simply, "Then, yes. But if Germany does not give us this answer, then what?"

"Then we stand alone. But we must have an answer soon, for the great decision depends on it."

Conrad did not make it clear then or later if he ultimately meant to go to war with Serbia regardless of the German reply, but for the moment it was understood that the decision for war or peace would lie with Imperial Germany. Both men were well aware that in October 1913, at the height of tensions during the Second Balkan War, Wilhelm II had assured the Austrian Foreign Minister, Count von Berchtold, that:

> If His Majesty Franz Josef demands something, the Serbian Government must yield, and if she does not, then Belgrade will be bombarded and occupied until the will of His Majesty is fulfilled. You may rest assured that I stand behind you and am ready to draw the sword.

The note to which Franz Josef had made reference had gone out over the signatures of both Tisza and Berchtold and in the name of Franz Josef, although Tisza never saw the final draft and Franz Josef had given his consent with grave reluctance. The contents were wholly those of Count Berchtold, and more completely reflected his views than it did those of the Emperor or the Prime Minister. In it Berchtold declared the disputes between Serbia and Austria-Hungary to be "unreconcilable," and declared in the same language that he had used to the Emperor, that it was an "imperious necessity" for the Dual Monarchy to "destroy with a determined hand the net which its enemies are attempting to draw over its head." In a cover letter signed by the Emperor himself, Berchtold was even more explicit, arguing that "the Sarajevo affair . . . was the result of a well-organized conspiracy, the threads of which can be traced to Belgrade," declaring that Serbia must be "eliminated as a power factor in the Balkans."

The note was hand-carried to Berlin by Count Alexander Hoyos, who directed Berchtold's secretariat and was his most trusted subordinate. In addition to delivering the note, Hoyos was instructed to inform the German government that Vienna would ask Belgrade for specific guarantees of Serbia's future good behavior: should the Serbs refuse to make such guarantees, Austria-Hungary would begin military action against them. Hoyos was to ask for a definite, specific declaration as to whether or not Germany would support Austria-Hungary should the issue come down to open warfare.

News of the murders in Sarajevo was quickly communicated to the capitals of Europe. As the story broke it provoked the inevitable expressions of shock and outrage, but there was little sense that a major crisis was about to break across the Continent: assassinations had been part of the European political landscape for hundreds of years. Overseas only passing notice was taken of the murders of Franz Ferdinand and Sophie. The lives of government officials and private citizens alike continued without noticeable disruption: balls and receptions, parliamentary sessions, diplomatic communications, business meetings, work in the offices and shops, toil in the factories and labor in the fields all went on much as they had before the Sarajevo tragedy.

And yet. . . .

There was a detectable undercurrent of tension running through the Chancelleries and Foreign Ministries of Europe, as if somehow this time the situation might be different. The question being asked everywhere was not if Austria-Hungary would react to the Archduke's assassination, but rather what form Austrian retribution against Serbia would take. Serbian complicity was taken for granted, and all of the Great Powers believed that the Dual Monarchy was fully within its rights in inflicting any reasonable punishment on her openly antagonistic neighbor.

Nobody could truly foresee that Armageddon was about to fall upon the Continent. Three times in the past decade—in 1905, 1909, and 1913—there had been an imminent threat of war, and each time common sense had prevailed, as the diplomats produced workable compromises and solutions to the crisis at hand. There seemed to be no justifiable reason to believe that this time would be different. What set this crisis apart from its predecessors was that in the previous incidents no one really wanted to go to war; this time, one of Europe's Great Powers was prepared to provoke a Continent-wide conflagration in order to assert what it believed to be its rightful place in the world. The fate of the peace of Europe, more fragile than anyone really knew or understood, was about to fall into the hands of men who had no use for it.

Chapter II

THE VIALS OF WRATH

"The vials of wrath were full."

Winston Churchill's Apocalyptic allusion was all too appropriate. For four decades, France had been yearning for, praying for, planning for the day of revenge, when Alsace and Lorraine would be reunited with *La Patrie*, and the old score settled with the hated *Boche*. Austria-Hungary, decaying from within, saw the moment arrive when she could strike out at the nation that seemed to be the source of all her tribulations. Russia, still stung by the defeats of the war with Japan in 1905 and the humiliation of the Bosnian Crisis of 1908, was determined to regain her lost prestige at almost any cost. But above all, Germany, full of arrogant bluster, was ready to embrace a war— any war—that would solidify the political and economic hegemony over the Continent which she saw as being her inevitable right and was being irrevocably eroded. Caught up in a tangled skein of alliances and counter-alliances, the Great Powers of Europe stood on the brink of the abyss, unable or unwilling to see the precipice before them, failing to understand that should one of them jump or fall into it—or worse yet, should one of their number push another into it— they all, like prisoners chained together, would be pulled in. Of all Europe, only Britain was bound to no other nation by any compact or alliance—save the 1839 treaty that guaranteed the neutrality of Belgium.

As the antagonisms grew, so did the armies, until young men by the hundreds of thousands had donned the uniforms of their homelands. Thousands of cannon and howitzers, hundreds of thousands of rifles, and millions of rounds of ammunition, had been accumulated in the armories of Europe. Never in history, before or since, has the world seen such a peacetime concentration of armies and armaments as was found in Europe in the summer of 1914, an aggregation which continued to grow as the nations nursed their grievances. . . .

Reflecting on the first years of the 20th century from the perspective of the first years of the 21st, it is stunning to look upon the world of that time, what today is commonly called the Edwardian Era, a world that often seems so far removed from the present that it is frequently difficult to believe that it is only now passing from living memory. The values, beliefs, motives, the very pace of life seem nearly incomprehensible today. Barry Pitt, writing in the introduction to John Keegan's *August, 1914*, caught the essence of this seeming unreality when he wrote:

> Dimly can be perceived a life which seems to bear no relation to the present one, conducted apparently to a different rhythm, by a different species of being, reacting to a totally different scheme of behavior. Bewhiskered monarchs write stiff family notes to each other before going out to shoot stag or bird, tiara'd queens whisper behind their fans, frock-coated statesmen hurry from capital to capital and debate in solemn enclave (occasionally one is shot), while the tight-collared and cloth-capped masses alternately riot or cheer, fortified the while on ale, wine, or porter, at a penny a pint. Away in a far corner a square of British infantry in blue and scarlet repels cavalry charges or hordes of fanatical natives. Perhaps the most astonishing aspect. . . is that the sun seems to have been shining all the time.

Yet though this time has often been portrayed as Golden Age or *Belle Epoque*, except for the privileged minority of the upper classes, it was not. The Europe of 1914 was, as astonishing as it may seem today, still very much a feudal society: class utterly defined the pre-1914 European world. The method of making the distinctions between the classes varied from country to country, but within any society the boundaries were usually quite clearly defined and enforced, never more so than when distinguishing between "we" and "they." Usually the classes fell into three categories—the working, or lower class; the middle class; and the upper class, or aristocracy. The class to which a man or woman belonged was determined by birth: people generally remained in the class in which they were born. Mobility was for the most part discouraged and restricted, usually by tradition, occasionally by law. There were, however, exceptions, especially from the middle to the upper class, as merchants, tradesmen, and industrialists amassed vast fortunes which demanded the attention if not the respect of the aristocracy, and allowed them a narrow *entrée* into more refined social strata. Also, it was not unknown for the line between the lower and middle classes to occasionally become blurred. For the most part, however, the barriers between the classes remained impermeable.

It was not an era of unbridled confidence, innocence, stability, or security, although it has often been portrayed as such. This is not to say that these qualities were not present; they were, but in an ongoing state of flux. People were more confident of their standards, believing in their values, secure in the ideas of Progress, aided by its handmaiden Science. However, equally present were doubts about the future, created by a complicated system of military alliances coupled with ever-growing expenditures for armaments; protests and demonstrations over frequently appalling working conditions and hours as well as often grossly inadequate wages for the working classes; and violent confrontations between protesters and police, or strikers and strike-breakers, clashing in street brawls, while anarchists and nihilists carried out a haphazard rash of bombings and assassinations. A new form of hatred and fear manifested itself in bloody confrontations between British police and the IRA, or Austro-Hungarian authorities and Serbian pan-nationalists, or Russian soldiers and Russian revolutionaries.

Yet it would be deceptive to depict the first decade of the 20th century as too closely resembling that of the 21st, for through all the tension and upheaval, there was a constant note of confidence running though the times. Thoughtful men and women everywhere, of all social classes, readily acknowledged that problems existed in society, though they might differ on how grave those problems were. However, even the anarchist with his bomb believed that the problems had solutions; it was only a matter of how and when they would be found. It was that sense of confidence that made the decade before August 1914 unique.

Perhaps most tellingly, these were the years of the music of Richard Strauss and Igor Stravinsky, the philosophy of Friederich Nietzsche and Henri Louis Bergson, the art of Cezanne and Seurat, the writings of Emil Zola and Bertrand Russell—all of them compelling, forceful, and dynamic, even revolutionary. It was a remarkable expression of art imitating life, the artists and thinkers transforming the external expressions of their disciplines as thoroughly as the external trappings of Western society were being transformed. The first decade of the 20th century was also the culmination of a hundred years of the most accelerated rate of change in society and technology that mankind had ever known. Between 1814 and 1914, humanity had gone from transportation, communication, production, and manufacturing methods powered by human or animal muscles augmented by wind and water to a world of steam engines, steamships, and steam-powered machinery. The new century was one of electric lighting and communications (though as yet electricity was common only in the cities, and then usually only in the middle and upper-class areas). By 1914 trucks, lorries, and motorcars powered by internal combustion engines were well on their way to supplanting horses as a means of transport.

In less than a century, mankind's rate of travel overland had more than trebled, while at sea it had more than quadrupled. Where in 1814 the best speed a traveler could hope for would be perhaps twenty miles an hour while riding in a horse-drawn coach, a railway passenger in 1914 would routinely reach speeds approaching seventy miles an hour on an express. A trip across the North Atlantic that once took more than a month was now accomplished in a week or less, and with a degree of safety and comfort unimaginable only a few generations before.

The accelerating rate of change was most marked in that last decade. In 1900 there had been fewer than 8,000 automobiles in the entire United States, but by 1910 there were close to a half-million. In 1903 the first flight of a heavier-than-air craft lasted 12 seconds and covered 852 feet; in 1909 Louis Bleriot had flown across the English Channel, a distance of twenty-six miles. The years between 1900 and 1910 had seen the introduction of the phonograph, wireless telegraphy, turbine-powered steamships, the electric light, the original Kodak "Brownie" camera, heavier-than-air flying machines, motion pictures—all of them as reliable apparatus rather than mere technical novelties.

This was the world which would witness revelations in the physics of Roentgen's X-rays, Marie Curie's radium, and Einstein's e=mc^2; in the psychology of Jung, Freud, Pavlov, and Adler; and in medicine where the secrets of vitamins, genes, and hormones would be unlocked. Science had been transformed from a dalliance for eccentrics into a systematic discipline, becoming the foundation of industry.

At the same time these changes unintentionally began an erosion in the nineteen-centuries-old faith in God as the source of all certainty and stability. The authority and infallibility of the Bible were no longer universally regarded as absolute, and the solid core of religious doctrines and dogmas that had bound Western civilization together was slowly crumbling. The industrial society that created and supported the multitude of innovations also built up new pressures in both prosperity and poverty, raising questions about the validity of the established order that churches could no longer answer convincingly, while growing populations and densely crowded cities created new antagonisms between classes, new problems for industry owners, and new opportunities for radicals and rabble rousers. Far from wallowing in its own decadence, as is all too often depicted, the Europe of the years before 1914 was dynamic, even exciting, driven by the momentum of centuries of accumulated tensions and energies—industrial, economic, and social—that created such contrasts of wealth and poverty, opulence and indigence such as no society had ever known before. It was this era that Mark Twain, despairing of its excess but blind to its potential, derisively christened the "Gilded Age."

What was a surprise to many a foreign visitor was that the cities of Europe, with allowances being made for national tastes and architectural peculiarities, were remarkably similar. Government buildings were usually constructed out of grey granite and designed according to some national ideal of "Imperial" architecture; commercial structures were similar, but often used red or yellow sandstone instead of granite. Smaller buildings and businesses, as well as houses, were most often slate-roofed, red-brick structures. This was the world where the small businessmen, bank clerks, accountants, brokers, bookkeepers, merchants, and shopkeepers worked, and where they lived with their wives and families. These were men and women who guarded their social station with as much determination as the aristocracy did their own, whose class was obsessed with respectability—always watchful never to say or do something that even hinted at a lack of good manners or proper breeding, or would somehow suggest that the individual involved was actually nothing more than a puffed-up member of the working class.

As a result they embraced the values of patriotism, education, hard work, and piety, and were as prim and proper as the upper classes were profligate. But while they might appear to be stolid and unimaginative, they were hardly docile: in Great Britain, the Liberal Party, which had just forced passage of the Parliament Bill that emasculated the House of Lords, had won its overwhelming majority in the Commons in 1908 because the middle class had wholeheartedly endorsed the Liberals' program of social reforms at home and imperial reforms abroad—reforms that the upper classes had doggedly opposed. In Germany, though the Social Democratic Party usurped the lion's share of the credit for social reforms passed by the Reichstag, those reforms came about only with the support of such middle-class bastions as the Christian Democratic Party.

Out in the countryside the brick and slate of the suburbs gave way to dressed fieldstone, half-timbering and thatch; the world of the landed gentry, of the manor house, the village church, *eglise*, or *kirche*, and the clusters of cottages, of vast fields of grass, wheat, barley, and heather, broken by stands of spruce and beech, birch and oak. Here men would listen for the call of the blackbird and the cuckoo, and sharpen their long-bladed scythes in anticipation of cutting the thick summer grasses. Here, life moved to a rhythm little changed for centuries, in a world of farmers, shepherds, blacksmiths, weavers and tanners—men who rose with the sun and retired with it. Their work was hard, for mechanization was still a dream for most. They worked the land and tended their animals much as their great-great-grandfathers had. Occasionally, a stolen afternoon would be spent fishing for trout in a nearby river, and most evenings would find the men rewarding themselves with a well-earned pint at the local pub or *bierstube*, but always there would be an ear cocked to the wind, an eye glancing at the sky, for all it took was one of those summer storms to roll in from the east to wash away an entire season's planting or sweep away a flock of sheep in a sudden flood. It was a world undisturbed by the comings and goings of the rich and powerful, and it had precious few days left.

There was a third landscape that existed in every country in Europe, but it was far removed from the glittering bustle of the capitals, the neatly ordered suburbs or the gently rolling countryside, both in geography and character. These were the industrial cities of Scotland, the Midlands, Le Creusot, the Ruhr, or St. Petersburg and Moscow, where the vistas were of apparently endless corrugated-iron factory roofs, forests of belching smokestacks, and endless warrens of sooty red-brick row houses that gave shelter to the men, women, and children who toiled their lives away in the textile mills or the steel works.

Most of these row houses had deteriorated to slums, where a family of eight might share two beds and a pair of thin blankets among them, with little or nothing in the way of sanitary facilities, and subsist on an inadequate diet that left the children stunted, pale and apathetic. Despite compulsory education laws, few children living in these slums ever completed even the most basic education: by the age of eight they would be working, usually in a textile mill, where their small and nimble fingers were best suited to work amid fast-moving mechanisms. Wages were rarely more than a few pounds, francs, marks, or roubles a week, and injuries and fatalities involving a child snatched into the maw of a great weaving or spinning machine were commonplace and considered unremarkable by management, since replacements were always readily at hand.

The adults fared little better, often working in mine shafts or before vast open-hearth steel mills for as little as a shilling an hour, in a twelve-hour shift with no lunch break (lunches were eaten at the workplace if at all), six days a week. Taking a day off without permission in advance could result in a worker being jailed in some industries. Disease was rife among them, chiefly tuberculosis, and limited and meager diets often resulted in stunted bodies and minds. (It is a matter of official record that the minimum height requirement for the British Army was of necessity reduced in 1900 from five feet, three inches to five feet.) What most industrial workers today take for granted were the merest pipe-dreams: paid holidays, health care, pensions, and sick leave were ideas that hadn't yet been formulated, let alone articulated.

The labor unions had made some inroads in alleviating the worst of the workers' lot, but poverty and its accompanying deprivations were still the rule in most industrial workers' lives. A blacklist even existed in some industries: a worker dismissed for labor agitation could be barred from rehire, sometimes just within a certain city, sometimes within the entire industry. To souls such as these, hopelessness was a permanent condition: somehow, all the great material and technical progress that had been the hallmark of the Victorian Era had done little to ameliorate the lot of the people whose labors had made them possible. It was a social and economic imbalance that would produce pressures on European society, like a head of steam in an overheated boiler, which, unless given some sort of outlet, threatened to blow that society apart. While some of Europe's more perceptive politicians, journalists, and social leaders understood this, none of them could predict what sort of incident would trigger the explosion.

The one great constant of European politics for more than forty years had been the enmity that France bore toward Germany. The humiliation of the peace settlement that Germany imposed on France at the end of the Franco-Prussian war—it was far more harsh than the terms Prussia had dictated to Denmark or Austria just a few years previously—left a great wound on the French spirit, which, coupled with what Frenchmen regarded as the territorial mutilation of France when the provinces of Alsace and Lorraine were annexed to the German Empire, made revenge the driving force behind French military and diplomatic policy for the next four decades.

Cobbled together from the ruins of the Second Empire and the Paris Commune, the Third Republic found itself friendless, bankrupt, and with a German Army occupying France that was giving every indication of being prepared for a long stay; not since Napoleon had crushed Prussia at Jena and Auerstadt had peace terms between two European powers been so harshly punitive. The defeat had humiliated Frenchmen in every possible way: the myth of French martial prowess—and by implication, French virility—assiduously nurtured by the French since the days of the First Empire, had been shown to be merely a hollow boast; the nation was burdened with an indemnity that was deliberately intended to cripple France's economy for as much as twenty years; and the provinces of Alsace and Lorraine, cherished by Frenchmen as the loveliest in all France, had been torn from the French body politic and incorporated into the newly formed German Empire. That the Prussian King, Wilhelm I, and his Chancellor, Count Otto von Bismarck, chose to proclaim the formation of that Empire in the palace at Versailles merely added insult to injury.

For almost twenty years, France existed in a sort of diplomatic limbo, a condition carefully engineered by Bismarck, who successfully wooed away all would-be allies of the French Republic with a carefully thought-out array of treaties and agreements. It was only in 1890, when the new Kaiser, Wilhelm II, blundered and failed to renew the secret Reinsurance Treaty of 1887 with Russia, that an opening appeared in the diplomatic wall surrounding France. The treaty had guaranteed German neutrality in the event Austria attacked Russia, and Russian neutrality in the event that France attacked Germany. By failing to renew the treaty, Wilhelm caused the Russian Tsar, Alexander III, to fear that Russia might face the same sort of diplomatic isolation that had surrounded France. Wilhelm regarded himself as being as adroit at international diplomacy as Bismarck; despite his undoubted intelligence, he possessed not one whit of Bismarck's political acumen.

It was a folly for which Wilhelm would one day pay dearly, for within four months of the lapse of the Reinsurance Treaty, a French naval squadron paid a formal visit to Kronstadt, Russia's main naval base on the Baltic Sea. At a reception given for the officers of the visiting French ships, Alexander III stood bare-headed at the playing of the "Marseillaise," the anthem of Revolutionary France that had been banned in Russia for nearly a century. It was the beginning of the end of France's isolation, for within six months a formal alliance had been concluded between France and Russia. Two more unlikely partners could not be found—autocratic, arch-conservative Imperial Russia and liberal, regicidal Republican France—but a mutual fear of German ambition and power drove them to make common cause.

The conclusion of the alliance with Russia also marked the beginning in an historic shift in French policy regarding her other traditional rival, Great Britain. In 1896, a small French military expedition set out from Brazzaville in the French Congo, marching eastward on a twenty-four-month trek toward a small mud fort on the Upper Nile called Fashoda. Under ordinary circumstances the French column would have attracted little if any attention outside France, but in this case its objective was inside the boundaries of the Sudan, a territory the British had just acquired, expending considerable money and manpower to do so. The British government suspected that the French move toward Fashoda was the first step in a French plan to assert control over the southern half of the Sudan. A crisis loomed and there was talk of war when suddenly, the crisis evaporated. What had happened was that the commander of the British expedition to the Sudan, General Sir Herbert Kitchener, made a show of force before the fort at Fashoda, but with that curious mix of intuition and common sense that would characterize so many of Kitchener's decisions, decided not to resort to arms to decide the issue. Had he done so, the French position would have been completely untenable, not only at the fort but in Europe as well: the Royal Navy was prepared to sweep its French counterpart from the seas and impose a close blockade on France which she would have had no hope of breaking. In exercising restraint, Kitchener gave the French and British governments the opportunity to work out a compromise, whereby British suzerainty over the whole of the Sudan was reaffirmed, while the French troops at Fashoda were allowed to withdraw with honor, hailed at home and abroad for their courageous and daring exploits as explorers.

What made the entire incident significant was the willingness of both sides to avoid open conflict. While the French were indeed anxious to expand their empire in Africa—in the two decades immediately following the Franco-Prussian War France more than doubled the size of her overseas holdings—it was realized in Paris that a war with Great Britain would be the wrong war with the wrong foe. Only Germany could profit from a war between France and Britain; certainly a war fought over a few thousand square miles of African jungle would do nothing to help restore Alsace and Lorraine to France.

And that was the rub: all of France's focus, both of her policies and of her energies, were directed to the return of the two "stolen provinces." Victor Hugo, in the years immediately following the Franco-Prussian War, declared that:

> France will have but one thought; to reconstitute her forces, gather her energy, nourish her sacred anger, raise her young generation to form an army of the whole people, to work without cease, to study the methods and skills of our enemies, to become again a great France, the France of 1792, the France of an idea with a sword. Then one day she will be irre-sistible. Then she will take back Alsace-Lorraine.

There would be no single dominating political figure in France in the decades that followed the Franco-Prussian War to guide French policy toward the day of *revanche*—an endless procession of governments rose and fell, formed and dissolved in those years, as the same few score of ministers seemed to play musical chairs with their Cabinet posts, establishing the pattern that the Third Republic would follow for its entire existence. However, the idea expressed by Hugo was so strong, so compelling, that it became part of the emotional and spiritual core of every Frenchman, and so the unconscious urge to follow policies that would give life to Hugo's dream was always present. Any honorable means to that end would be embraced, including the putting aside of ancient rivalries, rivalries that now seemed pointless in the face of the clear and present danger across the Rhine. Her strength reviving, France knew that Germany, with her larger population and far greater industrial base, was merely biding her time before seeking to crush France once and for all. The sensibility displayed over the Fashoda incident began to work its way into France's relations with Britain in other areas.

The timing was fortuitous, for Great Britain, looking over France's shoulder at the Teutonic giant that had sprung up in Central Europe, began to feel a growing concern. By 1903, with the Boer War settled and anti-British sentiments having vanished from the mercurial French press, the British monarch, King Edward VII, announced his intention of paying a state visit to France and meeting French President Loubet on French soil. The announcement created an uproar, but the visit was one of the pivotal points in the two nations' history. The French people, who still harbored mixed feelings about royalty, and who had been raised on centuries-old traditions of regarding "perfidious Albion" as a natural enemy, were at first indifferent or sometimes openly hostile toward the British monarch. However, four days of appearances by Edward at state banquets, troop reviews, luncheons, theaters and the opera, transformed the populace. Always charming, smiling, gracious and tactful, Edward laid to rest the illusion of the British ogre. His efforts were rewarded a year later as, after much hard work by ministers of both governments in settling disputes, France and Great Britain signed a *rapprochement*, the Anglo-French Entente, in April 1904.

While the Entente was not a formal alliance with Britain, it was almost as valuable. By defining spheres of overseas influence, the Entente eliminated many of the past causes of friction between France and Great Britain. It allowed the French to concentrate more of their army in France, as well as bring several far-flung squadrons of warships home to French waters. Further, it gave France a sense of security, knowing that should war erupt with Germany again, her colonies were secure.

Another consequence of the Entente was that having tacitly acknowledged Germany to be the most likely foe of either nation in any future war, France and Britain began, a year after the Entente was signed, a series of conferences between the General Staffs of the two nations' armies, to coordinate operations between the French Army and any expeditionary force the British might send to the Continent. While the talks were not diplomatically binding—they did not require

Britain to come to France's aid should France and Germany come to blows—it was now possible for France to focus solely on the coming rematch with Germany. In less than a generation, the diplomatic and military position of France had been transformed in ways that Bismarck and the first Kaiser could never have imagined: a powerful, if ponderous, ally to the east, *rapprochement* with Britain in the west, and a rapidly reviving army. It would take a prodigious effort, for her population was barely two-thirds that of Germany's, her industrial base less than half. However, for France the gauntlet thrown down in the Hall of Mirrors at Versailles in 1871 still lay on the floor, an open affront to French national honor that demanded an answer.

The Empire of Austria-Hungary in 1914 was a far cry from that of the days of the 17th century when the House of Hapsburg overshadowed every other power in Europe, but it was still the largest nation on the continent, save for Russia. It was a collection of minorities: within its boundaries lived 40 million people, three fifths of whom were Slavs—Serbs, Czechs, Poles, Montenegrins, Bosnians, Slovaks. Political authority, though, was held by two other minorities, the Austrians, who were ethnic Germans, and the Hungarians, who were Magyars. The form of the government reflected their ascendency: it was a dual monarchy, with the Emperor (*Kaiser*) of Austria also being the King (*König*) of Hungary. The two minorities uneasily shared power within the structure of the government, and the Slavs were carefully excluded, lest by sheer numbers they should shunt their German and Magyar overlords aside.

That a nation of Slavs not under Austro-Hungarian suzerainty should exist on Austria-Hungary's own borders was an affront to the Empire's sensibilities. Worse, that nation, the kingdom of Serbia, became the focus for all the nationalistic aspirations of the subject Slav peoples with Austria-Hungary's borders. Serbia happily embraced this role, for the Serbs had ambitions of their own that could only be achieved at Austria-Hungary's expense. The Serbian dream was the creation of a Great Southern Slav Kingdom, built around Serbia and her capital of Belgrade, which would tear away from their Hapsburg masters the Empire's southern provinces of Bosnia, Herzegovina, and Montenegro. Masses of propaganda extolling Slav nationalism, accompanied by acts of political agitation and outright terrorism flowed from Belgrade to inflame the Empire's southern population.

Some sort of reckoning between Serbia and Austria-Hungary was inevitable. How, when and in what manner, would be determined by the Austrians, in the form of the Emperor-King, Franz Josef. Eighty-four years old, the Emperor had reigned for sixty-six years, a span of time that had seen many defeats and many fruitless victories. During those years, he tried tenaciously to maintain Austria-Hungary's status as a Great Power, even while outside events was eroding it away: the provinces of Lombardy and Venice were lost to Italian unification, while defeat at the hands of Prussia in 1866 marginalized Austrian influence in a coalescing Germany. Having lost so much, Franz Josef was determined to lose no more, and long refused to dilute his authority by altering the structure of the Austro-Hungarian government to allow the Slavs a voice in how they were to be ruled.

Franz Josef's nephew and heir, the Archduke Franz Ferdinand, thought otherwise. He was convinced that the best way to preserve the Hapsburg monarchy would be to radically restructure the Imperial government from a Dual Monarchy into a form of "Triple Monarchy," a sort of federation allowing the Slavs to share power with the Austrians and Magyars. As for Franz Josef, he would come to reluctantly embrace "Trialism" as the realistic means of preserving the House of Hapsburg, though as always when confronted by change and new ideas, his conversion came slowly.

There was a third way, although both the Emperor and the Archduke refused to consider it—perhaps the only thing, other than preserving the Empire, that they agreed upon. That was the military option: a preemptive war that would crush Serbia and hold her and the Slavic agitators she harbored under the Austrian heel. It had the advantages of being quick, decisive, and at least in the short run, a sure result. The French ambassador to Vienna, Alfred Dumaine, wrote Paris in December 1913 saying, "People here are becoming accustomed to the idea of a general war as the only possible remedy." Twice in less than five years Austria had mobilized against Serbia, first during the crisis over the Austrian annexation of Bosnia in 1908–09, and then again in the Second Balkan War, in 1912–13. The Chief of the General Staff of the Austrian Army, General Count Franz Conrad von Hötzendorf, regarded Serbia as "a dangerous little viper" and sought to treat her accordingly. He had been thwarted in 1909 by the Emperor himself, as Franz Josef had no desire to see his sunset years marked by any more violence, and in 1913 because Austria-Hungary's ally Germany, for her own reasons, had refused to support any aggressive move by Austria against Serbia.

Both Conrad and Franz Josef chafed at the thought that because of the Empire's increasing decrepitude, Germany held a veto over Austria's foreign policy, but they were both astute enough to realize that influence could be used both ways. In some ways Germany needed Austria as badly as Austria needed Germany. Each nation was the other's only reliable ally: Italy's membership in the Triple Alliance with Germany and Austria-Hungary counted for little, as Italy's pretense to Great Power status was exactly that, a pretense, and all three partners knew that Italy's participation was a convenience to lend Italy a prestige she had not earned and so really did not deserve. Both the Austrians and the Germans were convinced—rightly as events would turn out—that Italy would abandon the alliance on the slightest pretext. Hence, without each other, both Germany and Austria-Hungary would find themselves diplomatically and militarily isolated. Everyone in the German government from the Kaiser down was aware of Austria-Hungary's bumbling bureaucracy and creaking military. Hopelessly tied to the methods and mentality of the mid-19th century, a by-product of the Dual Monarchy system, Austrian inefficiency was already a standing European joke that only appeared likely to get worse should Franz Ferdinand's concept of a federated Empire come into being. Already the Empire was a liability as well as an asset to Germany: any further diminution of Austro-Hungarian power would only serve as a drag on Germany's ambitions, a consequence which Germany would accept almost any risk to avoid.

Those ambitions were simple—to maintain the political, military, and economic preeminence on the Continent that Germany had gathered unto herself in the last quarter of the 19th century. The great threat to Germany's position was Imperial Russia, whose vast potentials in industry and resources were just beginning to be explored and exploited, but were so immense that even in their infancy it could be seen that they could someday dwarf those of

Germany if they were left unchecked. The spasm of revolution that had wracked Imperial Russia following the defeats of the Russo-Japanese War of 1905 had brought only a temporary halt to Russia's economic and political development, while long-overdue military reforms prompted by those defeats were beginning to take effect. Nothing had altered in any way, however, Russia's continued devotion to her self-appointed role as the "protector" of all the Slavs of southern Europe, including Serbia. While political and economic disruption and military reformation might render Russia temporarily impotent, if left undisturbed in sorting out her problems, before long Russia could well emerge as the new force to be reckoned with in Europe, certainly a force that Austria would find irresistible. So while in early 1913 Germany had no desire to see Austria-Hungary go to war with Serbia, before the year was out her attitude had changed, and though the German ambassador to Vienna, Baron von Tschirschky, despairingly wrote to Berlin, "I constantly wonder whether it really pays to bind ourselves so tightly to this creaking phantasm of a state which is cracking in every direction," the truth of Germany's position was summed up by the German Chancellor, von Bethmann-Hollweg, when he declared "Our own vital interests demand the preservation of Austria."

Nor was Austria unwilling to exploit Germany's vulnerability. Constant reiteration—and careful exaggeration—of the threat that Serbia posed to Austria-Hungary, and by implication the Triple Alliance, had caused the little Slavic kingdom to become almost as great a bogeyman to the Germans as to the Austrians, particularly to the German Emperor, Kaiser Wilhelm II, who was rather excitable by nature. Of course Wilhelm, along with his generals, was looking not merely at Serbia, but past her as well, to Russia. They could sense the inevitability of a shift in the European balance of power once the Russian reforms had taken hold, and so began urging Austria to take decisive action against Serbia before that time came. In mid-May 1914 the Chief of the German General Staff, General Helmuth von Moltke, met with his Austrian counterpart, Conrad von Hötzendorf, in Karlsbad, where they discussed joint strategy. Conrad later recorded in his diary that von Moltke had "expressed the opinion that every delay meant a lessening of our chances" in a war against Serbia and Russia. Two weeks later Kaiser Wilhelm met with Archduke Franz Ferdinand at one of the Archduke's estates in Bohemia, where they deliberated over what Austria's best method of dealing with Serbia would be. Both men agreed that Russia could not be ignored, but it was Franz Ferdinand's considered opinion that Russia's internal problems were still too great for the Tsar to contemplate going to war over Serbia.

A month later, the Archduke was in the mountains of Bosnia, observing army operations. The maneuvers had a two-fold purpose: not only were they meant to test the readiness of units stationed in the Empire's southern military districts, they also were intended to intimidate the Serbian government, by flexing what was hoped would be perceived as an iron fist inside the velvet glove of peacetime maneuvers. At the same time, in what was meant as a placating gesture to the people of Bosnia, one which would, it was hoped, mute the threat implied in the army maneuvers, Franz Ferdinand consented to visit the Bosnian capital of Sarajevo on June 28, 1914, accompanied by his wife, Sophie. . . .

So it was that when the news of the two murders in Sarajevo broke across the capitals of Europe, the leaders of the Great Powers braced themselves for Vienna's reaction, which was sure to be violent. Still, no one expected that a showdown between Austria-Hungary and Serbia would amount to more than a tempest in a teapot; certainly no one imagined that it could grow into more than a localized confrontation. Everyone knew that Serbia would be punished, and for the most part believed that she should be punished: there was little sympathy for the tiny kingdom at that point—its actions had been far too provocative for far too long. Austria-Hungary was perceived to be well within her rights to exact a severe judgement against the Serbs, and most of the peoples and leaders of the Great Powers were prepared to stand thoughtfully aside as Vienna thrashed Belgrade.

Apart, almost aloof, from all of this stood Great Britain. Her staff talks with France notwithstanding, there was no binding commitment on the part of the British Empire to intervene in a European war on anybody's side. There was nothing in the *contretemps* between Vienna and Belgrade which remotely threatened or even involved British interests. In the summer of 1914, the focus of the British government—and the British people—was not on the Continent, but instead on the northern quarter of Ireland, which threatened to explode in civil war. Home Rule for Ireland had finally passed through Parliament and into law, and the six predominantly Protestant counties of northern Ireland had declared their refusal to recognize any attempt at rule from Catholic Dublin. When using the Army to coerce the six counties to accept Dublin's authority was deliberated, the Government was informed that the loyalty of the officers and other ranks was by no means guaranteed: it was likely that units would refuse to obey *en masse* if the order were given to open fire on the protesting Ulstermen.

It was this crisis which held the attention of the Cabinet of Prime Minister Herbert Asquith during the month of July 1914. While the gravity of the crisis that had erupted in Central Europe was fully appreciated in London, Asquith was convinced that there would be no cause for Britain to become involved. He had reason for such confidence, given how, when Europe had stood on the brink of war in the previous decade, the Great Powers had ultimately stepped back as diplomacy intervened; there was no reason to believe the same solution would not prevail again. Equally important to Asquith's reasoning was that the crisis seemed likely to be confined to Austria and Serbia, or possibly Austria, Serbia, and Russia. Should war come, and Germany and France become involved, there was still nothing to compel Britain to become a combatant. Foreign Minister Sir Edward Grey made it perfectly clear that the terms of the Entente, as well as the naval and military staff talks between Britain and France, had in no way committed Britain to act on France's behalf in the event of a European war. For a number of reasons, then, the war, if war came, could almost certainly be contained, limited to the Balkans: there was every reason to believe that there would be no cause for all of the Great Powers to leap first to arms, then at each others' throats.

Despite the later perception of Europe being a "powderkeg" or "tinderbox" awaiting only a spark before it erupted in a Continent-wide conflagration, none of the Great Powers were in a headlong rush toward self-destruction. The vials of wrath were indeed full, but they were not yet full to overflowing. All of the Great Powers—France, Russia, Austria-Hungary, Great Britain, and Germany—were prepared to accept a war with one or more of the other Great Powers, if that war were thrust upon them, in order to attain their national policies, or maintain their territorial integrity, national honor, or national identity. Provoking a war in order to achieve those ends was something else entirely, however—for all but one of them. For one of the Great Powers of Europe had, for half-a century, embraced war as a legitimate means of achieving national goals, not as a last resort when all other options had been exhausted, but as the preferred method of accomplishing those goals. Wars had given birth to this nation, and its leaders believed that only war could sustain it, along with the position of Continental pre-eminence to which those conflicts had brought it. Of all the nations of Europe, only one truly wanted to go to war: Imperial Germany.

Chapter III

COUNSELORS AND KINGS

The first head of state to learn that Austria-Hungary was considering going to war with Serbia was the German Emperor, Kaiser Wilhelm II, a man who was simultaneously one of the most intriguing, baffling, fascinating, and repulsive—not to say preposterous—of all modern European monarchs. Many, though by no means all, of the blunders, misunderstandings, evasions and outright deceptions that would take place over the next thirty days would be a consequence of or attributable to Wilhelm's erratic personality, incessant warmonger-ing, and incipient paranoia. Historian William Manchester once tellingly remarked that, "Time has blurred the sharp edges of Wilhelmine Germany, but it hasn't done much for the image of Wilhelm himself." Part Caesar, part buffoon, at one moment a wise, conciliatory statesman, the next a childish autocrat prone to temper tantrums, Wilhelm's mercurial nature would loom large in the waning weeks of peace that followed the murders in Sarajevo.

The German Empire's third Kaiser, Wilhelm II, would also be its last. Born in Potsdam in 1859, Wilhelm was the son of the tragic Friedrich III, whose abbreviated reign was cut short by throat cancer, and Princess Victoria, the eldest daughter of Queen Victoria of Great Britain. Brought up in a strict and authoritarian household, Wilhelm was by all accounts a remarkably intelligent young man, but also noticeably unstable. At birth he suffered an injury to his left arm, which

consequently never developed properly, remaining withered and minia-
turized; the humiliation caused by this disfigurement—along with his
efforts to compensate for it—would prove to be the underlying cause of
much if not all of Wilhelm's bombastic and sometimes irrational
behavior throughout his life. His education, first at the Kassel
Gymnasium and then at the University of Bonn, was marked more by
his willingness to only exert himself in subjects he liked than for consistently brilliant performance, despite his readily apparent intellect. It was
a trait which would mark much of his reign as well.

Wilhelm became emperor of Germany in 1888 when Friedrich III
died after only ninety-nine days on the throne. Unlike his father, who
had hoped to transform Germany into a constitutional monarchy along
the lines of Great Britain, the new Emperor was a convinced autocrat,
firmly believing that he reigned by Divine Right, a belief that had been
carefully cultivated by conservative and reactionary elements at court
and within the Imperial government. Consequently, Wilhelm had little
use for parliaments in any form, and regarded his own Reichstag as
little more than a collection of interfering windbags. Tragically for
Wilhelm, and eventually for Europe as a whole, the peculiar nature of
the Imperial German constitution gave the Kaiser ultimate authority in
almost every aspect of Imperial policy, so there was little the Reichstag
could do to exert a moderating influence on him.

At the time of Wilhelm's accession Otto von Bismarck was still
Reich Chancellor, and the guiding power behind Germany's foreign
and domestic policies. While still a powerful force in German politics,
the aging Bismarck was unable to wield the same sort of influence
over the new Kaiser as he had over Wilhelm I and Friedrich III.
Believing—incorrectly—that the first two Kaisers had been little more
than rubber stamps for Bismarck and his policies, Wilhelm II began
to make it known that henceforth the policies, foreign and domestic,
of the German Empire would be his, not the Chancellor's, a situation
the headstrong Bismarck found intolerable. A two-year-long battle of
wills ensued, but the outcome was foregone: in early 1890 the tired
and aging Bismarck was dismissed from office, his place taken by a
succession of non-entities who frequently found themselves and their
decisions overwhelmed by the force of the Kaiser's personality.

The overarching characteristic of Wilhelm's persona was his

bombastic militarism: an observer once remarked that "he never stopped playing war." It would be no exaggeration at all to say that he genuinely loved the panoply and trappings of war, if not actual warfare itself. He militarized everything: his personal servants were assigned military ranks, as were his ministers and many government functionaries. Wilhelm almost always appeared in public in uniform—his personal wardrobe contained over two hundred uniforms and required the full-time services of twelve valets. One of his favorite diversions was to attend test shootings at the target range at Meppen, in Hanover, owned by Krupp, the mammoth armaments manufacturing firm based in Esssen. There he could enjoy the sights and sounds of real artillery pieces firing, real shells exploding, real targets being obliterated. In no small way Wilhelm's rampant militarism was a way of compensating for the handicap—emotional as well as physical—of his withered left arm. A just as important thought was that it was also an expression of a rising paranoia in his character, a trait he shared with many other Germans, both within and without the government. The ententes concluded by Great Britain with France and Russia in 1904 and 1907 were recognized by every other European power, including Austria-Hungary, as nothing more than diplomatic resolutions of long-standing disputes, misunderstandings, and mutual irritations, leaving each government involved to pursue more pressing issues at home and abroad. Not so Wilhelm or his government—or indeed much of the German nation. Because the ententes had been concluded between the two nations that Germany regarded as her most likely enemies in any future war, it appeared to Wilhelm, who was suspicious by nature, that the British had joined the French and Russians in an effort to diplomatically and military isolate Germany, "encircling" her with hostile powers. Consequently, his aggressively militaristic posturing was an attempt to intimidate those Powers whom he believed had maliciously aligned themselves against Germany.

Thus, every public event, be it a banquet for a visiting foreign dignitary, the unveiling of a new monument, or the dedication of a new public building, was a forum for Wilhelm to espouse the virtues of military strength and preparedness. To Wilhelm it was a simple equation, really: the German Empire had come into being through feats of German arms; only overwhelming military strength could ensure the Empire's continued existence. Wilhelm was fervent in his efforts to continue increasing the strength of Germany's army throughout his reign, and he was even willing to risk antagonizing and permanently alienating Great Britain by attempting to build a German battlefleet that could challenge the supremacy of the Royal Navy in order to enhance Germany's—as well as his own—power, prestige, and influence, a decision which would ultimately cost him and his Empire dearly.

Wilhelm first learned of Vienna's warlike intentions on the morning of July 5, when the Austrian Ambassador to Berlin, Count Ladislaus Szögyény-Marich called the German Foreign Ministry on the *Wilhelmstrasse*, announcing that he had a personal communication for Wilhelm from Emperor Franz Josef. An invitation to lunch with the Kaiser and the Kaiserin was immediately arranged, and Szögyény dutifully arrived at Berlin's New Palace at noon.

After introductions were made, the Count wordlessly handed the letter to Wilhelm, who read it in silence. It was, for Franz Josef, an astonishing communication, both for its bluntness and its belligerence:

> The crime against my nephew is the direct consequence of the agitation carried out by Russian and Serbian Pan-Slavists whose sole aim is to weaken the Triple Alliance and shatter my Empire. The bloody deed was not the work of a single individual but a well-organized plot whose threads extend to Belgrade. Though it may be impossible to prove the complicity of the Serbian Government, there can be no doubt that its policy of uniting all Southern Slavs under the Serbian flag encourages such crimes and that the continuation of this situation is a chronic peril for my House and my territories. My efforts must be directed to isolating Serbia and reducing her size.

Franz Josef then closed the letter with a pointedly direct question for Wilhelm: what would Germany do should Austria-Hungary choose to "punish. . . this center of criminal agitation in Belgrade?"

By the polite, restrained standards of pre-war diplomacy, Franz Josef's letter was a bombshell. There were none of the delicately structured phrases or careful circumlocutions to which diplomats were devoted, giving them room for maneuver and compromise; nor was there any hint of any desire for arbitration by anyone in Vienna. Instead Franz Josef was announcing that he was prepared to give Field Marshal Conrad the green light to launch an offensive intended to crush Serbia, then, once the war was over, he was determined to reduce Serbia to geographic and political insignificance. The note did not even seek German approval for such an action—all that it asked was a clear answer whether or not Germany would stand with Austria-Hungary once war on Serbia was declared.

The choice that Wilhelm would make in replying to Franz Josef would be the defining moment for him and Germany. Arrogant, dynamic, erratic, brash, impetuous, enamored of warfare and all things military, the Kaiser in many ways personified his Empire. Unlike Austria-Hungary, whose five centuries of history and tradition allowed Franz Josef to wear the crown of the Dual Monarchy with a quiet self-assurance, the German Empire was very much the *arriviste* among the Great Powers of Europe, of which made Wilhelm painfully self-conscious. He once remarked to King Victor Emmanuel of Italy that in "All the long years of my reign, my colleagues, the Monarchs of Europe, have paid no attention to what I have to say."

Between 1865 and 1871, the kingdom of Prussia, under the guidance of King Wilhelm I and his ambitious and astute Chancellor, Otto von Bismarck, had fought a series of short, sharp wars with, in succession, Denmark, Austria, and France. The result of these "wars of unification" was that a collection of thirty-eight small kingdoms, duchies, principalities, and free cities were amalgamated into the German Empire, with Wilhelm I crowned as its first Emperor, or Kaiser. These feats of arms gave the newborn empire military and political supremacy in Central and Western Europe, while a penchant for hard work and efficiency that was the complete antithesis of the Austrians allowed German workers and industrialists to spawn an economy that was second only to that of the British Empire.

Yet, despite these achievements, as well as their accomplishments in science, medicine and music, the Germans still felt that the other European powers weren't giving them their due respect. When Wilhelm himself complained that when the British aristocracy toured the Continent, they would flock to Paris and shun Berlin, he was only giving voice to a slight shared by all of his countrymen, who could never comprehend the vast appeal that the vibrant, decadent French capital had over Germany's stuffy and strait-laced chief city. The philosophies of Nietzsche and Treitschke, that of the *Übermensch* and the arch-nationalist, fed a growing belief among the Germans that Teutonic blood was superior, and that by right Germany was entitled to primacy of place in the world order. German diplomacy became characterized not by endeavors at cooperation and conciliation but by outright threats and blandishments of force intended to extract concession through intimidation. Barbara Tuchman succinctly described it this way: "In German practice [Theodore] Roosevelt's current precept for getting on with your neighbors was Teutonized to, 'Speak loudly and brandish a big gun.'"

It was an attitude predictably guaranteed to alienate rather than endear, and the more overtly it was displayed, the more Germany's neighbors began to believe that one by-product of the easy victories of 1865, 1866, and 1871 was a form of national self-delusion regarding Germany's proper place in the world. The frequent German assertions of superiority became ever more strident with each iteration. When the Boxer Rebellion broke out in China in 1900, the German troops dispatched by Wilhelm to relieve the besieged European embassies in what was still called Peking were charged by the Kaiser to model their conduct on Attila's Huns when they met the Chinese in combat. (It was a poor choice, as "Hun" became a pejorative that would haunt the Germans for the next half-century.) Clamoring for their "place in the sun," when Germany entered the last mad scramble for colonies in Africa and the Far East, ultra-nationalistic societies such as the *Alldeutscher Verband* (Pan German Union) and the Navy League believed that the other European powers were obligated to simply concede to Germany on demand what those nations had acquired through outpourings of blood and treasure. It appeared to her neighbors that Germany was determined to deliberately affront even those powers who had been disposed to be friendly. In 1905, despite earlier attempts by Great Britain in 1899 and again in 1901 to form an alliance with Germany, the Reichstag, responding to the megalomaniacal goading of Admiral Alfred von Tirpitz, passed a law authorizing the construction of a High Seas Fleet that would challenge the supremacy of the Royal Navy, a threat to which Great Britain could never be reconciled nor could ignore. From that date onward, British naval and military planning was formulated with the idea that the most likely of Britain's enemies in a European war would be Germany.

Beguiled by their own bluster, neither the German people nor their leaders understood the antagonisms their actions and attitudes provoked. Of course the continued hostility of France was taken as inevitable, it never having occurred to the Kaiser or Reichstag that to continue to administer Alsace and Lorraine as occupied territories, rather than formally incorporating them into the German Empire, merely poured salt in France's great open wound. What was inexplicable to the Germans was how such dissimilar nations as republican France and autocratic Russia could formulate an alliance—or how Great Britain could achieve an *entente* with both of her traditional foes in order to focus her energies on defending against what was perceived as the greater Teutonic threat. Even while German bombast was driving such unlikely partners into understandings, the only explanation that seemed acceptable to the Kaiser and his people was that the nations surrounding Germany were formulating a policy of political and military encirclement (*Einkreisung*) of Germany in order to deny the Germans their rightful place as masters of the world.

It was with the thought of breaking that circle, either by diplomatic or, preferably, military means that German policy was formulated. The most famous and extreme extension of that policy would, of course, be the Schlieffen Plan, which supposedly would enable Germany to defeat France in a military campaign lasting not more than six weeks, allowing the entire might of the German Army to then be turned on the presumably hapless forces of Imperial Russia. However, it wasn't necessary to go to that extreme—any diplomatic setback severe enough to give Russia cause to rethink her commitment to the Franco-Russian alliance would effectively break it down, ending the dreaded encirclement of the Reich.

It was with this eventuality in mind that Wilhelm pondered his reply to Franz Josef's letter. At first Wilhelm was cautious, deferring any decision until he had consulted with his Chancellor, von

Bethmann-Hollweg, about what Wilhelm termed "serious European complications"—which meant, of course, the question of what Russia's reaction would be. As the afternoon passed, though, Wilhelm displayed one of those mercurial shifts in attitude which were the despair of his Foreign Ministry as well as most of his European neighbors. Suddenly becoming more bellicose in his attitude toward Serbia when, after lunch he was pressed by Szögyény for a firm reply, Wilhelm assured him that Austria could "rely on Germany's full support" for whatever actions Austria chose to undertake, adding that in his opinion such action "must not be long delayed." Concerns about Russia were quickly dismissed: according to Szögyény, Wilhelm said that "Russia's attitude will no doubt be hostile, but for this we have been prepared for years." Austria could rest assured that Germany, "her old, faithful ally, would stand at her side." Wilhelm concluded by flatly declaring that "Russia is in no way prepared for war."

It was a pivotal, fateful moment in history: without restraint or condition, Wilhelm had given Austria-Hungary what amounted to a "blank check" of support in Austria's plan to extinguish Serbia. Should his assessment of Russian capabilities be wrong, he was risking war between Germany and Russia, and in so doing, risked war between Germany and France, Russia's ally, as well. After his lunch with Szögyény, the Kaiser met with his minister of war, Field Marshal von Falkenhayn, and other military advisors, informing them of Franz Josef's note, Austria's intentions toward Serbia, and his own decision to support his fellow monarch. He was quite blunt in informing them that if "the Russians refused to tolerate this, Austria would not be disposed to give way." The officers all agreed that the Kaiser's decision had been the proper one: not only was Russia unprepared for war, it seemed unthinkable that the Tsar would openly side with a band of regicides. Even if he did, the German Army would defeat the Russian Army so resoundingly that the debacles of the Russo-Japanese War in 1905 would seem a mere bagatelle by comparison. Wilhelm, in yet another of his wide swings of emotion, suddenly grew cautious and inquired of Falkenhayn whether the German Army was prepared should something go wrong and war break out. Falkenhayn assured the Kaiser that the army was "ready for all eventualities," then asked if any preparations should be made.

Wilhelm considered this for a moment, then declared that a war with France and Russia was unlikely—there was no need for the army or navy to take any action.

Meanwhile, Count Szögyény had cabled Vienna with a summary of his conversation with the Kaiser, emphasizing Wilhelm's unconditional endorsement of any action the Austrians chose to take against Serbia. Arriving at the Austrian Foreign Ministry at almost the same time was a second cable, this one from Count Hoyos, Foreign Minister Berchtold's personal representative who had been meeting with Arthur Zimmermann, Germany's Undersecretary of State. Hoyos' telegram made it clear that the Kaiser's decision accurately reflected the prevailing opinion in the *Wilhelmstrasse*, further bolstering Berchtold's militant position. In Vienna, it was clear, the "war party" now had a firm grip on the reins.

Astonishingly, the following morning, when Wilhelm's decision was communicated to his Imperial Chancellor, Theobald von Bethmann-Hollweg, the Imperial Chancellor wholeheartedly endorsed it. This was a lapse of judgment, if indeed a lapse it was, which the Chancellor would be unable to explain for the rest of his life. Von Bethmann-Hollweg's failure, if not outright refusal, to moderate Wilhelm's sweeping assurances of support made to Ambassador Szögyény was the first great turning point in the developing crisis. By offering Germany's unqualified support to Austria in whatever course of action Vienna chose to take against Serbia, Wilhelm effectively gave up any opportunity Germany might have had to exert a moderating or restraining influence on Austria-Hungary. Given Wilhelm's impetuous nature, that he should fail to grasp the significance of what he had done is not surprising; that von Bethmann-Hollweg should allow this affirmation of German support for Austria-Hungary to stand appears to be an inexplicable dereliction of duty. The Chancellor himself later tried to excuse this lapse by saying that he felt, given the present mood in Europe, Austria-Hungary had a unique opportunity to strike at Serbia, while the rest of the Continent was still angry and sympathetic over the assassinations.

Here von Bethmann-Hollweg was being disingenuous: while Wilhelm was most assuredly not a politician, the Chancellor was the consummate political animal. Consequently, he understood the complexity and fragility of the political circumstances entangling

Austria-Hungary, Serbia, and Russia, and knew that an Austrian attack on Serbia was virtually certain to provoke a Russian declaration of war on Austria, compelling Germany to go to war with Russia in support of her Austrian ally. He knew all this and was fully prepared to risk such a war, for he was playing a very cagey game. Using the Kaiser's declaration that the preservation of the Hapsburg monarchy and the territorial integrity of Austria-Hungary were vital to Germany's own interests as a smokescreen, von Bethmann-Hollweg was privately looking to external events to distract attention from the German Empire's internal stresses, which he believed threatened to bring down the Empire.

Theobald von Bethmann-Hollweg had become the Imperial German Chancellor in 1909, succeeding Bernhard von Bülow. Originally planning a career in law, he studied at Strasbourg, Leipzig and Berlin, but, apparently motivated by a family sense of duty (von Bethmann-Hollwegs had been serving the state in some capacity since the middle of the seventeenth century), he ultimately chose instead to enter the Prussian civil service. His first position of note was his two-year appointment as the Prussian Minister of the Interior in 1905, followed by two years as state secretary in the Imperial Office of the Interior. It was during this time that von Bülow began grooming von Bethmann-Hollweg to be his successor as Chancellor. When he succeeded von Bülow in July 1909, von Bethmann-Hollweg adopted a political outlook which, for a German aristocrat, was rather liberal for that day, and worked quite hard to maintain a sense of social and political cohesion between the increasingly vocal liberal elite on one hand and the conservative Junker aristocracy, as well as the military, on the other. He was constantly being confronted by political extremes from both left and right, and while he tried to govern by compromise and conciliation, he too often appeared to swing from one view to the other, so that neither liberals nor conservatives entirely trusted him.

The German Army High Command in particular viewed von Bethmann-Hollweg with undisguised suspicion, specifically for his repeated attempts to control the Imperial budget by limiting the expenditures for armaments and expansion of the standing army. He also ran afoul of the German Navy in 1912 and when, after almost three years of painstaking negotiation with the British, a compromise was reached putting a brake on the horrendously expensive naval race, it was unceremoniously crushed by the Secretary of the Navy, Admiral Alfred von Tirpitz, who in turn was supported by the Kaiser.

Despite his aristocratic heritage and preferences—he was never genuinely enthusiastic for parliamentary government—von Bethmann-Hollweg accepted that he had to work with the growing democratic elements within German society and politics. He was convinced that in order to preserve the entity of the German Empire, a constitutional monarchy, however distasteful the idea might seem to the Kaiser and the more reactionary aristocracy, was inevitable. To the Chancellor, the 1912 elections, which had resulted in the return of 110 socialist deputies to the Reichstag, nearly a quarter of the legislature's membership, was a vision of the future. It was a warning that the rising power—and threat—of the working classes could no longer be ignored, and he attempted to appease the more radical liberals with election reform and social legislation lest they start openly agitating to abolish the monarchy outright.

This then was the background of von Bethmann-Hollweg's decision to unquestioningly endorse the Kaiser's decision to issue the "blank check" to Austria-Hungary; he feared any action—or inaction—which might result in a loss of prestige for the House of Hapsburg, for it could be perceived as a weakening of Imperial authority, the precursor to Austria-Hungary's disintegration. Revolution in Vienna might then, as it did in 1848, spread to Berlin, bringing down the German Empire. Von Bethmann-Hollweg knew that in the situation that was developing, war with Russia was almost inescapable, but he also believed that it was a war Germany could, and would, win. War with Russia (and possibly France) would have the added benefit of being widely, if not universally, popular at home, reviving public support for the monarchy and the institutions of the Empire, restoring some measure of political and social stability—that is, the maintenance of the social and political *status quo ante bellum.*

Reassured by his chancellor's endorsement of his decision, Wilhelm announced on the afternoon of July 6 that he would proceed with his planned summer cruise of the Norwegian fjords, followed by the annual exercises in the North Sea by the German High Seas Fleet. When he departed Berlin the next morning, he declared to a senior navy official that "he did not believe there would be any further military developments." It was a belief in which he was encouraged by both von Bethmann-Hollweg and the Foreign Minister, Gottlieb von Jagow, who was a near-non-entity, weak-willed and lacking ambition or vision, cheerfully prepared to rubber-stamp any decision made by his superiors. It was important to get the Kaiser out of the way, for von Bethmann-Hollweg and von Jagow in Berlin, along with Berchtold and Tisza in Vienna, were about to engage in a monstrous deception of the whole of Europe. No one was to know that Austria-Hungary and Germany were each preparing for war—Austria-Hungary for war with Serbia and possibly Russia, Germany for war with Russia and possibly France. Above all, the Tsar must be given no reason to suspect that war was looming on the horizon.

It is difficult not to not feel a certain sympathy for Nicholas II, Tsar of Russia: knowledge of the sad fate which awaited him and his family in 1918 causes him to be surrounded with an air of tragedy. Yet the great tragedy of Nicholas II was not that he and his family would be brutally executed by the Bolsheviks simply because he had been the Tsar, but rather that he had ever been the Tsar at all. Fundamentally a good, decent man who was devoted to his wife and family, he was con-scientious and dedicated, and took his responsibilities very seriously, even if he executed them poorly. He would have made an ideal Austrian or German mid-level civil servant, an admirable factory manager in France, or a perfect bank supervisor in England. As the Tsar of All the Russias, the Supreme Autocrat ruling over a nation of more than one hundred million people during the greatest crisis in his nation's history, he was doomed by his very nature to tragic failure.

Nicholas was born on May 18, 1868; his father was Emperor Alexander III, his mother the Danish-born Empress Maria Fyodorovna. Taught by a succession of royal tutors, Nicholas' formal education was completed before he reached the age of twenty. He was not an extraordinarily bright man, though he was far from stupid—Barbara Tuchman's characterization of him as having "an intellect so shallow as to be almost entirely surface" is erroneous to the point of being slanderous. What would plague his rule was not his intellectu-al limits, rather those of his character. While he believed that he ruled by Divine Right, what Nicholas lacked was that iron will required of anyone who aspires to rule as an autocrat.

To much of Russia and the world, Nicholas' father was the embodiment of a Russian monarch: physically imposing, resolute and authoritarian in nature, it was clear to anyone whom he met that he was truly born to rule. Nicholas, for his part, lived in his father's shadow, never insisting that he be properly taught how to reign and rule, in anticipation of the day when he would become Tsar, and never making any serious effort to learn those necessities on his own. At the same time, Alexander was simply too busy to spend time instructing Nicholas in the duties which he would one day inherit. Consequently, when he came to the throne in November 1894, after Alexander unexpectedly died from liver disease, Nicholas was completely unprepared for his accession. Just twenty-six years old, Nicholas had been something of a royal playboy, keeping a mistress (one of the dancers in the Imperial ballet), and spending his time indulging in the pursuits of the day enjoyed by royalty the world over: parties, theater, hunting, shooting and sailing. Few of his predecessors had ever ascended to the Romanov throne as poorly prepared as Nicholas for the duties and responsibilities of being Tsar. (Just as "kaiser" is in German, "tsar" is a rendering of "Cæsar" in Russian, bringing with it all the power and pitfalls that the name implies.)

Accession to the throne did bring some notable changes in him. He abandoned his mistress and his playboy ways, and the same year he became Tsar he married Princess Alix of Hesse-Darmstadt, the granddaughter of Britain's Queen Victoria. From beginning to end, their marriage was unquestionably a love match, and again had Nicholas been anyone but the Russian Emperor, their romance would have been memorable only for its strength and devotion. However, Alexandra, who took the name when she converted to Russian Orthodoxy upon accepting Nicholas' proposal, became something of a religious fanatic, devoutly believing in autocratic principles, even more convinced than was the Tsar himself that he ruled by Divine Right. As a result Alexandra brought considerable pressure to bear upon Nicholas to resist the rising tide of sentiment among the Russian people for more representative and responsible government among Russia's upper and middle classes, instead cultivating a passionate belief in the loyalty of the Russian masses. Nicholas, admittedly, required little persuasion: tradition-bound and suspicious of foreign influences, he had little use for the institutions of western democracy.

Because of her German birth, Alexandra was unpopular with the Russian aristocracy. (In those days, one of the most vicious insults one Russian could hurl at another was to call him a "stupid German.") Their antipathy grew as it became clear that she exerted a greater influence over her husband than did any of the Russian elite. Here Nicholas' own character began to betray him: solitary and shy, he had no intimate friends, no one with whom he could ever, even for a moment, cease to be Tsar and simply be Nicholas Romanov. No one that is save his wife; they had four daughters, all of whom they adored, before the birth of the long-awaited Tsarevitch, the heir to the throne, Alexis.

Alexis had hemophilia, however, an incurable and often painful condition where uncontrolled bleeding would occur when he received an injury, no matter how minor. It was a condition beyond the doctors of the day to cure (it still is), but for reasons never fully explained, an obscure Russian monk, Gregory Rasputin, possessed the ability to contain and ultimately halt the Tsarevitch's bleeding incidents when they occurred. In 1905 Rasputin was presented to the Royal couple, and soon his ability to relieve the effects of Alexis' frequent attacks gave him tremendous influence over Alexandra. This influence grew as the Tsarina became convinced that he was not only a gifted spiritual healer but that he was also the voice of the loyal Russian peasantry.

The Tsarevitch's condition gradually undermined Alexandra's health while at the same time exacerbating her already high-strung personality. Emotionally she became increasingly unstable and sometimes hysterical, while physically she became something of a hypochondriac. As her own condition deteriorated, Alexandra increasingly turned to Rasputin for comfort, counsel and guidance, and in turn passed on his advice to the Tsar, who, already influenced himself by the monk's power to comfort his son, usually accepted it without question. At the same time, the Tsarina was becoming something of a religious mystic herself, and as her religious convictions grew so did her belief that preserving the autocracy—concentrating absolute power in the hands of the Tsar—was the only way to preserve the Russian Empire. It was a belief that Nicholas shared as well, though his reasons were more pragmatic. He was convinced that the only alternative to autocratic rule was socialist revolution, and he held constitutional monarchies such as that of Great Britain, where his English cousins reigned but did not rule, in the deepest contempt. Nicholas' advisers agreed with him, believing that the Russian Empire, as much in its way an ethnic patchwork-quilt as was Austria-Hungary, could only be held together by author-itarian rule: liberal or democratic government would only lead to the Empire's dissolution.

The problem was that Nicholas was an ineffective ruler: by its nature autocracy demands that the monarch play an active, vigorous role in the day to day functioning of his government. This Nicholas never did. He was never able to enforce cooperation between his ministers, yet would not suffer a dilution of his own power by appointing a proper Prime Minister. The sheer size of Russia and the massive scale of the bureaucracy required to run it, along with the multitude of complex issues confronting the empire was a burden which would have taxed the energy of Peter the Great, let alone the narrow shoulders of Nicholas II.

Russia was in the midst of an unprecedented industrial expansion throughout Nicholas II's reign, and with economic modernization came the problems of any emerging industrialized nation: poor working conditions and low wages led to violence between workers and industrialists, which often saw the army brought in to restore order. Unions lacked recognition and rights, while worker morale was low—discipline and productivity both suffered as a result. In the countryside, tensions also grew between nobles and peasants, as the newly liberated peasants (Alexander II had freed the serfs in 1878) sought to claim some of the lands they had formerly worked for the nobility for themselves.

It was Nicholas himself who caused the unrest to escalate into revolution in 1905. Determined that Russia should receive a share of the spoils as the European powers carved up China in the wake of the Boxer Rebellion at the turn of the century, Nicholas' expansionist policy in Manchuria and Korea ran afoul of Japan's imperialistic ambitions in 1904. The result was the Russo-Japanese War of 1904–05, where Russia suffered an ignominious defeat at the hands of the upstart power of Japan. The international humiliation was terrible, as an apparently modern European army and navy had been crushed by a supposedly inferior Oriental race. At home, the war destroyed much of monarchy's credibility: protests began when in 1904 over one hundred thousand workers in St. Petersburg went on a four-day strike to protest the declining value of wages. An appeal was made to the Tsar, but in January 1905, when a peaceful march was made on the Winter Palace, it was greeted with gunfire from formed troops: more than one hundred of the petitioners were killed and hundreds more wounded. The incident became known as "Bloody Sunday" and sparked the 1905 Revolution, a convulsion across Imperial Russia where strikes spread around the country and mutiny erupted in the army and navy.

Nicholas grudgingly responded by granting basic freedoms which the rest of Europe had long taken for granted: freedom of speech and assembly, freedom of conscience, and an end to imprisonment without trial. Additionally, he announced, no new laws would be enacted without the approval of the Duma, a elected, representative body with consultative authority. The first serious cracks in the facade of Russian autocracy had appeared, though they were quickly papered over.

When the Duma attempted to assert a legislative authority it did not possess by demanding sweeping social and agrarian reform, Nicholas dissolved it, as he did with its successor. By the time the Third and Fourth Dumas were seated, Russian parliamentarians had learned their lessons and moderated their demands and their rhetoric. However, the damage had been done: Nicholas now had the reputation of being the unrepentant opponent of any form of responsible government in Russia.

More pointedly, the failures of the Russian Army and Navy in the Russo-Japanese War, along with the mutinies that accompanied the 1905 Revolution, had saddled Russia with the burden of appearing feeble, having become a *quantite negligibles* in European politics. If for no other reason than to restore the Empire's lost prestige, Russia—and Nicholas—could never again afford to appear weak or irresolute. Nicholas had no love for regicides, but he understood, when news reached St. Petersburg that Austria was preparing to go to war with Serbia, that if Russia were to retain her role of leadership with the Slavic peoples of the Balkans, she would have to stand beside the Serbs.

In giving shape to this determination, Nicholas relied heavily on his Foreign Minister, Sergei Dmitrievich Sazonov. In the summer of 1914 Sazonov was fifty-four years old, having served as Russia's Foreign Minister since 1910, earlier holding a series of appointments in Russian embassies in London, Washington and the Vatican. He was the Tsar's Deputy Foreign Minister when Alexander Izvolsky was forced to resign in disgrace in 1910 in the aftermath of the crisis following Austria-Hungary's annexation of Bosnia-Herzegovina; Sazonov immediately stepped into his erstwhile-superior Izvolsky's vacant position.

From the outset Sazonov was determined to bind the three Entente Powers—France, Russia, and Britain—closer together, encouraging both military and naval cooperation in an effort to contain an increasingly belligerent Germany; at the same time he was not blind to the benefits of improving Russia's relations with Germany wherever possible. Wilhelm II's refusal to renew the Reinsurance Treaty, with its implication that Russia had been marginalized in international affairs, still rankled in Moscow, particularly after the humiliations of the Russo-Japanese War seemed to confirm that opinion. Sazonov understood the need to reassert Russia's international position, but was careful to do so only when he was confident of success; wrapping Imperial Russia in the mantle of the protector of the Slavic peoples of the Balkans seemed to be a realistic beginning. However, knowing in 1912 and 1913 that the military reforms instituted in the wake of Russia's defeat by Japan were only just starting to take effect, he advised the Tsar to keep Russia out of the Balkan Wars, counsel of considerable wisdom which Nicholas gladly accepted and followed.

In July 1914, though, the situation was once again changing. Russia's rail network was vastly improving, her armaments industry was growing at a prodigious rate, and improvements in equipment and training were transforming the Russian Army into an even more formidable force than it had been in 1905. (The Japanese had been able to defeat the Russian Far East Army not because of any marked demonstration of military skill: in open combat, the Russians and Japanese usually fought each other to a standstill. What doomed the Russian Army in Korea and Manchuria was that the Russian Navy had performed so miserably: the Russian Army was dependent on a single, often-unreliable trans-Siberian railway track for its supply, so when the Japanese naval victories cut off all possibility of resupply by sea, the collapse of the Russian Army was a foregone conclusion.) Moreover, the political realities of 1914 were such that Russia could no longer avoid her self-appointed responsibilities in the Balkans: standing aloof from Serbia while the little kingdom was menaced by Austria-Hungary would be certain to lose for Russia what remaining influence it had with the other Slavic nations.

Still, Sazonov was not looking for a war with Austria-Hungary. Ever the realist, he fully expected that the Dual Monarchy would resort to some form of military action, and was willing to communicate this to Vienna. What Russia would find intolerable would be any campaign that threatened Serbia's national identity: Russia would allow Serbia to be punished, she would not stand idly by while Serbia was crushed.

Yet that was precisely what Vienna planned to do. On July 7, after reading the cables from Berlin sent by Counts Szögyény and Hoyos, Prime Minister Tisza convened the Council of the Ministers of the Dual Monarchy. With Germany pledged to support Austria-Hungary, there seemed to be no obstacle to a settling of accounts with Serbia, and within an hour the Council had decided to go to war. Tisza, echoing what he knew would be old Franz Josef's sentiments, demanded that no attack on Serbia take place until and unless an ultimatum had been issued to Belgrade and duly rejected. The minutes of the meeting make for chilling reading, for they are the preamble to Austria-Hungary's death sentence:

> All present except the Royal Hungarian Prime Minister hold the belief that a purely diplomatic success, even should it end in a glaring humiliation of Serbia, would be worthless and that therefore such a stringent demand must be addressed to Serbia that will make refusal almost certain, so that the way to a radical solution by means of military action should be opened.

Barring something miraculous, Austria-Hungary and Serbia were going to go to war. The question now was how many of Europe's Great Powers would follow them.

Chapter IV

WAR PLANS

Emboldened by the Kaiser's assurances, which were quickly confirmed by the German Chancellor, the Austrian government began preparations for its strike against Serbia. At the behest of Count Tisza, the Council of Ministers hastily convened a meeting on July 7, quickly confirming Berchtold's determination to avoid seeking a diplomatic solution to the growing crisis, believing that "even. . . a glaring humiliation of Serbia," would fail to properly assert the dominating position which Austria-Hungary intended to assume over the small Balkan kingdom. The Council concluded that "such a stringent demand must be addressed to Serbia that will make refusal almost certain, so that the road to a radical solution by means of military action should be opened."

Then, despite the almost frantic haste with which the Imperial government had made its decision to go to war, the legendary Austro-Hungarian inertia set in: the next two weeks would be spent preparing the ultimatum to Serbia, but not, curiously, preparing for war. The old Emperor was, in part, to blame for some of the delay: Franz Josef insisted on observing all the details of diplomatic protocol, and refused to order a mobilization before the ultimatum was drafted, sent, and rejected. This was not hypocrisy on the part of the Emperor, however: if there was the slimmest chance that Belgrade might accept Vienna's ultimatum, no matter how humiliating, and so prevent a war from beginning, Franz Josef was willing to pursue it.

At the same time, there was an air of unreality about the almost lackadaisical attitude Vienna adopted toward actually formulating the ultimatum to Serbia. It was almost as if all the urgency in the crisis had been in making the decision to go to war, but none was in the effort needed to implement that decision. It was a curious attitude, for the Austrians were aware that time was not on Vienna's side: swift action against Serbia would be readily understood and appreciated by a sympathetic Europe as just retribution for the murders of Franz Ferdinand and Sophie. It was possible that should Austria-Hungary strike fast, hard, and decisively, the war with Serbia might be over before Russia could effectively intervene. If so, it might be possible to persuade St. Petersburg to refrain from any retaliatory action against Vienna, or to stay out of the conflict entirely. However, the longer Vienna prevaricated, the more the tide of sympathy would ebb, and should Austria-Hungary take too long in exacting its retribution, the more it would appear to the rest of the Continent that Vienna had merely manipulated the incident for its own political ends, rather than as a measure of justice meted out in the name of the slain Archduke and his wife.

On July 9, Berchtold took the report of the Council of Ministers' decision to present Serbia with an unacceptable ultimatum as a pretext for war to the old Emperor. As Tisza knew he would, Franz Josef insisted that all the diplomatic formalities be observed. That same day, von Jagow, the German Foreign Minister, was pressing Count Szögyény in Berlin, telling him that "the proposed action against Serbia. . . should be taken without delay." On July 12, the German Ambassador to Vienna, Count Heinrich von Tschirschky, appeared in Berchtold's office, determined "principally to impress on the Minister once more, emphatically, that quick action was called for." This was the first of a succession of similar visits which would take place over the next week, always with Tschirschky telling Berchtold the same thing—stop wasting time!

It was in one of these meetings that an incident occurred which cast a starkly revealing light on the attitude toward the crisis which then prevailed in Vienna. Count Heinrich von Lützow, a career diplomat with a distinguished service record, dropped in on one of the Berchtold-Tschirschky exchanges and upon hearing them discussing the coming war with Serbia, declared unequivocally that it would lead to a Continent-wide conflict—in his opinion it was "sheer fantasy" to believe that Russia could be kept out of any war involving Austria-Hungary and Serbia. At that point, an unidentified aid of Berchtold's piped up: "So what can happen to us? If it goes wrong, we lose Bosnia and a piece of East Galicia." Or as William Jannen, Jr. put it in *The Lions of July*, "The Hapsburgs, after all, had been picking up and losing pieces of Europe for centuries." Apparently Vienna believed the coming fight with Serbia would be yet another such dynastic property struggle. If so, it was a fatal attitude.

What was becoming clear to the Germans was that Austria-Hungary was completely unprepared for the war she was trying to provoke. Berchtold, in the day between the Council of Ministers' meeting and his audience with Franz Josef, had done nothing in the way of preparing the ultimatum which was to be presented to Belgrade—no rough drafts, no outlines, no list of possible terms, nothing. The next two days were then spent negotiating with Count Tisza over whether the communication sent to Belgrade would take the form of a note followed by an ultimatum, or simply that of an ultimatum. Realizing that there was no political support among the Austrians or the Hungarians for anything short of an ultimatum, on July 15 Tisza accepted the inevitable and set another meeting of the Council of Ministers, this one to give approval to the final draft of the ultimatum, to be held on Sunday, July 19.

In the eyes of the Germans this apparent dawdling was wasting more than just time: not only was the opportunity for a quick, decisive blow against Serbia slipping away, but there was also the fear—in Berlin—that the longer Austria-Hungary took to prepare and deliver the ultimatum, the more the likelihood grew that one or more of the other European powers might learn of it and propose arbitration to resolve the crisis. It was an offer which Serbia would surely embrace; should Austria reject it, she risked losing her image as the injured and aggrieved party and suddenly appearing as a bully intent on harming a much smaller, weaker neighbor. For Germany, intent on using this latest Balkan crisis for her own ends, arbitration would mean the ruin of the plans and ambitions of many of her political and military leaders, among them the Chancellor and the

Chief of Staff of the German Army; it simply could not be allowed to happen.

Fortunately for them, arbitration was equally unacceptable to Berchtold as well: he would go to any length to see his determination to crush Serbia carried through. Since any request to Austria-Hungary for arbitration would have to come through the Foreign Ministry, and Berchtold controlled the Foreign Ministry, he was in a position to not only ignore any such requests, he could also ensure that no word of any such request would reach the other ministries of the Dual Monarchy. In Berlin, von Bethmann-Hollweg and von Jagow were prepared to do the same with their own government. As a result, a quiet collusion between Berlin and Vienna took place whereby a facade of "business as usual" was presented to the outside world while Austria girded herself for war and Germany prepared to support her.

The deception was quite simple: so many of each nation's senior government officials were away from their respective capitals on summer holidays that to all appearances the crisis simmering in the Balkans was only the most minor affair. With so many of the powerful decision-makers away from their offices, the likelihood of war would appear to be so minimal as to be almost non-existent.

The Kaiser, of course, was cruising the fjords of Norway. Von Bethmann-Hollweg, it was reported, had retired to his country estate—what no one knew was that he was frequently traveling in secret to Berlin. Admiral von Tirpitz, the Naval Secretary, was on holiday somewhere in Switzerland; von Jagow, the Foreign Minister, had returned to Berlin on July 9, but that same day the Minister of War, Field Marshal von Falkenhayn, had left for the country; von Moltke, the Chief of the General Staff, was taking a cure in Karlsbad. As the Bavarian Minister to Berlin reported to Münich, these circumstances would, it was believed, allow the Imperial German government to:

> . . . immediately upon presentation of the Austrian ultimatum in Belgrade . . . claim that the Austrian action had been just as much of a surprise to it as to the other Powers, pointing out the fact that the Kaiser is on his northern journey and the Chief of Staff and the War Minister are away on leave of absence.

The situation in Vienna echoed that of Berlin: Emperor Franz Josef had removed himself to his hunting lodge at Bad Ischl; Berchtold and Tisza had each left the capital for one of their country estates; and before he departed Vienna the Foreign Minister had advised General Conrad "It would be a good thing for you and the War Minister to go on leave for a while so as to keep up the appearance that nothing is going on."

Absent from Vienna or not, the next three weeks should have been Conrad's shining moment. Instead it became something of an embarrassment, both to the Dual Monarchy and its Imperial German ally, as the legendary Austro-Hungarian bureaucratic inertia nearly turned what was one of the fundamental functions of Imperial government into something close to a shambles, namely the mobilization of the Austro-Hungarian Army.

Field Marshal Count Franz Conrad von Hötzendorf remains an elusive figure for history to judge. Before the Great War he was widely regarded by military professionals as a shrewd strategist and planner, yet during the war he lost almost every campaign that he commanded. The question remains whether the dubious quality of the Dual Monarchy's army undermined Conrad's brilliance, or if his abilities were simply vastly over-rated before they were actually put to the test. On balance, the evidence seems to support an answer of either, or both.

Certainly he gave every indication of being an energetic, forward-looking senior officer, the very antithesis of the stereotypical, hidebound military reactionary who has become the popular caricature of a First World War general. A small man who never appeared to be completely comfortable in his uniform, at the age of sixty-two he was appointed to the posts of Chief of Staff and Commander-in-Chief of the Austro-Hungarian Army in the summer of 1906. One of the most progressive military men of his day, he was an early and vocal advocate of such novel concepts and technologies as signals intelligence and aerial reconnaissance. From the moment of his appointment Conrad worked hard to transform and modernize the Austrian Army, but was frequently hampered by a combination of a lack of funds and the legendary lethargy of the Imperial bureaucracy.

At the same time, however talented he was as a military commander, Conrad was rather naive politically. Utterly confident that the Austro-Hungarian Army was more than a match for Serbia's forces, he was constantly advocating a so-called "preventative" war against the smaller Balkan kingdom. Likewise, because of an unresolved dispute with Italy over the Tyrol and the city of Trieste, on more than one occasion he wanted to go to war with the Italians. The truth was that Conrad had a very poor grasp of politics, and seemed to misunderstand the realities of how war and politics—as well as their consequences—were intertwined in the Balkans.

In 1911, during Italy's war with Turkey, Conrad's agitation for war with Italy resulted in his being dismissed from his post; he was recalled in December the following year, unrepentant. It was in the July Crisis that his calls for military action against Serbia finally found a receptive audience in the person of Foreign Minister Berchtold. Like Berchtold, Conrad had been a friend of the murdered Archduke, so for him, as with the Foreign Minister, a settling of accounts with Serbia was something of a personal matter as well as a question of national policy.

While Conrad's prewar reputation was built mainly on his talents as a theoretical strategist, his first real test came in the weeks following the Sarajevo murders, as Austria-Hungary's Army mobilized during the last half of July. It cannot be said that he acquitted himself well: the process reflected the single greatest flaw in Conrad's tenure as Chief of Staff—inadequate contingency planning. The mobilization would be poorly managed and the forces assembling on both the Serbian and Russian fronts would be inadequate and unprepared.

"Mobilization" is a term which today is frequently misused and poorly understood. A century ago, however, its meaning and implications were familiar to every man, woman, and child living in Europe. "Mobilization" was the sum of the methods and mechanisms by which a nation's standing army prepared itself for action against an enemy in the event of a war—or a crisis which threatened to escalate into a war—while at the same time it was being expanded and reinforced by an influx of reservists. The primary responsibility of any nation's General Staff, once it had drawn up its war plans, was to create the mobilization timetables and schedules appropriate to each plan which would enable those plans to be put into effect.

Each of the Continental Great Powers possessed relatively large standing armies, modeled along similar lines. These armies would be built around a professional officer corps and a body of a few thousand non-commissioned officers—the corporals, sergeants and warrant officers, all long-term professionals who were the backbone of any army. The requisite number of troops which would bring the army up to its established peacetime strength were supplied by conscription, that is, a draft for which every able bodied young man between the ages of eighteen and twenty-one was eligible. In the summer of 1914, France had 777,000 soldiers in uniform, while Austria-Hungary's Army numbered 450,000; Germany could field 840,000 officers and men, Russia had 1,430,000 men of all ranks under arms.

These numbers were far from arbitrary, as several distinct calculations had entered into their formulation: the minimum force necessary to defend the nation against a surprise attack; the size of the garrisons in towns and cities scattered across the country; the requirements for fortifications along national frontiers; in some nations the army also served as a national police force. Most importantly, though, in wartime the standing army would serve as a framework for a vastly expanded force, the skeleton to which the sinews and muscles of the reserve forces would be attached. Mobilization would allow the armies to grow to hitherto unimagined proportions: fully mobilized, the German Army would, for example, expand from 840,000 officers and men to a force of 2,300,000.

The young men who had been called up—"conscripted"—to serve in the army would spend two years (three in France) in uniform. In theory almost all fit young men of the requisite ages were obligated to serve; in practice that never happened, the limitations usually being financial. The Germans, for example, usually only called to the colors 50% of the young men of any given "class" (a designated year of eligibility for service); France, who had a significantly smaller population than her Teutonic neighbor and so had to exert greater efforts to match Teutonic numbers, usually called up around 85% of her eligible young men; the other European Powers' armies fell somewhere between these two.

Once he was given his conscription notice, the soldier-to-be would report to his local army depot, where he would be given a uniform and kitted out, and begin his military training in the infantry, artillery, or cavalry. Once his term of service was complete he would be released from active duty and returned to civilian life. However, for a number of years, usually until he reached the age of forty, he would remain on the army rolls as a trained reservist, required to participate in annual exercises designed to keep his martial skills fresh against the day when he would be called back to the colors.

Should the army be ordered to mobilize, a flood of telegrams would sweep the country, ordering the reservists to report to their assigned army depot on a specific day at a specific time. There they would once again be given uniforms and equipment, formed into units under the command of a "cadre" of professional officers and NCOs from the standing army, and shipped off to the front aboard a collection of troop trains moving according to meticulously calculated timetables: some troop trains traveled along major trunk lines separated by intervals as short as two minutes.

It was expected that upon arrival at their destinations—the forward-most point of the rail-line, known as the "railhead"—these reserve units would be unloaded and formed up, and would then be used primarily for duties that offered little opportunity for actual combat. They would occupy conquered cities, towns, and villages; guard supply routes and lines of communication; hunt down partisans; man fortifications; and occasionally take over a quiet sector opposite the enemy in order to gain some "front line" experience. Taking over these responsibilities, of course, freed the active-duty troops for operations against the enemy. It was a quite logical and practical system, well thought-out, designed to make the most effective use of the manpower which the army had at its disposal.

All of this was dependent on the right troops and equipment arriving at the right places at the right times. Senior officers and their staffs could only begin to execute their operational plans when they were certain that the troops on which those plans relied would be available. Thus came about the military's obsession with railroad timetables, routes, and schedules: a handful of misdirected or tardy trains would have a ripple effect throughout the whole of the railroad network, snarling the entire system and essentially paralyzing the army. (In Germany, the Army even had the authority to determine the routes new-laid rail-lines would follow in order to expedite the mobilization process.) While all of the armies regarded a smoothly functioning mobilization as essential to their war plans, a mobilization order was not a war plan itself—it did not automatically commit a nation's army to battle, but merely delivered the troops, organized and prepared for action, where they were needed.

Austria-Hungary's mobilization was based on two operational plans which were mutually non-supporting, if not actually mutually exclusive, "Plan B" (Balkans) and "Plan R" (Russia). The critical factor, as it would be with the Schlieffen Plan, was geography: Austria-Hungary's frontier with Russia lay to the north, while Serbia lay to the south. Any attempt to implement both plans simultaneously would require the Empire to divide its forces, leaving them under strength and inadequate to undertake offensive action on either front.

The Austrian Army comprised forty-eight divisions organized into twenty-four corps, which would then allow the Austro-Hungarians to put six armies in the field. In Plan B, three of these armies were to be used to invade Serbia, the other three posted along the Russian border to contain any Russian offensive. Plan R called for greater strength in the north, with two armies left to watch over Serbia. Conrad was banking on the slowness of Russia's mobilization to allow him enough time to mass the forces necessary to launch an offensive against Serbia, then once the Serbian Army was routed, withdraw some of the pursuing Austro-Hungarian forces and transfer them to the northern frontier.

When events would make it apparent that the Russian mobilization was moving far more quickly than he expected, Conrad would find himself unable to decide which strategy he would adopt, Balkan or Russian, and instead attempt to pursue both, by trying to hastily turn many of the troops headed south toward Serbia northward into Galicia. There were no plans for such eventualities: the requisite logistical groundwork had never been laid, so railway schedules and timetables did not exist, supply arrangements had not been made, equipment was misdirected or lost; in the resulting chaos the bulk of the troops being moved were stranded at one time or another somewhere between the two fronts. As the Germans, and eventually his own government, began pressing Conrad to make some sense out of Austria-Hungary's mobilization, he repeatedly begged for more time, which Vienna was grudgingly forced to grant him, which had unforeseen political as well as military consequences.

There is some question as to whether the delay in the Austro-Hungarian mobilization was due solely to inefficiency and poor planning, or if there was also an unwillingness on Conrad's part to actually fight the war he had been so long advocating. This would not have been the first time in history where a peacetime general talked bravely while the guns were silent, only to turn timorous and hesitant when they began speaking in earnest. What is known for certain is that Conrad's strategic indecision left Austria's mobilization in tatters.

Russia, like Austria-Hungary, faced two potential adversaries, in her case Austria-Hungary and Germany, and so had developed two strategies for a war on her western frontier, Plan "G" and Plan "A" (also known as "Plan 19"). Unlike Austria-Hungary's planning, which required her army to be irretrievably committed to a northern or southern strategy before mobilization could begin, Russia's plans allowed for more flexibility, both politically and militarily.

Plan G was drawn up around the premise that as soon as war was declared, Germany and Austria-Hungary together would mount a major offensive against Russia, striking out of East Prussia and Galicia deep into Russian Poland. Russian forces posted along the frontier were to delay the advancing German armies as long as possible, inflicting as many casualties as possible, buying time for the Russian Army. It was a classic Russian strategy, which only Russia's vast geography permitted her to adopt, of trading space for time. That the Russians would be compelled to endure a succession of local defeats was accepted as inevitable and necessary. The time so dearly bought would allow the Russian Army to complete its mobilization, where it could bring its massive preponderance in manpower down upon an enemy already deep within the Russian homeland, the enemy's lines of communication and supply routes already dangerously overstretched.

The officers who created Plan A were not so sanguine about sacrificing Russian territory—and manpower—in the opening days of the war as were the creators of Plan G. Devised in 1910 by General

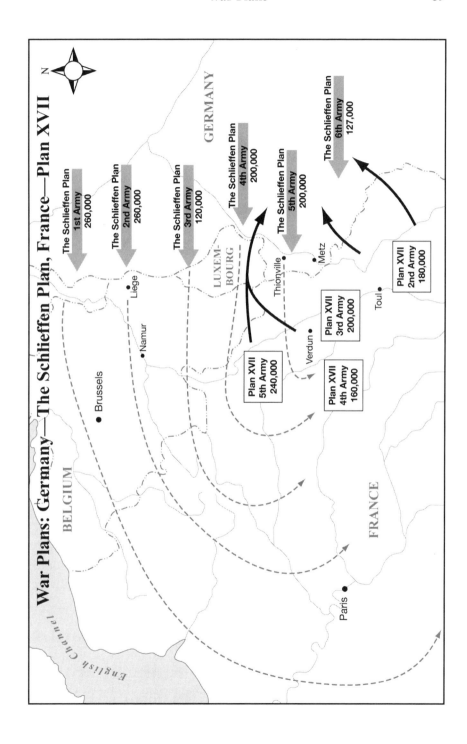

War Plans: Germany—The Schlieffen Plan, France—Plan XVII

G. N. Danilov, as Russia's expanding railway network and growing industrial base made noticeable improvements in her military capabilities, it meant to put those improvements to good use. Plan A assumed that Germany would begin the war by launching her opening offensive against France rather than Russia. As originally drawn up, Danilov's strategy was for Russia to disrupt the attack on her ally with an assault of her own: the two Russian armies deployed along the Russo-German border (19 corps, hence the alternate name "Plan 19") should immediately invade East Prussia. The defense of the Galician border with Austria-Hungary was to be left in the hands of the garrisons of the chain of fortresses guarding that frontier until the mobilization was complete.

France had exerted a considerable influence on the development of this plan. Much of the capital which was funding the growth of Russia's industry and railroads was coming from French financiers via the French government, who insisted on having a say on how the money was spent and where. At French insistence priority was given to the Russia's western railways and those industries which could most directly support the Russian military. Simultaneously, joint conferences between the Russian and French General Staffs were marked by rather heavy-handed French pressure on the Russians to launch an offensive against Germany as quickly as possible, even if it meant doing so before Russia's mobilization was complete, in order to draw German strength away from the west and the French Army.

While there was some merit, both politically and militarily, to Plan A, not all of Russia's senior officers were prepared to endorse it. Austria-Hungary, they believed, was a far greater threat to Russia than Germany, given her proximity to the Ukraine, a major source of Russia's raw materials as well as her food supply. In 1912 Plan A underwent a substantial revision: only two armies, rather than four, were to attack East Prussia, with the other two moving southward to defend Russia from the Austro-Hungarian Army.

If Russian strategy was realistic, though somewhat ambitious, that of their French ally was nothing short of preposterous. Part of the insistence by the French General Staff on an early Russian offensive into East Prussia was motivated by nature of France's own war plan, the now-infamous Plan XVII. For over ninety years "Plan XVII" has been synonymous with military ineptitude; given all the evidence, it is still difficult to arrive at any charitable judgement about it.

The objective of Plan XVII was deceptively simple—the recapture of the "stolen" provinces of Alsace and Lorraine. There was nothing flawed in the objective, but rather in the methods by which it was to be achieved. All military planning proceeds from certain assumptions made about the capabilities of each belligerent's soldiers, their training, equipment, weaponry, and logistical support. It is further assumed that those assumptions have a foundation in reality: Napoleon, the *ne plus ultra* ideal of French generalship, repeatedly warned his subordinates of the dangers of "painting pictures;" that is, taking for granted that their troops would always act in a certain way while the enemy acted in another. (Napoleon himself ultimately fell prey to this delusion at Waterloo.) Plan XVII was constructed around an entire series of "painted pictures" as the French General Staff, still stinging from the defeat of 1871, thrashed about for ways of inflicting an equally humiliating defeat on Germany.

The plan's primary architect was General Ferdinand Foch, one of the most outspoken and controversial instructors at France's *Ecole supérieure de guerre*, the French equivalent of the *Berliner Kriegsakademie* or the U.S. Army War College. Foch was a passionate advocate of offensive warfare, arguing vociferously (and with substantial justification, it must be admitted) that only offensive operations were decisive in warfare. While historical example was on his side, the consistent flaw in his reasoning was oversimplification. True, offensive warfare is the only genuinely decisive strategy, but its decisiveness lies not in the offensive itself but in its application: where and when an offensive is launched—and for what objectives. Merely attacking for the sake of being on the offensive, in the hope that the moral effect of the assault would somehow be decisive, is not of itself decisive, and frequently accomplishes nothing.

Nevertheless, Foch, along with his protégé and fellow instructor, General Loyzeaux de Grandmaison, found a large and willing following within the French officer corps. This was due in part to the emotional appeal of their arguments: 1871 had been more than merely a wound to French vanity, it had raised genuine doubts about French courage—it was an affront to French honor. The timorous deployments of Napoleon III and his generals, indecisively huddling their troops in the shadows of France's fortresses, had irretrievably handed the strategic initiative to the Germans, who made swift use of the unexpected gift and defeated the French armies in detail. No small part of Foch's passionate advocacy of the offensive was his determination to never allow such a *contretemps* to recur. An army on the offensive always possesses the initiative, which combined with French martial prowess, Foch believed, would prove irresistible.

At this point Foch and de Grandmaison departed from military theory and entered the realm of the spiritual—and foundered badly. While Napoleon was on one hand ignored, on the other he was given too much credence. Bonaparte's famous epigram "The moral is the physical as three is to one" was taken far too literally by Foch, de Grandmaison, and their acolytes. They embraced the belief that within every Frenchman existed something they called the *élan vital*— a uniquely Gallic fighting spirit capable of overwhelming any enemy by its sheer power; with it a French *poilu* was assumed to be more than a match for a German *soldat*. The sight of an inexorably advancing French Army, determined, resolute, unshaken by casualties, in appearance the embodiment of the irresistible force, would, it was believed, completely unnerve German defenders, who would either surrender or flee. (This peculiarly Gallic capacity for self-delusion would persist well into the war: as late as 1916 the French high command had convinced itself—without any supporting evidence whatsoever—that for every two Frenchmen who died in action, three Germans had been killed.)

For all that, Foch and de Grandmaison were professional army officers, not mystic dreamers, so there had to be some basis for their assumptions—and there was. Historians have perpetuated the myth that Foch, and in particular de Grandmaison, were the fathers of a "cult of the offensive," which had as its dogma that willpower alone could prevail over firepower. Nothing was further from the truth: they were not ignorant of the potency of modern weaponry, both small arms and artillery. Their fallacy lay in their theories about the application and effectiveness of firepower. Clinging to the Napoleonic dogma of shock action, where the massed French troops would decide the action *à la bayonette*, they ignored the devastating effects of modern firepower. When confronted with the accumulated evidence from the Russo-Japanese War and the Balkan Wars of the dreadful supremacy that firepower now gave a defending force over any attacker possessing less than overwhelming strength, they dismissed it with a combination of bigotry and professional arrogance. The evidence was invalid, they argued, because those were wars fought by peoples who were racially, culturally or martially inferior to the French. More specifically, they overestimated the effectiveness of field artillery (perhaps understandably, as the French 75mm field gun was far and away the finest gun of its type at the time), while underestimating that of heavy artillery.

Likewise, they underestimated the effectiveness of the machine gun, what Britain's General J. F. C. Fuller once described as "the concentrated essence of infantry," but in this they were far from alone. None of the armies which would go to war in 1914, not even Germany's, fully appreciated the tactical significance of either heavy artillery or machine guns. Instead, Foch, de Grandmaison and their adherents believed that French infantry, imbued with that peculiarly Gallic *elan vital,* would be able to advance irresistibly under the protection of a hail of small arms fire from the infantry's rifles, covered by a furious barrage of shells from the 75mm field guns raining down on the enemy's positions.

From a purely technical perspective, Plan XVII was not completely unrealistic. Four French armies would advance into Alsace-Lorraine, passing to the north and south of the Metz-Thionville fortress complex, avoiding the carefully prepared killing grounds on which the Germans had worked since 1871. The southern wing of the attacking force would capture first Alsace and then Lorraine; the direction of advance for the northern wing would depend on the actions of the German Army. If the German Army was attempting to strike into France via Luxembourg, the northern wing would protect the left flank of the southern as it liberated the two "stolen" provinces. Should the Germans advance out of Metz-Thionville, the northern wing would strike northeastward, behind it, taking dead aim on the Ruhr, the heart of industrial Germany.

It was a strategy that in another time, in other terrain, might have stood every chance of success. In 1914, in foothills of the Vosges

Mountains of eastern France, it was doomed to failure, condemned by a lethal combination of topography and technology. The ridgelines of the Vosges run generally northwest to southeast: Plan XVII called for the French armies to advance at nearly right angles to them, thereby creating a series of natural defensive lines for the Germans. When mated with the deadly efficiency of modern small arms and artillery, these positions would be nearly impregnable, consigning the attacking French armies to a succession of costly and uncertain frontal assaults.

The great irony of Plan XVII is that it was an outgrowth (if not an entirely logical one) of two earlier plans, which, if either had been adopted and implemented in 1914 might have produced a sharp, even decisive defeat for the German Army in the first weeks of August. Plan XV, which was drawn up in 1903, had anticipated a German attack in the west as the opening stroke of any war involving Germany and Russia. In response it outlined an initial defensive strategy along the Franco-German border, which would be followed up when the opportunity presented itself for a counter-strike into Lorraine. Its successor, Plan XVI, was similar, however its deployment placed more French reserves in the north, where they could be positioned against a German movement into Belgium.

The French high command was not ignorant of the possibility that the Germans might attack France through Belgium, but in a dreadful miscalculation they assumed that the Germans would lack the numbers to mount an offensive in any significant strength there, while still holding the line in Alsace-Lorraine and simultaneously defending against the Russians in the east. For the Germans had already decided that in order to bring the maximum weight to bear against the French, the reserve units which had heretofore been relegated to secondary duties would be committed to the front lines, giving the German Army a superiority of strength in what was to be the most ambitious of all of the pre-war plans of any of the Great Powers. This plan has become probably the most widely debated and least-understood operational plan in military history—the Schlieffen Plan.

Taking its name from its principal architect, Field Marshal Alfred von Schlieffen, it was a strategy which attempted to resolve the dilemmas and contradictions inherent in Germany's geographic and strategic position in Europe. Drawing up his first draft for the plan in 1905, the same year he was appointed Chief of the General Staff, von Schlieffen began by assuming that a war on two fronts—with France in the west and Russia in the east—was inevitable. It was a not unreasonable assumption, although it was over-simplistic. The continued hostility of France was a given, as long as the provinces of Alsace and Lorraine remained under German rule. Russia was more problematic: the Hohenzollern and Romanov monarchies had been close friends, even allies, far longer than France had been allied to Russia, and there were no long-standing antagonisms between the two nations barring the path to resuming that friendship. Preparing for the possibility of war between Germany and Russia was sensible; assuming that hostility would be inevitable was not only naive, it was dangerous.

Nevertheless, the greater threat to Germany, as von Schlieffen saw it, was the Russian Army: it was enormous, and given the size of Russia's population, its manpower reserves were virtually inexhaustible. Inevitably, the bulk of the German Army would have to eventually be deployed in the east to stand against the expected Slavic onslaught. However, within its immensity, the Russian Army suffered a weakness which von Schlieffen perceived as an opportunity: the sheer size of Russia coupled with a relatively poor railway network meant that it would take a much longer time for the Russian Army to mobilize and concentrate than would its western European counterparts.

Railways were the key to it all: in the first decade of the 20th century the Russian rail network could barely sustain the movement of 200 trains each day into the whole of Russian Poland and Galicia, trains on which Russian armies would depend for movement and supply. The Germans, in contrast were moving more than 650 trains a day just over the bridges in the city of Cologne alone. Von Schlieffen calculated—more or less correctly, as it turned out—that at least six weeks would be required for the Russian mobilization to field forces in sufficient numbers to mount major offensive operations in Poland or Galicia, whereas Germany's mobilization could be accomplished in as little as three days.

In these six weeks von Schlieffen saw a window of opportunity. It was not an opportunity to deal a decisive blow against Russia,

War Plans: Austria-Hungary—Plan B and Plan R,
Russia—Plan A and Plan G (post mobilization)

Baltic
Sea

• Kongisberg

Plan A—Northwest Army Group
1st Army 210,000
2nd Army 206,000

Plan G—Northwest Army Group
1st Army 210,000
2nd Army 206,000
4th Army 204,000

N

GERMAN EMPIRE

RUSSIA

Tannenberg •

• Warsaw

• Brest-Litovsk

POLAND

Kiev

Plan A—Southwest Army Group
4th Army 204,000

Plan G & Plan A—Southwest Army Group
3rd Army 226,000
5th Army 240,000
8th Army 256,000

Tarnow
•

Plan B—Northern Forces
1st Army 200,000
2nd Army 200,000
3rd Army 180,000

Cracow
•

Gorlice
•

Plan R—Northern Forces
1st Army 200,000
2nd Army 200,000
3rd Army 180,000
4th Army 160,000

• Vienna

• Budapest

AUSTRIA-
HUNGARY

RUMANIA

Plan B—Southern Forces
4th Army 160,000
5th Army 180,000
6th Army 160,000

Plan R—Southern Forces
5th Army 180,000
6th Army 160,000

Bucharest •

•
Belgrade

•
Sarajevo

SERBIA

BULGARIA

• Sofia

Adriatic Sea

MONTENEGRO

ALBANIA

OTTOMAN
EMPIRE

disrupting her mobilization or achieving some near-unassailable strategic position, or even preparing defenses in the east which would make any attack on German soil prohibitively expensive, Russia's vast reserves of manpower notwithstanding. Instead von Schlieffen saw a chance to crush Russia's ally France with a single, sledgehammer blow. In order to do so he would commit the vast bulk of German forces to an offensive in the west, with an overwhelming assault on Paris as its objective, leaving only enough troops in East Prussia to conduct a holding action against the Russians while the Tsar's army completed its mobilization. Once France had been defeated the armies in the west would board troop trains bound for East Prussia, where they would face the anticipated Russian menace.

However, to attack France with sufficient strength and speed to ensure her defeat within the six-week window which von Schlieffen believed would be available, Germany could not launch the assault across the Franco-German border. The terrain was too difficult: the heavily wooded ridges and valleys of the Vosges Mountains, coupled with a limited road and rail network in that region, made rapid strategic movement impossible, while the same ridges and valleys which made a mockery of Plan XVII would in turn offer their defensive advantages to the French, effectively negating the superior German numbers. As von Schlieffen saw it, there was only one practical route to invading France which would allow the Germans to employ their superior numbers with sufficient speed to ensure the decisive result he sought: the German Army would have to launch its invasion through Belgium. The plains of Flanders were the route to victory.

Once he had settled on this basic premise, formulating the operational outline of the plan was a relatively simple process. Six German armies, each consisting of five or six two-division corps, would advance through Belgium and into France in a carefully coordinated wheeling motion, much like a swinging door, with Luxembourg as the hinge. The army on the extreme right, designated the First Army, would sweep as far west as possible before turning southward to fall on the vulnerable French left. Von Schlieffen's oft-quoted remark, "Let the last man on the right brush the Channel with his sleeve" summed up the essence of this wheeling movement.

To make up the numbers he believed were necessary to overwhelm the French—a minimum of sixty-six divisions—von Schlieffen proposed a radical innovation in the deployment and employment of reserve units. Placing more confidence in the quality of his reservists than did his French counterparts in theirs, he proposed that reserve units be employed as front-line troops from the beginning of the invasion. This would, he believed, provide the critical margin of superiority in numbers which would allow the German Army to outflank and envelop the French.

While the six armies of the German right wing thrust across Belgium, a seventh army, positioned to protect the Franco-German border, would attempt to draw the French Army into the difficult Vosges terrain, exposing the rear of the French forces to the *feld-grau* juggernaut thundering down from the north. Accomplishing this was imperative, for careful study of the French railway system led von Schlieffen to conclude that it would be impossible for the French Army to withdraw from the Vosges and turn to meet the advancing German right wing in time to avoid its own encirclement and destruction.

At the same time, von Schlieffen expected that the First Army would also capture the French capital. The disruption caused by the fall of Paris would be simultaneously psychological and physical, for not only was the city the heart and soul of France's national identity, it was also the central hub of the national railroad network. Taking Paris would make the difficult task of shifting troops between sectors almost impossible, further diminishing the French Army's ability to defend France.

From the start a potential weakness existed in von Schlieffen's plan: the rigidity of the timescale made little allowance for any difficulties in maintaining supply and communication to the far-flung armies of the right wing. There was the real possibility that they could march out of contact and into exhaustion before the supporting services caught up; the supporting units would be stretched to the breaking point as it was. Supplying these troops was not an insurmountable problem, but it would require exceptionally well-coordinated staff work to achieve. Phase lines and army boundaries were carefully drawn to mark the expected pace of advance, specific roads and rail-lines assigned to each advancing army, precise calculations of the rations and fodder needed for the troops and horses moving across Belgium were carefully worked out. No detail, however insignificant-seeming, was overlooked: by the time von Schlieffen's staff had finished their work, every last Belgian road and railway were assigned to the support and supply of one or more of the six armies on the right wing.

At the same time, overriding every other consideration, was the fundamental premise on which von Schlieffen's plan was constructed— speed. For the plan to succeed it was vital that France be given no time to react to the German Army's massive sweep through Belgium. Therefore, it was essential that Germany's mobilization be completed, the troops quickly concentrated on the Belgian border, and the offensive be launched as soon as the required forces were assembled, all as rapidly as possible: von Schlieffen anticipated the six German armies assigned to invade Belgium and Luxembourg would go into action within hours of arriving at their railheads. The speed with which the German forces would fall upon the French left, combined with their massive weight, would ensure the collapse of the French flank, allowing the advancing German armies to sweep around and behind their beleaguered Gallic foes, completely destroying the French Army.

There was, however, one problem with the Schlieffen Plan, which no amount of staff work planning or swift deployment could overcome: it simply would not—could not—work.

The fatal flaw which rendered the plan unworkable was the city of Paris. To much of the world, Paris was the "City of Light," of romance, gaiety, *joie de vivre* and *fin de siecle* decadence. It was the city of the Moulin Rouge and the Folies Bergere, the Eiffel Tower and the Louvre, Notre Dame and the Left Bank of the Seine—in short, the embodiment of all of its clichés. To military men, however, Paris presented a far different face, that of the most heavily fortified city in the world.

While by no means defended by fortifications as modern as those which guarded Liege and Antwerp in Belgium (which would compel the German Army to develop new artillery designs which dwarfed anything yet produced) the defenses of Paris were still formidable. Although some of the fortifications dated back to the mid-19th century, most had been constructed in the years after the Franco-Prussian War. Though far from invulnerable, they were still fortifications, which could offer a not inconsiderable measure of protection to any defending force—and the garrison in Paris and its environs was formidable, consisting of nearly 100,000 regular and reserve troops. This was too large a force for any invader to merely bypass or ignore: if the First Army attempted to pass east of Paris, the garrison would lie on its right flank, poised to strike a crippling blow at any moment. Should the First and Second Armies try to envelop Paris, that same garrison would be positioned to drive a wedge between the two armies, cutting the supply and communications systems of either or both. Because the French capital was so heavily protected, it was impractical to try to besiege the city: despite the age of some of the defenses, they were in total too deep and too numerous to allow for a serious investment. So in order to negate the threat of Paris and its garrison, additional forces would be needed to contain it.

By von Schlieffen's calculations, it would require a minimum of eight army corps to "mask" Paris and protect the flank of the First Army should it move east of the city, or to protect the flanks of the First and Second Armies should they attempt to envelop the French capital. And on that point the entire plan fell apart. In 1905, when von Schlieffen first concocted the plan, the necessary eight corps were not available—they simply did not exist. By 1912, when the plan underwent its final revision, peacetime expansion of the German Army had created the additional eight corps, but did not resolve the dilemma.

The problem was not in manpower but in logistics: the opening movements of von Schlieffen's plan stretched the capacity of the German railroads to its limit so there were no trains available to move the extra eight corps and no place on the tracks to put them if there were transport. In Belgium the situation would be even worse: the Belgian road network would already be overloaded by the advancing armies and their supply and support columns. There would be no room for an additional eight corps to march, let alone be supplied. In short, even though the eight corps needed to mask Paris were available, there was no place to put them, and no way to get them to the front where and when they were needed.

For seven years von Schlieffen labored to find a solution to the problem and in the end was compelled to admit to failure—it was literally insoluble. And for all of his labor—von Schlieffen's creativity was more the product of hard work than inspired genius which had typified von Moltke the Elder—he could ultimately offer no other solution to Germany's strategic dilemma, save for having the German Army stand on the defensive in both east and west, an alternative he abhorred for its lack of a definitive objective and resolution. Year after year the Schlieffen Plan was revised and refined, becoming ever more precise and exact, but still fatally flawed. von Schlieffen retired in 1912 and was replaced by Helmuth von Moltke, nephew and namesake of the great Prussian general who was the victor of 1865, 1866, and 1871; the plan was bequeathed to the new Chief of Staff, already institutionalized as Germany's sole option should war erupt between her and Russia or France. Von Moltke, chronically gloomy and pessimistic, in his turn lacked the intellectual and moral courage to scrap the plan and adopt a defensive strategy for the German Army. Rather than create and develop alternative plans, he continued to refine and rework the Schlieffen Plan in the hope that by some miracle it might succeed should it ever be put into operation. Most critically, von Moltke was more sensitive than von Schlieffen to the likelihood that launching the German attack on France through neutral Belgium would almost certainly bring Great Britain into the war against Germany. Von Moltke was constantly brooding over the relative decline of the Fatherland's strength compared to that of the rising power of France and Russia: he knew perfectly well that Germany could never also confront the might and resources of the British Empire and hope to win. However, in the timorousness of his despair, von Moltke refused to alter the fundamental strategy of the German Army: the war, when it came, was already lost, and von Moltke knew it.

Just as she stood aloof from the web of Continental alliances, Great Britain stood apart from the other Great Powers in that the British Army possessed no master plan for its deployment and operations should war break out on the Continent. Since the end of the Napoleonic Wars British governments had pursued its diplomatic and military aims independently of any other Great Power, forming no long-standing alliances, a policy revealingly defined in 1895 by the then-Prime Minister, Lord Salisbury, as "Splendid Isolation." The only standing treaties to which Great Britain was signatory were the 1839 international agreements which guaranteed the neutrality of the Netherlands and Belgium.

However, as the 19th century gave way to the 20th, Splendid Isolation was a policy which began to lose its validity as the waxing power of Imperial Germany loomed ever greater in Continental Europe. Since 1905, there had been joint staff conferences between the Imperial General Staff and the French Grand Quartier-General, as part of the Anglo-French Entente. The substance of these talks centered around the idea that in the event of a German invasion of France, a British Expeditionary Force of some 160,000 would be brought across the Channel and take up positions on the French left flank. It was a not-inconsiderable force, for though its numbers barely equaled two German corps, man for man the soldiers of the B.E.F. were unquestionably the best soldiers of their day, possibly the finest soldiers in history. Long-term professionals to a man, for whom military service was a vocation not an interruption of civilian life, they trained and drilled to an exacting standard unmatched by any Continental army. Know as "Tommies" after the prototypical "Thomas Atkins" who served as the exemplar in completing their forms and paybooks, they were armed with the bolt-action rifle, the legendary Lee-Enfield .303 SMLE Mark III. Their standard of marksmanship was to place fifteen aimed shots into a man-sized target at two hundred yards in the span of one minute. When they went into action, the Tommies would lay down such an intense and accurate volume of fire that their foes would be convinced they were armed with machine guns.

The same year that the Army began staff talks with the French, the Royal Navy moved the preponderance of its strength to its North Sea ports, where the newly formed Grand Fleet could neutralize any threat from Imperial Germany's High Seas Fleet. It was a redeployment that circumstances had made inevitable. The ententes reached with Russia and France effectively diminished their threat to British seapower, while the passage of the German naval laws of 1900 and 1905 had institutionalized the naval arms race between Britain and

Germany. With the two fleets more or less evenly matched technologically, the Royal Navy's numerical preponderance assured its supremacy should the two fleets come to blows. Having chosen to openly challenge Britain's economic strength and naval might, the German government had driven the British from the position of a possible ally and certainly a benevolent neutral to that of a potential foe. Clearly London had positioned its military resources to oppose any aggressive move Berlin might make in the west, and however much the Kaiser, the Chancellor and the Foreign Minister might decry Germany's "encirclement" (*Einkreisung*), it was a position brought into being in no small part by their own efforts.

However, these were strategic decisions that did not in any way commit Great Britain to any irrevocable course of action should a crisis break out in Europe and war threaten the Continent. Successive Governments, Conservative and Liberal, had repeatedly emphasized to their French counterparts that the staff talks were in no way binding militarily or diplomatically. If it were determined by His Majesty's Government that the British Empire's interests were best served by remaining neutral, this would be the course of action that would be followed. A German attack on France did not guarantee that British Tommies would fight alongside French *poilus*. Only if a Continental crisis presented a threat to British honor and British interests would His Majesty's Government intervene. Among the Great Powers of Europe, only Great Britain held sole sway over her own destiny.

The stage was set then for a tragedy of truly terrible proportions: in the summer of 1914, all but one of the Great Powers of Europe had drawn up mobilization plans from which they could put into motion their opening strategies. At the same time, none of those plans would, by their implementation, irrevocably commit that army and nation to war. None of them, that is, save for one: Germany. Alone among the Great Powers, Germany's mobilization plan was so closely linked to the actual attack the German Army would launch that it became inseparable from it: once the German Army mobilized, it was irrevocably committed to war.

Chapter V

AN ULTIMATUM FROM VIENNA

While the Kaiser's government seethed with impatience throughout June 1914, the Emperor's government lapsed into typical Viennese *schlamperei* and appeared to dither over the ultimatum to be sent to Belgrade. The Austrians found the Germans' attitude incomprehensible: what was the rush? The ultimatum would be sent, the Serbs would reject it, then Austria-Hungary would declare war on Serbia. The outcome was a foregone conclusion, the whole diplomatic charade was simply a sop to the proprieties of the rest of Europe, with a nod to the sensibilities of the Emperor.

Berchtold, who as Foreign Minister had the primary responsibility for drafting the ultimatum, was being very cagey. His duty was to formulate a document so punishing, so humiliating, that no nation with a shred of self-respect could accept its terms. On July 14, Ambassador Tschirschky cabled his superior, von Bethmann-Hollweg, saying that "The Note is being composed so that the possibility of its acceptance is practically excluded." However, at the same time, there was always the chance, however unlikely and remote, that Serbia would accept the Austro-Hungarian terms. This meant that those terms, however harsh, must be enforceable, and at the same time allow Vienna to eventually strip Belgrade of all but the most nominal independence. Likewise, the note could not be so overtly punitive in nature and in tone that it would appear to the rest of Europe that it was in fact merely the pretext for a fight. Clearly,

Austria-Hungary was the aggrieved party as far as the assassinations in Sarajevo were concerned: the Dual Monarchy must continue to hold the moral high ground, appearing to be seeking justice, not pursuing vengeance. Therefore, Berchtold worked with a crafty hand, sharpening a condition here, barbing a phrase there, like some pinstriped, frock-coated Frankenstein (himself, fittingly enough, an Austrian) working in his Transylvanian castle to create his diplomatic monster. As he worked, Berlin fumed and fidgeted.

What Tisza, Berchtold and the rest of the Viennese government did not understand—what they had no way of knowing—was the degree of duplicity to which *Berlin* was now subscribing. Although von Bethmann-Hollweg, von Jagow and the other senior officials of the German Foreign Ministry would deny having specific knowledge of the contents of the Austrian note to Serbia, in truth Berlin was kept fully informed of Berchtold's progress in drafting the ultimatum. The ambassadors of the other European powers posted in Berlin were subjected to a systematic campaign of lies originating in the Foreign Office, while simultaneously those same falsehoods were being repeated through the German ambassadors to the various European capitals. Over and over again, when pressed for any knowledge of what Austria-Hungary intended to do with Serbia, the *Wilhelmstrasse* and its representatives assured their listeners that to the best of the German government's knowledge, there was no cause for alarm: how else could the Kaiser, the Chancellor and most of the senior officers of the Army and Navy be away from Berlin on holiday? In short, the situation was serious, but far from critical.

In typical Viennese fashion the situation was critical but far from serious. The same lies being told by the German Foreign Ministry were being repeated by its Austro-Hungarian counterpart: in a July 10 cable to Berlin Count Tschirschky recounted how:

[Prime Minister Tisza] would gladly follow the [German] government's suggestion that the press be used to sway public opinion in England against Serbia—Count Szögyény sent a telegram concerning this matter. But in his opinion this must be done carefully so as not to alarm Serbia prematurely. The war minister will be going on holiday tomorrow, and Baron

Conrad von Hötzendorf will also be leaving Vienna for a time. As Count Berchtold confided in me, they are doing so deliberately in order to avoid causing any alarm.

On July 18, Russian Foreign Minister Sergei Sazonov summoned the Austrian ambassador to his office to ask for the latest news of the Dual Monarchy's intentions toward Serbia. The ambassador, Count Szápáry, reassured Sazonov that Austria-Hungary had no malevolent intentions toward the Serbian kingdom. Sazonov would later recall the Count's demeanor as being "as gentle as a lamb."

Yet no one was entirely fooled—everyone in Europe knew that something was going on in Austria-Hungary. The question which so far defied an answer was precisely what—and why was it taking so long? The delay was increasingly vexatious for von Bethmann-Hollweg, who was carrying his deception to extremes which Vienna never suspected. Not only was he lying to the governments of Europe about the severity of the Serbian crisis, he was telling the same lies to the Kaiser. For three weeks Wilhelm would cruise the fjords of Norway, blissfully unconcerned about the approaching confrontation between Austria-Hungary and Serbia, reassured by telegrams from Berlin that the situation was nowhere nearly so serious as to require his presence and personal attention. What was really happening was that both von Bethmann-Hollweg and von Jagow were keeping the Kaiser out of the way. His annoying habit of involving himself in the affairs of state would only make it more difficult to maneuver the Serbian crisis toward the ends which both men hoped to achieve. In one of his more pragmatic moments Wilhelm might unexpectedly comprehend the direction in which the crisis was headed, and make Germany's support of Austria-Hungary conditional to the Dual Monarchy acting with moderation, or even revoke that support entirely, shattering the Chancellor's hopes for a war.

Von Bethmann-Hollweg also worried that Sir Edward Grey, the British Foreign Minister, might formally propose arbitration as coming from Grey, such a suggestion could not be ignored. The German Chancellor personally despised Grey, but professionally he was compelled to respect him, not only because he represented the power of the British Empire, but also for his stature within the European diplomatic community.

Sir Edward Grey had earned the respect of the chancelleries of Europe during his first decade in office by negotiating the Anglo-Russian entente in 1907, which swept aside generations of friction between the two Empires, and for his skillful chairmanship of the Six Power Conference in London in 1913, which had averted an earlier Balkan crisis from expanding into a general European war. Grey was also known for his probity—he would never knowingly, deliberately lie to a fellow diplomat. He would, if confronted by an uncomfortable truth, find a way of sidestepping it rather than resort to falsehood. He had developed a knack for talking around the perimeter of an uncomfortable subject, gradually approaching it in an indirect, almost elliptical fashion which never gave offense, yet never completely evaded an issue. Grey would never dream of stooping to the sort of deception currently being carried out in Berlin and Vienna.

Speaking for His Majesty's Government, Grey recognized that Austria-Hungary was unquestionably the aggrieved party in the crisis, and that "the merits of the dispute between . . . [Austria-Hungary and Serbia] were not the concern of His Majesty's Government." The British Empire's interest in the coming ultimatum was "simply and solely from the point of view of the peace of Europe." To that end, Great Britain would attempt to influence Serbia to accept whatever demands Austria-Hungary might make, providing "that they are moderate and made reconcilable with the independence of the Serbian nation." In this he echoed the position taken by Russia's Foreign Minister, Sazonov, who had told Count von Pourtalés, the German ambassador to St. Petersburg, that Vienna's note to Belgrade ought not take the form of an ultimatum—but more importantly Russia would not permit any outright annexation or dismemberment of Serbia.

What Grey, Sazonov, and their French colleague Pierre Viviani, who carried the portfolios of both the French Prime Minister and Foreign Minister, could not know was that the Austrian note to Serbia was never meant to be a basis for negotiation. It would require full and complete capitulation by Serbia on all of its terms. Here Berchtold's subtle hand was once again at work, in an effort to avoid the charge that the note would be, in truth, an ultimatum. The note would state that the only immediate consequence should Belgrade fail to comply was a rupture in diplomatic relations between the two nations, not that a state of war would automatically be presumed to exist. The actual declaration of war would follow in a matter of days, if not hours, but in the meantime, all of the diplomatic niceties and legal technicalities would be scrupulously observed. When war came it would do so with the most impeccable legal trappings. Berlin, of course, was kept fully informed not only of the note's contents but also of the details of how it would be delivered. Nothing would be left to chance. War was the inevitable outcome, it was just a matter of ensuring that to the rest of the world it appeared as if war was thrust upon Austria-Hungary rather than having been the Dual Monarchy's goal all along. This pleased von Bethmann-Hollweg and his colleagues, who desperately wanted this war; indeed they had been planning for it for years.

On Sunday, December 8, 1912, a most extraordinary meeting took place at Potsdam Palace, outside Berlin. At 11 o'clock that morning, the Kaiser met in council with Admiral Alfred von Tirpitz, the Naval Secretary; Admiral George von Müller, the Navy Chief of Staff, and his assistant, Vice Admiral Heeringen; and Field Marshal Helmuth von Moltke, Chief of the Great General Staff. The Kaiser read to them a report sent by the German ambassador in London, Prince Lichnowsky, on the current political situation. The gist of the report was that, according to the Prince, Richard Haldane, acting on the behalf of Sir Edward Grey, the British Foreign Minister, had informed Lichnowsky that should Germany attack France, Great Britain was prepared to come to France's defense: a French defeat would so badly upset the European balance of power in Europe that it would be intolerable to British interests. When he had finished reading the report, Wilhelm announced that he found the message a welcome relief, for it made clear to everyone the true anti-German position of the British government. The Kaiser took particular pleasure in pointing out what he believed was Great Britain's open hostility toward Germany, especially when a number of high-ranking government officials had been, as he put it, "lulled into a false sense of security by the recently friendly English press."

Wilhelm went on, declaring that Austria-Hungary must come to a reckoning with Serbia if she wanted to maintain control of the Slavs living inside Austria's borders. Acknowledging Russia's self-proclaimed role as protector of the Slavic peoples, and citing a remark by Russia's Foreign Minister Sergei Sazonov that Russia would launch an attack straight into Austrian Galicia should the Austrians march into Serbia, he stated without hesitation that war would then inevitably come to Germany. It was hoped that in such an event Bulgaria, Romania, and Albania—possibly even Turkey—would make common cause with Germany against the Russians. Such a combination, should it be brought about, would free even more German troops to be launched in the attack on France using the Schlieffen Plan.

Then, demonstrating that even at that time he was aware of the perils of the Plan's violation of Belgium's neutrality, the Kaiser turned to von Tirpitz and said, "Naturally, the fleet will have to prepare for war against England." Von Tirpitz agreed, pointing out that, given Haldane's statement, the possibility of a war against Russia alone, an idea von Tirpitz had long advocated, could no longer be considered realistic. Once war was declared, German submarines would begin attacks on British troop transports sailing for Belgium, concentrating around the Scheldt Estuary or near Dunkirk; mines would be laid in the Thames.

At this point Field Marshal von Moltke spoke up, announcing that, "The sooner war comes, the better!" He also insisted, however, that when the decision to go to war was made, Germany should be in a diplomatic position where she could issue an ultimatum to either Russia or France, or even both, constructed in a manner which would trigger the war but at the same time place the onus of blame on the two allies. The Kaiser unhesitatingly seconded von Moltke's declaration, and gave instructions that the German press be manipulated toward this end. Von Tirpitz did point out that the Navy would prefer to see a major war delayed by one to two years in order to complete current construction. Von Moltke, who had always been somewhat contemptuous of the Navy, retorted that even then the Navy would not be ready, while, because of limited finances (which he implied was due to the money wasted on the High Seas Fleet) the Army's situation would continue to worsen *vis-a-vis* France and Russia, who were rearming and re-equipping their armies at a furious pace.

On that somewhat discordant note, the council adjourned. While no real decision to go to war by a specific date had been made, it was clear from the nature of the comments made by everyone present that the meeting had been no idle discussion: a policy of aggression was being formulated and refined. It unmistakably represented the direction which German foreign policy—as well as its objectives—was expected to take in the years to come. Now, in the high summer of 1914, the war which Wilhelm and his ministers had so calmly discussed eighteen months earlier was almost upon them.

On July 18, the same day Sazonov was being reassured by Count Szápáry that Austria-Hungary had no malevolent intentions regarding Serbia, the note to Belgrade was ready to be delivered. Momentarily, Berchtold held his hand, though not out of any sense of mercy or forbearance for Serbia, but rather for the very best of Machiavellian motives. At that moment the President of the Republic of France, Raymond Poincaré, was departing for a state visit to Russia to reinforce the diplomatic and military ties between Paris and St. Petersburg. Poincaré, like so many of his countrymen, never resolved to the loss of Alsace-Lorraine, was irredeemably hostile toward Germany, and by extension toward Germany's ally, Austria-Hungary. The visit would last from July 20 to July 23; therefore, in Berchtold's considered opinion:

> We should consider it unwise to undertake the threatening step in Belgrade at the very time when the peace-loving, reserved Tsar Nicholas and the undeniably cautious Herr Sazonov are under the influence of the two who are always for war, Isvolsky [Russia's ambassador to Paris] and Poincaré.

Better to wait, Berchtold believed, until Poincaré had departed from St. Petersburg and was at sea on his return journey to France, a time when he would only be in the most limited communication with Paris and his Cabinet. Accordingly, the timing of the delivery of the note was set for five p.m. on July 23. Later, to ensure that Poincaré was well and truly on the high seas when the note was delivered, the time was pushed back until six p.m. In Berlin, von Bethmann-Hollweg continued to stew and fidget at this latest delay, but he could not deny the cleverness of Berchtold's timing.

The note was duly delivered to the Serbian Foreign Ministry at precisely six p.m. on July 23 by the Austro-Hungarian ambassador, Baron Wladimir Giesl von Gieslingen. Copies were circulated in the Foreign Ministries of Europe the following morning. Not since the Ems Telegram which precipitated the Franco-Prussian War in 1870 had such a potentially explosive document been presented by one European government to another. Austria-Hungary's note caused gasps of incredulity in Europe's capitals, and left the Serbian government in Belgrade in a state of shock. After opening with the expected self-justifying preamble which were characteristic of all such documents, the note leveled a devastating accusation:

> It results from the depositions and confessions of the criminal perpetrators of the outrage of the 28th of June that the Serajevo assassinations were planned in Belgrade; that the arms and explosives with which the murderers were provided had been given to them by Serbian officers and functionaries belonging to the *Narodna Odbrana* [the Black Hand]; and finally, that the passage into Bosnia of the criminals and their arms was organized and effected by the chiefs of the Serbian frontier service.

In short, Serbia was being accused of officially assisting in planning and conducting the murder of Franz Ferdinand and his wife. It had been one of the Balkans' worst-kept secrets that some Serbian government officials had connections to the Black Hand organization; it did not automatically follow, however, that the Serbian government supported the terrorist group as a matter of policy, yet that was the accusation Vienna was leveling against Belgrade.

However, a charge of such enormity was necessary to justify what was to follow: a list of ten demands, each carefully crafted to erode some measure of Serbia's independence, the sum being the reduction of Serbia to little more than vassalage to the Dual Monarchy. It was the product of Foreign Minister Berchtold's grim determination to crush Serbia once and for all time. Any publication, book, or newspaper "which incites to hatred and contempt" of Austria-

Hungary was to be suppressed; teaching materials in Serbian schools containing "propaganda against Austria-Hungary" were to be destroyed and replaced with texts of which the Dual Monarchy approved; army officers and government officials of all ranks "guilty of propaganda against the Austro-Hungarian Monarchy" were to be purged; specific individuals were listed who were believed to be heavily involved in anti-Austrian agitation and terrorism—they were to be arrested and turned over to Austrian authorities.

The demand with the most profound implications was the requirement for the Serbs: "To accept the collaboration in Serbia of representatives of the Austro-Hungarian Government for the suppression of the subversive movement directed against the territorial integrity of the Monarchy"—in other words, subordinate Serbia's police forces to those of Austria-Hungary. Should Serbia comply, the net result would effectively reduce the kingdom into the position of a client state of the Dual Monarchy.

In a move clearly intended to salt the wound, the Serbian government would also be required to issue a formal apology in the form of a declaration published in the official government newspaper and issued as an Order of the Day to the Serbian Army in the name of the Prince Regent, Alexander. The Note even went so far as to dictate wording, which was humiliating to the point of insult:

> The Royal Government of Serbia condemn the propaganda directed against Austria-Hungary—i.e., the general tendency of which the final aim is to detach from the Austro-Hungarian Monarchy territories belonging to it, and they sincerely deplore the fatal consequences of these criminal proceedings.
>
> The Royal Government regret that Serbian officers and functionaries participated in the above-mentioned propaganda and thus compromised the good neighbourly relations to which the Royal Government were solemnly pledged by their declaration of the 31st of March, 1909.
>
> The Royal Government, who disapprove and repudiate all ideas of interfering or attempting to

interfere with the destinies of the inhabitants of any part whatsoever of Austria-Hungary, consider it their duty formally to warn officers and functionaries, and the whole population of the Kingdom, that henceforward they will proceed with the utmost rigor against persons who may be guilty of such machinations, which they will use all their efforts to anticipate and suppress.

This was the language a victorious Power might use in dictating terms to a vanquished foe, which is what in essence Serbia was. Pitifully under-equipped and outnumbered by more than four-to-one, the Serbian Army was in no position to withstand a determined Austro-Hungarian attack. All Serbia could do was search for a way of complying with Austria's demands while preserving at least some shred of national dignity; and there was precious little opportunity for that, as the time limit on the note was forty-eight hours. Once that lapsed, no one knew for certain what Austria-Hungary would do; clearly the threat of war was more than implied if never quite explicit.

Sir Edward Grey for one had never seen anything like it. In a meeting of the British Cabinet, he declared it to be "brusque, sudden, and peremptory." It was, he said, "the most formidable document ever addressed by one state to another." Nicholas II called the Austrian note "outrageous," and his Foreign Minister, Count Sazonov, was even more blunt with Count Szápáry. When the Austrian ambassador presented a copy of the note to Sazonov, the Russian minister blurted out, "I know what it is—you mean to make war on Serbia and this is just a pretext!" Szápáry replied, not without some truth, that Austria-Hungary had been extraordinarily tolerant of Serbian provocation for years: if war was what Vienna wanted, there was no need of a pretext. Sazonov responded in turn by declaring, "What you want is war and you have burned your bridges! . . . You are setting fire to Europe!" The Austrian emperor, Franz Josef, certainly understood what was about to transpire: convinced that Russia would regard the Note as an open challenge, he told Berchtold, "Russia will not accept it. There will be a huge war."

Russia was, in fact, Serbia's one hope. Often lost in the flurry of telegrams flying back and forth between the capitals of the Great Powers is a communication from the Serbian Prince Regent, Alexander, directly to the Tsar, Nicholas II, appealing for Russia's protection. Admirably subdued in its tone, it has that curious dignity possessed by someone who knows their cause is lost and sees no shame in begging for rescue.

Belgrade, July 24 1914

The Austro-Hungarian Government yesterday evening handed to the Serbian Government a note concerning the "attentat" of Serajevo.

Conscious of its international duties, Serbia from the first days of the horrible crime declared that she condemned it, and that she was ready to open an inquiry on her territory if the complicity of certain of her subjects were proved in the investigation begun by the Austro-Hungarian authorities.

However, the demands contained in the Austro-Hungarian note are unnecessarily humiliating for Serbia and incompatible with her dignity as an independent State.

Thus we are called upon in peremptory tones for a declaration of the Government in the "Official Journal," and an order from the Sovereign to the army wherein we should repress the spirit of hostility against Austria by reproaching ourselves for criminal weakness in regard to our perfidious actions.

Then we have to admit Austro-Hungarian functionaries into Serbia to participate with our own in the investigation and to superintend the execution of the other conditions indicated in the note.

We have received a time-limit of forty-eight hours to accept everything, in default of which the legation of Austria-Hungary will leave Belgrade. We are ready to accept the Austro-Hungarian conditions which are compatible with the position of an independent State as well as those whose acceptance shall be advised us by your Majesty.

All persons whose participation in the "attentat" shall be proved will be severely punished by us. Certain of these demands cannot be carried out without changes in our legislation, which require time. We have been given too short a limit. We can be attacked after the expiration of the time-limit by the Austro-Hungarian Army which is concentrating on our frontier.

It is impossible for us to defend ourselves, and we supplicate your Majesty to give us your aid as soon as possible. The highly prized good will of your Majesty, which has so often shown itself toward us, makes us hope firmly that this time again our appeal will be heard by his generous Slav heart.

In these difficult moments I voice the sentiments of the Serbian people, who supplicate your Majesty to interest himself in the lot of the Kingdom of Serbia.

Alexander

It was an appeal which Nicholas, despite all appearances of cosmopolitan breeding and western sophistication, could not ignore. To the core of his quintessentially Slavic soul, he believed in his role as the protector of the Slavs as part of his divine appointment as Tsar. A gentle man to whom violence was abhorrent, Nicholas sought a way to discourage Austria-Hungary from mobilizing her army and marching on Belgrade. To this end he instructed Count Sazonov to request an extension of Vienna's deadline; simultaneously Sir Edward Grey in London was asking for the same thing. Both men were hoping that a delay in the note's expiration might give them sufficient time to bring diplomatic pressure to bear on Vienna and Berlin to accept an offer of arbitration.

The Austrian's rejection of Sazonov's request was blunt: Ambassador Szápáry quickly disabused the Russian Foreign Minister of the "mistaken idea" that Austria's informing the Great Powers of the content of her note to Serbia had been done:

With a view to learning their opinion of the case. All we intended was to inform the Powers of our step and thus conform to international etiquette. We consider our action an affair which concerns exclusively us and Serbia.

Grey's treatment was even more brusque, even ominous: he was simply ignored. The Kaiser's ministers wholeheartedly endorsed Vienna's intransigence, as Berlin's sense of urgency grew, and Ambassador Szögyény cabled Berchtold on July 24 that "Here every delay in the beginning of war operations is regarded as increasing the danger that foreign powers might interfere."

Unprepared to accept the idea that one of the Great Powers was driving another into a war which threatened to grow beyond any nation's ability to contain, Grey and Sazonov then turned to the Serbs, hoping that a mollified Austria-Hungary might moderate her belligerence and accept a negotiated settlement. To that end they urged the Serbs to make every concession possible to the Austrians—in Grey's words, "give a favorable reply to as many points as possible within the time limit." This was von Bethmann-Hollweg's nightmare come true—Grey was specifically suggesting a reconvening of the Six Power Conference in London which had so successfully defused the Balkan Crises of 1912 and 1913. Here Grey was playing the diplomatic game with consummate skill, for the same six representatives who had sat at the earlier conferences were still in London: Austria's Prince Mensdorff; Russia's Count Benckendorff; Grey's personal friend Paul Cambon, France's ambassador; Imperiale of Italy; and Prince Lichnowsky of Germany. Having lived and worked in close proximity to each other for years would serve the conference admirably by minimizing the sort of personal frictions which sometimes grew out of unfamiliarity. As Grey saw it, Germany was the key: if Berlin accepted an invitation to the conference, Vienna could not afford to refuse. Consequently, Grey approached Lichnowsky first. The Prince, who had been kept ignorant by the *Wilhelmstrasse* of the intrigues in Berlin and Vienna, took at face value the claim that the German government was as surprised as any other by the nature of the Austrian ultimatum. So it was in good faith that he accepted Grey's invitation, declaring in a telegram to von

Jagow that "I see in it the only possibility of avoiding a world war." He went on to warn the German Foreign Minister of the danger of snubbing Grey: "Grey will not bestir himself again. . . . Once more I urgently advise the acceptance of the English proposal."

Sazonov had a further, detailed suggestion that was even more specific: once concessions were made, Serbia should abandon any idea of actually resisting an Austrian invasion, should it come to that, permitting Belgrade to be occupied and seeking the protection of the other Great Powers through arbitration. Count Szápáry's protests to the contrary notwithstanding, Sazonov regarded the crisis as an international issue, convinced that a war between Austria and Serbia would soon spread beyond the Balkans. In this he was presenting not only his own views but those of the Tsar as well: both men keenly believed that Russia had a moral responsibility to protect Serbia's independence. Sazonov was prepared to submit the whole matter to an international panel of arbitration, composed of representatives from France, Italy, Germany, and Great Britain; the Tsar suggested that it go before the International Court in the Hague.

The Serbian government was in an impossible position, and knew it; the ultimatum would expire before the proposal could be formally issued, even should Austria-Hungary accept arbitration. Within hours of receiving Austria-Hungary's ultimatum, the Prince Regent and his ministers concluded that they would have to submit to the Dual Monarchy's demands: to do so would at least preserve something of Serbia's national identity; resistance would most likely only result in Serbia being obliterated from the map of Europe. By noon on July 25, Russia, France and Great Britain were all informed that the government in Belgrade was prepared to accept all of the Austro-Hungarian conditions, with only minor reservations.

What followed next could have been a scene straight out of a Gilbert and Sullivan comic opera, had it not been so tragic for Serbia. The Dual Monarchy's note demanded a reply, and under the accepted rules of diplomatic etiquette, a verbal response was insufficient and could not be considered legally binding. Accordingly the Serbian ministers spent the next several hours struggling with the wording of their response to the ultimatum, typing and retyping drafts, scrawling last-minute revisions and addendums across them, then retyping them once again. Part of the confusion lay in the fact that the reply was being drafted in Serb but translated and typed into French, the language of international diplomacy; adding to the chaos, despite the urgency of the situation, the typist selected was inexperienced and the typewriter itself kept breaking down. As the six p.m. deadline loomed closer, all thought of producing a flawless document was abandoned and the draft declared ready for delivery.

Another interlude of absurdity then occurred as no one was willing to take it to the Austrian ambassador. The Serbian government expected Austrian artillery stationed on the banks of the Danube opposite Belgrade to begin shelling the city the moment it was learned that Serbia's capitulation was less than total, and all of the ministers and secretaries were fearful of missing the last train south out of the capital. Finally the Prime Minister, Nikola Pašic—tall, gaunt, he was nearly seventy years old and had been a powerful figure in Serbian politics for nearly four decades—announced that he would deliver the reply.

At 5:55—five minutes short of the ultimatum's expiration—Pašic was shown into Baron Giesl's office, and with the solemnity due the moment presented Serbia's reply to the Austrian note, the document covered with misspellings, erasures, and last minute insertions written in ink. Giesl was a man of some considerable personal honor, and a loyal and conscientious officer of the Emperor; he was far from happy with his role in the unfolding charade. His recollection of the moment gives a hint that he believed that both he and Pašic deserved better:

> . . . the Serbian Prime Minister appeared in my office and gave me the answer of his government. . . . Pašic . . . was obviously conscious of the significance of the moment. His exceptionally intelligent eyes reflected a melancholy earnestness. When I asked him what the answer was Pašic replied in German, of which he had a full command: 'We accepted some of your demands . . . for the rest, we place our hopes on your loyalty and chivalry as an Austrian general. We have always been very satisfied with you.'

Giesl promised Pašic a quick reply, the two men shook hands, and the

Serbian Prime Minister departed.

Giesl's actions in the next few moments explain his discomfiture, and confirmed for the Serbs that the formulation and delivery of the ultimatum had been nothing but an elaborate ruse fabricated to provide Austria-Hungary with a *casus belli*, though Giesl himself was only acting on specific instructions from Vienna. Skimming over the Serbian reply, he noted the wording of Point Six:

> As regards the participation in this inquiry [into the assassination—which Serbia agreed to conduct] of Austro-Hungarian agents . . . [Serbia] cannot accept such an arrangement, as it would be a violation of the Constitution . . .

As instructed, he declared that as Serbia had refused to fully comply with all the demands of the note of July 23, diplomatic relations between Serbia and Austria-Hungary were immediately severed, and sent a previously prepared note to the Serbian Foreign Ministry stating as much. With that, he literally picked up his suitcase (the whole of the Austro-Hungarian Embassy staff were packed and ready to depart Belgrade) and set out for the railway station. There he caught the 6:30 p.m. train, the last train out of Belgrade bound for the Austrian border.

However, severing diplomatic relations was not a declaration of war. Berchtold had joined the Imperial household at Bad Ischl earlier that afternoon, and had impatiently waited in the office of Lt. Gen. Albert von Margutti, the Emperor's long-time aide-de-camp, while the hours passed with no word from Belgrade. Finally, as the clock struck six, he announced, "It is hardly likely that anything will come now. I am going out for a breath of fresh air." The Foreign Minister was barely out the door when the telephone rang, delivering the message that Giesl had left Belgrade: the Serbian answer had been unacceptable. Writing this information down as rapidly as possible, Margutti sent a messenger after Berchtold, then rushed over to the Emperor's villa, where he was immediately shown into Franz Josef's office. Silently placing his handwritten note before the old monarch, Margutti waited patiently for him to read it; he noticed that the Emperor's hands shook so badly that he could hardly put on his reading glasses. Finally after some minutes of silence, Franz Josef murmured, "Well, the breaking of diplomatic relations does not mean war."

This view was shared by Berchtold when he learned of the news from Belgrade. He immediately sent a telegram to the Serbian ambassador to Vienna, informing him that diplomatic relations were broken and authorizing the return of his passports. Simultaneously, he communicated the Emperor's authorization of the formal mobilization of the Austro-Hungarian Army. When news broke in Vienna, spontaneous demonstrations of support for the monarchy broke out across the city, as full-throated crowds waving the Imperial standard sang patriotic songs. Buoyed by the people's support and sensing that he might actually be on the verge of a bloodless triumph, Berchtold suddenly began entertaining the idea that there could still be a diplomatic solution to the crisis—a strange turnabout for the man who had insisted on war with Serbia almost from the moment the news had reached him of the Sarajevo assassinations. Preventing the war, which he had earlier disdained, now took on a particular urgency with Berchtold. Mobilizing the Austro-Hungarian Army would, he believed, intimidate the Serbs into full and unconditional acceptance of all of Vienna's demands. Knowing that both France and Great Britain hoped to avoid a major war, and believing that they would continue to do so at any cost (Berchtold was utterly ignorant of the fact that the Schlieffen Plan committed Germany to war with France regardless of French intentions) the Austrian Foreign Minister convinced himself that they, along with Kaiser Wilhelm, would exert a restraining influence on Russia, Serbia's only hope.

Once the order to mobilize the army was given, though, the situation would change dramatically: no longer would the confrontation between Serbia and the Dual Monarchy merely be an exercise in diplomacy. As Franz Josef had observed, severing diplomatic relations was not a declaration of war. Like reaching for the hilt of a sword, it was a gesture pregnant with possibilities and implications, none of which, however, posed an immediate danger. Once the gesture had made its point, it could be easily undone. Mobilization, however, was akin to actually drawing the sword—again, not an irrevocable act, but infinitely more threatening, fraught with the potential for mistakes, and far more difficult to withdraw without costly consequence. Now the pace of events would begin to accelerate.

By Monday morning, on July 27, it began to dawn on Berchtold Serbia's reply had begun to subtly reverse Europe's perception of the relative positions of the small Balkan kingdom and Austria-Hungary: now Serbia began to appear the victim and her powerful neighbor to the north the aggressor. The French newspaper *Le Matin*, conservative, nationalistic, and influential, voiced the opinion that

> Never had a people gone further along the path of concessions and even, let us use the proper expression, along that of humiliation. . . . In truth, the attitude of Austria passes understanding. She achieves a diplomatic victory, total, unhoped for, almost terrifying. And she is not content with it. She wishes to go still further.

As early as July 25, London's *Pall Mall Gazette*, frequently a voice for the Conservative Party, had taken the position that Austria-Hungary would lose the sympathy of Europe if her demands seemed intent on making war inevitable; now that was precisely what was happening. Even Sir Edward Grey, who had been shaken by the severity of Austria-Hungary's note, was amazed at the lengths to which Serbia was willing to go to accommodate the ultimatum. Now it was up to Austria-Hungary to decide if she wanted war or peace: for a few brief hours, the question hung in the balance.

The same day that Berchtold hesitated before stepping into the abyss, July 27, the Kaiser returned to Berlin. For three weeks he had been for all practical purposes completely cut off from events in Belgrade, Vienna, St. Petersburg, and, most critically, Berlin. Offering to cut short his sea-going holiday if his presence were required in Berlin, he was lulled into a sense of false security by the deceptive telegrams sent daily by the Chancellor. Von Bethmann-Hollweg urged him to continue to enjoy the splendors of the Norwegian fjords; the dispatches forwarded to the Kaiser by the *Wilhelmstrasse* were carefully chosen and edited. Wilhelm had no sense of the impending crisis: he continued to staunchly support Austria-Hungary and condemn Serbia, calling the small kingdom "nothing but a band of robbers that must be seized for crimes!" It was not until after the Austro-Hungarian ultimatum had been sent to Belgrade that he began to infer from reports in Norwegian newspapers that what had begun as a minor diplomatic contretemps was growing into yet another Balkan War—one which threatened to draw Germany into it. Although the Kaiser's memoirs could often be ridiculously self-serving, because his version is supported by those of other participants, his recounting of how he came to realize the gravity of the situation can be accepted at face value. The mixture of astonishment and anger he expresses at being so rudely and thoroughly deceived by the men who were responsible to him for guiding—and protecting—the Fatherland is startling.

> While I was on my summer vacation trip . . . I received but meagre news from the Foreign Office and was obliged to rely principally on the Norwegian newspapers from which I received the impression that the situation was growing worse. I telegraphed repeatedly to the Chancellor and the Foreign Office that I considered it advisable to return home, but was asked each time not to interrupt my journey. . . . When . . . I learned from the Norwegian newspaper—*not from Berlin*—of the Austrian ultimatum to Serbia and immediately after of the Serbian note to Austria, I started on my return journey without further ado. . . .

When Wilhelm arrived at the Potsdam station late in the evening of July 26, he was met by a pale, agitated, and somewhat fearful Chancellor. Von Bethmann-Hollweg's apprehension stemmed not from the dangers of the looming war, but rather from his fear of the Kaiser's wrath when the extent of his deceptions were revealed. The Kaiser's first words to him were suitably brusque: "How did it all happen?" Rather than attempt to explain, the Chancellor offered his resignation by way of apology. Wilhelm refused to accept it, muttering furiously, "You've made this stew, now you're going to eat it!" The next morning, Wilhelm was able for the first time to read in full the Serbian reply to Austria-Hungary's ultimatum. Once again his mood swung wildly, this time toward elation, for it seemed that there was no need to go to war after all. (For all of his endless martial posturing, Wilhelm was something of a coward: he loved playing at war, but actually fighting one was another matter entirely.) In a memorandum to Foreign Minister von Jagow, he wrote that the Serbian reply was "[a] brilliant performance for a time limit of only forty-eight hours. This is more than one could have expected. A great moral victory for Vienna; with it every reason for war drops away." He then instructed von Jagow to initiate arbitration between Vienna and Belgrade, with the condition that the Austro-Hungarian Army be permitted to occupy the Serbian capital during negotiations to assure Serbia's good faith.

Both von Jagow and von Bethmann-Hollweg were aghast at Wilhelm's instructions. The last thing that they wanted, along with Berchtold and Tisza in Vienna, was a peaceful resolution to the crisis—the sole reason it had been brought to such a critical juncture was expressly to start a war: Austria-Hungary meant to overwhelm Serbia, and Germany meant to exploit the resulting international uproar. Ignoring Wilhelm, von Bethmann-Hollweg cabled Tschirschky in Vienna on the morning of July 28 that he must "avoid very carefully giving rise to the impression that we wish to hold Austria back."

Predictably, Wilhelm's mood continued to change, his exultation deteriorating into anger over being deceived in so cavalier a fashion by von Bethmann-Hollweg and von Jagow. By nightfall his anger turning to belligerence, and naturally he focused it on his favorite target, Great Britain. Since his youth he had been afflicted by something akin to a chronic inferiority complex where his English cousins were concerned, envious of the pomp and grandeur of a 1200-year-old monarchy, with all the stability, nobility, and grace that were its trappings; where men and women carelessly and comfortably wore names and titles that were the very warp and weft of European history; a society that was relaxed, mature, and secure in its own longevity. Imperial Germany was none of these things, and yet Wilhelm craved them all—and because he could not have them, in the sourest of grapes he scorned, mocked, and sneered at them. When word of Sir Edward Grey's proposal for resumption of the Six Power Conference reached Berlin that afternoon, Wilhelm was almost contemptuous in his dismissal. Germany would participate, he declared, only at Austria's express request, and that was unlikely to be forthcoming, since "in vital matters people consult nobody."

The events in Berlin on July 27 would become one of history's watersheds, not because of the decisions made, but rather for the reasons for making them. They marked the passing of a political paradigm which had existed for nearly three centuries: that national and dynastic policies were synonymous, that monarchs and their ministers could create and carry out political agendas while being accountable to no one but themselves. No longer could the crowned heads of Europe, however autocratic in their rule they might be, act without reference to the people they ruled. In its place a new paradigm emerged, one of the public's perception of their government and its accountability—along with the confidence, or lack of it, those perceptions created. With it the nature of national and international politics for the rest of the 20th century and well into the 21st would be permanently altered.

In his refusal to accept von Bethmann-Hollweg's proffered resignation, the Kaiser may have been motivated in part by a desire to make the Chancellor face the consequences of his actions, but Wilhelm also knew that, despite their duplicity, he could not afford the political cost of dismissing both his Chancellor and his Foreign Minister in the middle of such a grave international crisis. To do so would raise questions in the Reichstag and the press about who was really running the German government, questions which could only further erode the German people's confidence in the monarchy, which while perhaps not as shaky as von Bethmann-Hollweg feared, was far from being as monolithic as was presented to the outside world. Wilhelm would appear weak and ineffectual, exposed to precisely the sort of ridicule he had always feared was being directed at him, weakening the moral foundations on which rested the Hohenzollern throne.

What mattered now was saving face, for the Chancellor, for the Kaiser, for Germany, for the German-Austrian alliance. Prestige, the euphemism for the power—military, economic or both—to compel, and if need be coerce, other nations into favorable or even preferential policies and actions, is the intangible yet real currency of diplomacy and international relations. Prestige was what was suddenly at stake in the crisis: Austria-Hungary's position as a Great Power was in jeopardy; so was Germany's credibility as a reliable ally.

Austria-Hungary could not afford to back down from her intransigent stance toward Serbia without appearing to have been too weak to have actually imposed her will on the smaller kingdom; Germany could not afford to withdraw her support of Austria-Hungary lest it create the impression that Germany had blundered in her initial offer of that support. The whole terrible drama now had to be played out to the bitter end.

The British government, and most specifically Grey, continued to press for arbitration throughout the day. Three times Ambassador Lichnowsky cabled warnings to Berlin, his growing frustration evident with each successive communication, as it seemed that the *Wilhelmstrasse* simply could not grasp that its apparent inaction was increasing the likelihood of war. He said in the first telegram

> Sir E. Grey had me call on him just now. It appeared to him that Serbia had agreed to the Austrian demands to an extent such as he would have never believed possible. . . . Should Austria fail to be satisfied with this reply. . . it would be absolutely evident that Austria was only seeking an excuse for crushing Serbia.

Later:

> I found [Grey] irritated for the first time. He spoke with great seriousness and seemed absolutely to expect that we should successfully make use of our influence to settle the matter. . . . Everybody here is convinced that the key to the situation is to be found in Berlin and that, if peace is seriously desired there, Austria can be restrained from prosecuting—as Sir E. Grey put it—a foolhardy policy.

Finally, just before dinnertime in Berlin:

> Our entire future relations with England depend on the success of this move by Sir Edward Grey [the proposed Six Power Conference]. Should the Minister succeed. . . I will guarantee that our relations with England will remain. . .

intimate and confidential. . . . Should Austria's intention of using the present situation to overthrow Serbia. . . become more and more apparent, England, I am certain, would place herself unconditionally by the side of France and Russia. . . . If it comes to war under these circumstances, we shall have England against us.

On one hand, Lichnowsky was exaggerating: Great Britain was not prepared to go to war over Serbia. British interests and British honor were not involved—that drama was still some days away, to be played out over the fate of another small kingdom. On the other hand, however, Lichnowsky was sounding a fair warning, advising Berlin that there were limits to how far Britain—along with the other Great Powers—could be pushed. London would tolerate a chastisement of Serbia: naked aggression by Austria-Hungary was another matter entirely. What Lichnowsky could not know, of course, was that war was precisely what von Bethmann-Hollweg and von Jagow wanted; and while the Chancellor rightly feared the might of the British Empire, the Kaiser, the rest of his ministers and his General Staff, confident in Germany's preponderance of power on the Continent, discounted it. The war, if it came, would be over before the British, with their seemingly insignificant army, could make their influence felt.

Meanwhile, Berchtold had overcome his earlier hesitation, and on the morning of July 28, exercising the authority granted to him by Emperor Franz Josef before the ultimatum had been sent, he drafted Austria-Hungary's declaration of war on Serbia. What occurred next was the final episode of the Austro-Serbian *opera bouffe*. With diplomatic relations severed between Belgrade and Vienna, there was no one in the Serbian capital authorized to deliver the Austro-Hungarian declaration of war. Baffled by the situation, which could only have occurred in Austria, Berchtold worried for several hours before hitting upon what he regarded as a clever, even brilliant solution. Noting that the Serbian government had evacuated Belgrade for the southern city of Nish, he sent two identical telegrams there, one addressed to the Serbian Foreign Ministry, the other to the Serbian Army Headquarters. They read:

Vienna
28 July 1914

The Royal Serbian Government not having answered
in a satisfactory manner the note of July 23, 1914,
presented by the Austro-Hungarian Minister at
Belgrade, the Imperial and Royal Government are
themselves compelled to see to the safeguarding of
their rights and interests, and, with this object, to have
recourse to force of arms.

Austria-Hungary consequently considers herself henceforward in state of war with Serbia.

Count Berchtold

Pašic at first thought the messages were someone's idea of a sick
joke—after all, who ever heard of a declaration of war via telegram?
Even worse than a hoax, they might be an act of Austrian
provocation, attempting to goad the Serbs into firing the first shots of
the war. Before long, however, he was able to confirm through the
French and British ambassadors that the war was real. Further confirmation, if any was needed, came the next morning, when Austrian
artillery batteries, taking up positions on the north bank of the
Danube, began shelling Belgrade.

Conforming to accepted diplomatic etiquette, Austria-Hungary
had duly informed each of the Great Powers that she had declared
war on Serbia at the same time the telegrams were sent to Nish. When
the news reached St. Petersburg, a pall settled over the Tsar's
government. Up to that moment Sazonov had still been working to
find a peaceful resolution to the confrontation, assuring Vienna that
he "was ready to go to the limit in accommodating Austria,"
suggesting that "there must be a way of giving Serbia a deserved
lesson while sparing her sovereign rights." Grey's proposal for
arbitration through the Six Power Conference was still on the table,
having been communicated to Berlin, Vienna, Paris, St. Petersburg,
Rome, and Belgrade the night of July 26. These efforts had gone far

in reinforcing the impression in Vienna and Berlin that Russia was not prepared to fight for Serbia. From the onset of the crisis Count Berchtold had been convinced that Tsar Nicholas, under pressure from France and Great Britain to avoid a war, and having little sympathy for regicides, would do little more than pay lip service in support of Serbia. It was a political calculation in which Prime Minister Tisza in Vienna, and Kaiser Wilhelm and Chancellor von Bethmann-Hollweg in Berlin all concurred.

As a result, the news broke like a thunderclap in Vienna and Berlin when word arrived from St. Petersburg that Russia's southern military districts were being mobilized. Russia was going to war.

Chapter VI

MOBILIZATION IN ST. PETERSBURG

From the onset of the confrontation between Austria-Hungary and Serbia, the brooding shadow of the Russian Empire had loomed over the two nations. To Serbia, Russia was the ultimate refuge, the powerful protector who could save the tiny kingdom from being crushed by the Austro-Hungarian Army. The Dual Monarchy, while not fearing a war with Russia, lacked the strength to overrun Serbia and at the same time defend herself from a Russian attack. Accordingly, to both nations the question of "What will Russia do?" was of paramount importance in the growing crisis.

The question was of no small concern to the rest of Europe as well, for should Russia choose to intervene on Serbia's behalf, it would become increasingly difficult, if not impossible, to confine the war to the Balkans. The cause of this concern was simple: Russia was France's ally, while Austria-Hungary was Germany's. Given the perpetual enmity between Teuton and Gaul (and Germany had openly courted war with France in 1905 and 1911), any conflict between their allies threatened to draw in Berlin and Paris as well, turning what might have been a regional conflict into a continent-wide war.

It was an open secret in the diplomatic world that the alliance between Russia and France was one of military and political convenience rather than ideological commitment: the two nations had nothing in common except a shared enemy, Germany. Both had become diplomatically isolated as a consequence of German political maneuvers, France at the hands of Bismarck in 1871, following her defeat in the Franco-Prussian War, Russia in 1890 by Wilhelm's refusal to renew the Reinsurance Treaty, which ended the Russo-German alliance. Even their regard of Germany as an enemy, real or perceived, was unequal. As long as the provinces of Alsace and Lorraine remained under German rule—"occupied" was how most French politicians phrased it—there would be no real peace between France and Germany, only an ongoing state of uneasy, heavily armed truce. Between Russia and Germany, however, no such deeply rooted enmity existed, there were no long-standing confrontations, no history of conflict between the two monarchies: more than a century and a half had passed since the last war between Romanov and Hohenzollern. Russia and Germany were rivals, not enemies.

What stood between Russia and Germany was ambition. In the last quarter of the 19th century, the fastest-growing, most dynamic economy in Europe belonged to Germany; by the end of the first decade of the 20th century, that distinction belonged to Russia. While Germany still wielded far more economic power than Russia, her economic domination of the Continent—and with it her military and political supremacy—was no longer assured. At the same time, her burgeoning population was becoming a concern, as the resources of the Fatherland's cities were being pushed to their limits. Emigration to North or South America was one solution, but that had the consequence of essentially depriving Germany of that portion of her population: once in the embrace of the United States or the Argentine, the sons and daughters who left the Fatherland behind were also effectively beyond Germany's political influence. With no colonial empire to speak of, the only direction Germany herself could expand was to the east. *Drang nach Osten* had been a theme in German politics for centuries, but by 1914 it had taken on an entirely new meaning, as the lands of Russian Poland, Lithuania, and Estonia were being eyed covetously by Berlin.

For St. Petersburg, the largest obstacle Germany presented to Russian ambition lay in her choice of allies. Austria-Hungary had for centuries resented and sometimes forcibly opposed Russia's westward expansion, particularly into the Balkans. Austria's refusal to support Russia in the Crimean War had opened a rift between the two nations which never really closed; it became permanent after 1877, when Britain and Austria combined to threaten Russia with war after Alexander II ordered his army to march on Constantinople. At the same time Russia found Austria's growing dominance in the Balkans particularly irksome, on both a temporal and spiritual plane, as it blocked Russia's own ambitions toward Constantinople and came at the expense of fellow Slavs. However, Russia could never feel sufficiently confident of resorting to war with Austria as long as the Hapsburg empire was allied with its Hohenzollern cousin: Austria-Hungary alone was a foe Russia could confront with real confidence of defeating, while Austria-Hungary and Germany combined was beyond Russia's power to successfully oppose.

As long as Otto von Bismarck was Chancellor of Imperial Germany, this situation was not as great a problem as it might have been. In a series of clever diplomatic moves he created a remarkably stable situation. The first was the League of the Three Emperors, created in 1873, which was a vague, but appealing, concept whereby the Emperors Wilhelm I, Franz Josef, and Alexander III agreed to act in a spirit of "brotherhood" and not undertake any foreign adventures which might impinge on the interests of one or the other monarchies. When the League lapsed in 1877, Bismarck then negotiated the Austro-German Treaty of 1879, an agreement of mutual assistance which would require Austria-Hungary and Germany to each stand beside the other as a co-belligerent should one or the other go to war with France or Russia. One of its key clauses was that the terms of the treaty could be invoked regardless of who actually started the war or why.

The Tsar's government naturally felt that this was a direct threat—Austria-Hungary could provoke a war with Russia and bring Germany into it with her, but Bismarck had anticipated this, and in 1887 he concluded his masterstroke, the highly secret Reinsurance Treaty with Russia. Reduced to its essence, the treaty stated that in the event of a war involving Russia and Austria-Hungary, Germany would only honor its alliance with the Dual Monarchy in the event that Russia attacked Austria-Hungary. Should the Austrians attack Russia, Germany would remain neutral in the conflict. Likewise, should France attack Germany, Russia would maintain her neutrality.

The terms of the treaty—even its existence—were kept a closely guarded secret, lest the Austrians believe that they were being summarily betrayed by their German ally. Yet for Russia and Germany it was an extraordinarily accomplished piece of diplomacy: it protected Austria-Hungary by assuring Germany's support in the event of a Russian attack, yet at the same time reassured Russia that Germany would not allow herself to be used as an instrument of Austro-Hungarian expansionism.

Bismarck's grand design collapsed in the wake of his dismissal in 1890 by the new Kaiser, Wilhelm II as one of the casualties of Bismarck's fall was the Reinsurance Treaty. Because the treaty's existence had been kept secret, no one in Europe expected what happened next. Russia and France, who both found themselves diplomatically isolated, were driven into an alliance. The process began on July 23, 1890, less than a month after Wilhelm allowed the Reinsurance Treaty to lapse, when a French naval squadron tied up at the Russian fleet anchorage of Reval, on the Baltic Sea. Invited by the Tsar, Alexander III, this mission was the opening move of the process which led to the Franco-Russian Alliance. Deprived of their only European ally, the diplomats of St. Petersburg had set about looking for another, and with Germany and Austria-Hungary already allied with each other and Great Britain still pursuing her policy of "Splendid Isolation," France was the inevitable choice.

This does not mean it was an easy decision: when Russia's then-Foreign Minister, Nicholas Giers, warned Wilhelm against allowing the Reinsurance Treaty to lapse, he did so with the words "The Tsar will be forced, against his own wishes, to ally himself with the French Republic." The two nations were almost the antitheses of each other: Russia, autocratic, Orthodox, xenophobic and underdeveloped, both economically and politically, shared little in common with republican, regicidal, Catholic, cosmopolitan, industrialized France. Yet as unlikely as they seemed as partners in alliance, both nations saw the wisdom as well as the need to make common cause against Germany. Consequently, Alexander found himself standing at attention in his own Peterhof Palace in St. Petersburg, at a state dinner given for the commander of the visiting French squadron, while a military band played the "Marseillaise," a revolutionary tune banned for a century within the borders of Russia. In turn, a few days later in Moscow the French Admiral, Pierre Gervais, stood and raised his glass, saying, "I drink to Holy Moscow, the great Russian nation, and its noble Tsar."

The negotiations took three-and-a-half years to accomplish, though the outcome was never really in doubt: on January 4, 1894, the alliance—popularly known as the Dual Entente—became official. The terms of the treaty were very specific, and would be modified and reworked several times over the next two decades as Europe's political, economic and military landscape shifted. In its earliest inception the treaty specified that any mobilization by Austria-Hungary would automatically trigger a simultaneous mobilization by France and Russia; subsequent amendments to the treaty set more precise conditions under which each nation would be required to come to the aid of the other. As it read in 1914, only if Germany mobilized her army would the two allies mobilize in turn—a mobilization by Austria would not be sufficient to trigger such a reaction.

While the treaty was supposedly a secret, neither France nor Russia went to any great pains to keep it so, for much of the alliance's value lay in its effectiveness as a deterrent to Germany; before long the general outlines of the Franco-Russian alliance were well-known across Europe. It also provided the rationale behind the Schlieffen Plan, and in every Continental crisis subsequent to the treaty's creation, the chancelleries of Europe kept a close eye on Germany's reactions, knowing that alone among the Great Powers, Germany's mobilization made war a certainty. Thus the underlying precept of European diplomacy for two decades was to prevent any crisis from reaching the point where Germany felt compelled to mobilize: the nations of Europe did not fear Germany so much as they feared the war that she would start.

The alliance with France had been emphasized most dramatically by the state visit to St. Petersburg by France's President, Raymond Poincaré, and her Premier, Rene Viviani, in the week before Vienna issued its ultimatum to Belgrade. The timing of the visit had been entirely fortuitous—it had been scheduled months before the Sarajevo assassinations—but was quite effective nonetheless.

The visit itself had been a huge success, which came as a surprise to almost all parties concerned. Poincaré in particular was not fond of

Russians, and specifically mistrusted the Russian Foreign Minister, Sazonov. Sazonov refused to put France's diplomatic interests ahead of Russia's, which Poincaré peevishly concluded was an indication that Sazonov did not take the alliance seriously enough. He was suspicious of munitions orders placed by the Russian Army with German arms manufacturers (Russian industry could not supply all the guns and ammunition required by the reorganized army, and French munitions manufacturers perversely refused Russian orders, claiming they were already working full time to supply the French Army, though they had little trouble supplying arms to other overseas customers), and feared, groundlessly, that the Tsar's court was pro-German. In the French President's opinion, the alliance with Russia existed solely for France's benefit, and it was time that the Tsar and his ministers were made to understand this. To Poincaré, whose ignorance of Russia was exceeded only by his lack of regard for her, the country was unstable—he would have heartily agreed with Winston Churchill's description of the Tsar's empire as a "quasi-Asiatic mass"—with, as he saw it, assassinations taking place with alarming frequency, and riots breaking out almost daily in the major cities, while corruption could be found everywhere.

Despite Poincaré's prejudices, for most of its four days, from July 19 to July 23, the visit was a success. An endless succession of state banquets, military reviews, religious services, and serious talks, the visit climaxed on July 23, with a massive military review and the commissioning of the newest class of Russian officer-cadets. At a dinner that evening aboard the battleship *La France*, the Tsar and Poincaré stood and exchanged toasts, reaffirming the strength and solidarity of the Franco-Russian entente, which was followed by an official communique announcing that "the two governments are entirely in agreement in their views on various problems which concern for peace and the balance of power in Europe has laid before the Powers, particularly in the East." A confidential summary of the visit compiled by the British Ambassador to St. Petersburg, Sir George Buchanan, drew attention to determination of the French and Russian governments to be firm with Vienna in their belief that as a result of any aggressive action by Austria-Hungary Serbia "would be justified in regarding as an attack on her sovereignty." He also felt it important to record Nicholas' and Poincaré's "solemn affirmation of obligations imposed by the alliance of the two countries." *La France* departed St. Petersburg at 11:00 p.m. local time—7:00 p.m. in Vienna and 6:00 p.m. in Belgrade. At that same moment, the Austro-Hungarian ultimatum was being delivered to the government of Serbia.

The Russian government officially became aware of the ultimatum sometime before noon on July 24, when the Austro-Hungarian ambassador, Count Szápáry, presented Sazonov with a copy of the note along with a detailed memorandum presenting the evidence Austria had gathered which implicated Serbia in the assassinations of Franz Ferdinand and Sophie. It was during this meeting that Sazonov had blurted out to Szápáry, "I know what it is—you mean to make war on Serbia and this is just a pretext." Szápáry attempted to reassure Sazonov that this was not the case, reminding him rather sharply that given Serbia's history of provocation the Dual Monarchy needed no pretext if it sought a war. The Russian Foreign Minister was not fooled for a second. Within minutes he had ushered Szápáry out of his office and began making telephone calls, the first being to the army Chief of Staff, General Nicholas Yanushkevich. Sazonov suggested that preparations for a partial mobilization begin, but only for those military districts bordering on the Dual Monarchy: the districts which shared borders with Germany would remain inactive. In his turn Yanushkevich instructed General Sergei Dobrolski, chief of the army's mobilization department, to prepare a proclamation of the partial mobilization, warning Dobrolski that "nothing must give Germany occasion to perceive. . . any hostile intent toward herself."

Sazonov then had a working lunch with the French and British ambassadors, respectively M. Maurice Paléologue and Sir George Buchanan. It was at this luncheon that the idea was first broached that Great Britain might make a declaration of open solidarity with France and Russia should Germany make any move that indicated military action in support of Austria-Hungary. It was Buchanan who later reported he privately believed there was "a good deal of truth" in Sazonov's contention that "if Germany knew beforehand that France and Russia could count on English support, she would never face the risks which such a war would entail." Buchanan, though, as a career diplomat, was a professional through and through, and while he knew that precisely this idea was being considered in London, as it was not Britain's official policy he carefully refused to say or do anything which might be misconstrued by either Paris or St. Petersburg.

Maurice Paléologue, for his part, possessed none of Buchanan's sagacity or restraint. He was a poor choice for ambassador to St. Petersburg—or anywhere else for that matter. His only two qualifications for the post were his unreserved support of the Dual Entente and his close personal friendship with President Poincaré. He was moody, depressed, chronically pessimistic, and an ego-maniac: his penchant for self-promotion and the most fantastic of self-aggrandizing lies was the stuff of legend in St. Petersburg. His Russian counterpart in Paris regarded him as a windbag and a liar, an impression Paléologue's tenure in the Russian capital did nothing to contradict. He lacked tact, discretion, and charm, the three most vital characteristics of any ambassador. His most grievous fault—and there are few worse for a diplomat—was his penchant for expressing his personal feelings and opinions as if they were the official policy of the French government. At the luncheon with Buchanan and Sazonov he repeatedly announced that Great Britain must support France and Russia should it become necessary for the two allies to stand up to Germany, each time making it clear that he expected Buchanan to spontaneously make such a declaration. Buchanan refused to be drawn, however, and he brought both men up short when he asked what the two men expected would happen if Russia, France, and Great Britain all warned Austria-Hungary against interfering in Serbia's internal affairs and Austria-Hungary ignored them. Looking pointedly at Sazonov, he asked if Russia would declare war on Austria-Hungary in such a case.

That silenced both Sazonov and Paléologue; the Russian Foreign Minister because he knew that such a policy had still to be decided by the Tsar and his ministers, the French ambassador because he was, for all his bluster and bombast, a coward. Paléologue spoke brashly, but he lacked the moral fiber to make hard decisions for which he might be held responsible. After a pause Sazonov replied to Buchanan, saying that this was the very question to be settled that afternoon when the Council of Ministers met.

That meeting began at precisely 3:00 p.m. It was a troubled conference: everyone present understood that financially—and possibly socially—Russia could not afford a war at that moment. Yet paradoxically, she could not afford politically—and possibly socially—to avoid war under any and all circumstances. The double-edged social threat was that should Russia not win the war, revolution could be a very real outcome at home; on the other hand, should Russia appear to be abandoning their fellow Slavs, the Russian people might still rise in revolt. Sazonov stated the situation clearly and concisely when he asserted that should Russia allow Serbia to become a vassal state of Austria-Hungary, Russian prestige and authority in the Balkans would "collapse utterly." Attempting to appease the Dual Monarchy and Germany over this latest Serbian crisis would only lead to later challenges and demands by the two monarchies. The critical argument, made by A. V. Krivoshein, the Minister of Agriculture, and arguably the most powerful man at the conference, was that the time had come to assert Russia's authority as a Great Power: to fail to do so now would almost certainly assure that she would not be able to do so in the future.

The ministers agreed with Krivoshein: over the next few hours they produced five recommendations of routes which Sazonov might follow in an effort to defuse the crisis before war was forced upon them, but they never wavered in their determination that if the issue did come down to a violent resolution they would not shy away from it. Their recommendations were, first, that Sazonov should make every reasonable effort to get Austria-Hungary to extend the time limit on the note, in the hope of a breakthrough toward arbitration. Second, that Serbia accept as many of the terms of the Austrian note as she could; if Vienna insisted on attacking, the Serbs should withdraw into the interior of their kingdom and appeal to the rest of Europe for protection. The third recommendation was that, if needed, a partial mobilization should be initiated in the military districts of Odessa, Kiev, Kazan, and Moscow—all districts bordering on Austria-Hungary—while no such activity would begin in the districts opposite Germany. Fourth, military units, stores, and supplies should be brought up to a state of full readiness; and fifth, the finance minister would begin withdrawing Russian funds, particularly gold, from German and Austrian banks. The tone of all of these measures, individually and in sum, was that while Russia was not actively seeking a war with Austria-Hungary, she was prepared to accept one should it be forced upon her. It was hoped that this was a message which was understood in Vienna.

It was this list of recommendations which lent the urgency to the efforts of Count Sazonov, and which found an echo in Sir Edward Grey, over the next five days to keep the crisis between Austria-Hungary and Serbia confined to those two nations, and if at all possible, avoid a war altogether. At the same time, perversely, Count Berchtold's goal was similar—localizing the crisis—but he also intended to localize the war it was meant to provoke. However, perhaps because of his ultimately malevolent intent, his methods were a good deal more ham-handed, and counter-productive.

Though he did not know it at the time, in attempting to bully Russia into staying out of the crisis, Berchtold had blundered badly. The closing sentence of his rebuke of Foreign Minister Sazonov's request for an extension of the Austrian ultimatum's time limit—"We consider our action as an affair which concerns exclusively us and Serbia"—was little short of a slap to the face of the Russian government. It implied that the Balkans were Austria-Hungary's exclusive sphere of influence, and that Russia had no right to take an interest in the affairs of the small Slavic states which nevertheless looked to her for guidance and protection. Events might have taken a very different turn if Vienna had reserved its bellicosity solely for Belgrade, but this affront had a particular effect on the Tsar who seemed to take it personally. While in the days to come he would make frequent, sincere overtures to Germany to avert a wider war, his feelings would consistently be far more belligerent toward Vienna than toward Berlin.

Prince Regent Alexander's telegram begging for Russia's support placed Nicholas in an awkward position: he regarded Russia's role as the protector of the Balkan Slavs as a serious responsibility, yet he was being asked to come to the defense of a regime which was being implicated in the murder of Austria-Hungary's heir apparent. As Nicholas had little sympathy for regicides no one would have accused him of bad faith had he abandoned Serbia; indeed, in both Vienna and Berlin it was expected that he would do just that. Likewise, he was no arch-militarist like the Kaiser; Nicholas detested confrontation of any kind.

That abhorrence had first manifested itself to the world in 1898, when Nicholas astonished Europe by proposing to convene representatives from all of the Great Powers in a great conference which would explore ways to slow what was already a frightening arms race. Russia had long been regarded as insatiably expansionist and aggressive even when not being actually warlike; a backward, barely civilized country that hid behind its facade of Western civilization a brutal and autocratic regime perpetually repressing the ignorant masses of its peasantry while its aristocracy lived in corrupt splendor. While there was a certain degree of truth in that perception, it was over-simplistic, for as the 19th century gave way to the 20th, Russia was one of the most dynamic nations on the planet.

Vast investments in Russian industries by the French government as well as French capitalists, originally meant to spur the growth of Russia's armament industry and so increase her military potential—which would in turn increase Russia's value as a deterrent to German aggression against France—had the unanticipated side effect of spurring the growth of the entire spectrum of Russian industries. While Russia's middle class, working class and industrial base were all minuscule when compared to those of Britain, Germany or France, they were expanding at phenomenal rates. At the same time, agriculture, which had long been the foundation of Russia's economy, was more productive than ever, as Russian wheat fed Germany, Great Britain, the countries of Scandinavia and even lands as far away as South America.

When he ascended the Romanov throne in 1894, it was Nicholas' naive hope that his reign would preside over unparalleled economic growth while preserving the autocracy of Imperial Russia. It would be his tragedy that he never realized the two goals were mutually exclusive. Nevertheless, he believed that the first step toward prolonged prosperity would be taken by releasing the Great Powers from the overbearing burdens of their bloated military budgets, and with this in mind he proposed the first Hague Conference. The idea had first been mooted by his then-Minister of War, General Alexi Kuropatkin, and its roots lay not in the strength of the Tsar's character, but rather in the weakness of Russia's army. What gave the proposal such vitality and made it so remarkable was the determination with which Nicholas embraced the idea.

The basic problem was that in the decade before the turn of the century, Russia's finances were too shaky to allow the Tsar to modernize his army—artillery was obsolete, rifles were too few, ammunition supplies were inadequate, all obstacles which even the Russian soldiers' bottomless supply of courage could not overcome. With all of the European powers stocking their arsenals with ever-newer weaponry, Russia had no hope of ever achieving anything like parity with Germany or Austria-Hungary, her most likely foes in any future war. If the arms race could be halted, or at least curbed to some degree, Russia could gain time for the capabilities of her infant industries to grow to the point where they might be able to begin to meet Russia's needs. This was the ruthlessly practical motive behind General Kuropatkin's suggestion.

However, once Nicholas embraced the idea, it took on a whole new dimension, as he believed that genuinely humanitarian benefits could come from the proposed peace conference. In addition to seeking ways to rein in the arms race, the conference could codify much of the conduct by which "civilized" armies and navies would wage war among themselves, prescribing their behavior not only against each other but toward civilians as well. While not achieving the lofty goals set by Nicholas, the first conference was deemed a success by almost all the nations that took part, mainly because it took place at all. The most significant development was the establishment of a permanent panel of international arbitration, soon to become formalized as the International Court of Justice, seated, fittingly enough, in the Hague.

However, Nicholas failed to achieve his primary goal, a meaningful check on the arms race, and so Russia continued to lag behind the rest of the Great Powers in both the quantity and quality of the arms with which her armies were equipped. While the sheer size of the Russian Army—more than one and a half million men in uniform, with a ready reserve of over twice that number on which to draw for reinforcements—was sufficient to exert a measure of real intimidation on the Powers in Europe, the Russian Empire stretched across nearly a fifth of the globe. The Russian transportation network was not yet capable of properly supporting Russian armies in Europe so supporting forces in the easternmost marches of Siberia and along the Chinese border was well-nigh impossible. This vulnerability was ruthlessly exploited by Japan in 1904, when the Russian fleet at Port Arthur, on the Korean peninsula, was attacked and crippled in a surprise attack by the Japanese Navy. In the twelve months that followed, the Russian fleet sent to break the Japanese blockade and relieve the beleaguered forces in Korea was annihilated at Tsushima Strait. The Japanese Army then inflicted a series of crushing defeats on the undersupplied Russian forces, eventually compelling a humiliating capitulation by the Tsar's government.

No sooner had a peace settlement been reached than Russia found herself wracked by revolution. A groundswell of social change was about to flow across Russia, but of more immediate concern for Nicholas was the diminution of Russian power and influence in European affairs as a consequence of Russia's humbling at the hands of the Japanese. Sweeping reforms of the military, in training, organization, and equipment, all based on the experiences of the recent war as well as careful examination of the other Great Powers' armies, were put in hand almost immediately, though it would be seven to ten years before they were complete and their full effect was felt. Nevertheless, it was a beginning.

Most critically weakened was Russia's ability to fulfill her role as the protector of the Slavic peoples of southern Europe. Assuming that mantle in the early 19th century, it was one she wore with increasing confidence as the years passed and the Ottoman Turks, overlords of the Balkans for three hundred years, grew ever more feeble, the Ottoman Empire's Balkan provinces gradually assuming the shape of independent states. In a succession of bloody, brutal wars fought in the last quarter of the 19th century between Russia and the Ottoman Turks, the independence of Serbia, Bulgaria, and Romania, all at one time former Ottoman provinces, was assured by Russia. It was inevitable then that these three nations should continue to look to Russia for protection and support.

However, the defeats suffered in the Russo-Japanese War left the Russian Army in such disarray that when Austria-Hungary forcibly annexed the principalities of Bosnia and Herzegovina in 1908, there was little Russia could do but fume and protest. Four years later, in the Second and Third Balkan Wars, Nicholas still did not feel confident enough in his army to match the threats of Austrian or German intervention with a counter-threat of his own. It was a continuation of this impotence on which both Austria and Germany had counted when the ultimatum was sent to Serbia on July 23.

Events now compelled Nicholas into a choice that he would have preferred not to have to make: at issue was not whether Russia would support Serbia, but rather what form that support would take. Would Russia answer with only diplomatic protests, or would she affirm her role as protector of the Slavs and threaten Austria-Hungary with war? There were strong, sound reasons for offering only diplomatic support: Nicholas might well be setting a dangerous precedent by appearing to embrace a regicidal, revolutionary regime in Belgrade; at the same time there was still sympathy for the Dual Monarchy among the other nations of Europe because of the perception that the assassinations were at least condoned if not actually sanctioned by the Serbian government.

Not only that, but a precedent for refraining from intervention had been set in 1878 between Franz Josef and Nicholas' father Alexander II. In that year the two emperors had reached an understanding that Austria-Hungary would not interfere when Russia resorted to force to against the Ottoman Turks after Sultan Abdul Hamid revoked the constitutional protections for the Christian minorities in the Ottoman Empire's Balkans possessions. Thus the basis for a *quid pro quo* between Austria-Hungary and Russia existed if Nicholas and Franz Josef chose to allow it. Moreover, there were no binding treaties or agreements obligating the Russian Army to fight on Serbia's behalf; should St. Petersburg stand aloof, the Serbs had no recourse to claims of bad faith.

Balanced against all of these arguments was the perception in St. Petersburg that Russia's stature as a Great Power was at stake. While Nicholas genuinely desired to avoid a war, there was a deep seated sense of anger and frustration throughout the Imperial government and the Russian people alike at the international humiliations which Russia had been compelled to endure in the years following the Russo-Japanese War. Nicholas shared these feelings, and while he was a peaceful man, he was also a proud man, and he believed that the time was coming for Russia to act.

That hour came in the morning of July 28, when confirmation of Austria-Hungary's declaration of war reached the Russian Foreign Minister, Count Sazonov. Rushing to Tsarskoe Selo, the Imperial retreat outside St. Petersburg, Sazonov informed the Tsar of the Austrian declaration, then asked him for instructions. Nicholas had already issued the orders for the "Period Preparatory for War" on July 25, even before Serbia's reply to the Austro-Hungarian ultimatum was known. Nicholas had warned all of Europe that Russia would not be "indifferent" to Serbia's fate, and the "preparatory period" was a significant step in affirming that stand. The declaration covered the whole of European Russia, not just the military districts facing Austria-Hungary, and they allowed the district commandants to take any and all steps they believed necessary to make their commands ready for war short of actual mobilization. Fortresses were garrisoned at wartime strength, depots were readied to receive the anticipated flood of reservists, transports for baggage and supply trains were requisitioned, and security measures including mail censorship were put in place. It was not war, it was not even mobilization, but it was a necessary step that would save a tremendous amount of time and labor should mobilization become a fact.

Still at issue was whether or not Serbia was worth the risk of war with Austria-Hungary and Germany. Tragically, the situation required far more political skill than Nicholas possessed—only a Bismarck, a Disraeli, or a Metternich might have mustered the subtle combination of intimidation, cooperation, and guile that could have avoided war altogether. Nicholas' solution was to order the partial mobilization of the Russian Army suggested by the Council of Ministers. The Dual Monarchy lacked the manpower to simultaneously attack Serbia in the south and protect her border with Russia in the north: the threat of an attack in Galicia would completely disrupt Austro-Hungarian strategy, compelling Vienna to call off her planned assault across the Danube and instead stand on the defensive, saving Serbia in the process. The Russian Army would not have to actually take the offensive against Austria-Hungary for the ploy to succeed. Its pending presence on the Dual Monarchy's northern frontier would be sufficient to force Conrad von Hötzendorf to take precautions against what the Russians *might* do. The Austro-Hungarian mobilization would take fifteen to sixteen days, Russia's would require twenty-five to thirty days. Yet even allowing for the fact that Austria had already begun a partial mobilization and had a week's head start, there would still not be sufficient time for von Hötzendorf to assemble his forces in the south, overrun Serbia, then withdraw, re-equip and reinforce them, and turn them around to move them northward to the Galician frontier in time to stand against the looming Russian menace.

At the same time, though, the threat to the Dual Monarchy could not appear to be so grave as to provoke Germany into taking action against Russia in order to support her ally. The terms of the 1879 treaty which had formed the alliance between Germany and Austria-Hungary had explicitly stated that if Austria-Hungary mobilized her army in response to a Russian threat, Germany would mobilize as well, a course of action which, given the operational requirements of the Schlieffen Plan, made a continent-wide war a certainty. It was a significant point in the Tsar's reasoning that Austria-Hungary had been the first to mobilize her army: though only a partial mobilization as yet, it was a circumstance under which the treaty obligations did not require Germany to mobilize as well. The challenge was to make the Russian threat to Austria-Hungary appear to be both legitimate and yet limited.

Nicholas believed a partial mobilization of the Russian Army, only in the military districts where Russia shared a common border with Austria-Hungary, was the solution. It would be the sort of classic exercise in diplomatic bluff and counter-bluff that had been carried out by the monarchies of Europe for centuries. Forcing the Austrians into redeploying their armies while refraining from an actual attack would hopefully demonstrate the limited nature of Russia's intentions: as long as Austria-Hungary did not attack Serbia, Russia's armies would not cross the Austrian frontier. At the same time, the districts along the Russo-German border would remain quiescent, hopefully demonstrating to Berlin the limited nature of St.

Petersburg's intentions.

It was a course of action which the Tsar's Foreign Minister, Minister of War, Chief of Staff and the Council of Ministers as a whole approved. There was every reason to believe that it would work, for the German Foreign Minister, von Jagow, had earlier recognized such a move as a legitimate political ploy, informing the Russian, French and British ambassadors in Berlin that Germany would not feel compelled to respond in kind should Russia only mobilize in her southern military districts.

It is unclear at this distance (and the documentary record is very vague at this point) whether von Jagow was being truthful or deliberately provocative. Given the atmosphere of deception then hovering over Berlin, the latter seems entirely likely, as the German Army had been hoping to try conclusions with its Russian counterpart for a number of years, while the Chancellor was looking toward a war with Russia as an escape route from the rising tide of domestic problems. If this was so, then the German government was carrying out a dreadful deception of its own ally, for Austria-Hungary most assuredly did not want a war with Russia. (Years after the tragedy of the summer of 1914 von Jagow would claim that he honestly believed that a wider war could have been averted, and blamed the ensuing catastrophe on "the damned system of alliances." However, von Jagow was also as firmly convinced as anyone else in Berlin that Germany and Russia would inevitably come to blows, and like the rest of the German government, civilian and military, felt that the sooner it came the better.)

Still, Nicholas would not take any chances: he understood that there was always the chance Germany—or even Austria-Hungary— would call his bluff. Therefore two mobilization decrees were prepared, one directing the partial mobilization in the south, the other a full mobilization along the whole of Russia's western frontier. At the same time, Nicholas made it clear to his generals that no further actions were to be taken without his express consent—there would be no "incidents" which either Germany or Austria-Hungary could use as a pretext for war. Nicholas was understandably astonished when, as word of the partial mobilization decree reached his General Staff, he was informed that no plan existed for such an operation.

General Yuri Danilov, the same General who had created "Plan G" (or "Plan 19") had been away from St. Petersburg on leave when the crisis broke on July 24; he was the Russian Army's Quartermaster General, responsible for the logistics which formed the basis for Russia's mobilization plans. Upon his recall, Danilov learned of the pending partial mobilization, and was horrified: as he explained the situation to the Tsar, the basic assumption underlying Russian planning for any war in the west had been that it would be fought against both Germany and Austria-Hungary. A partial mobilization could be initiated, but should the need for a full mobilization arise, its movement schedules and timetables would be seriously, even dangerously, disrupted. The reasons for this were partly technical, partly political.

The technical reasons involved the allocation of forces and the limited resources available to move them into position and support them. The districts which shared borders with Austria-Hungary would muster a total of thirteen corps, while Russian plans called for a minimum of sixteen for any operations against Austria; the balance of the forces were to have come from the districts facing Germany. Should the international situation deteriorate to the point where a complete mobilization became necessary, those three corps—and the vital troop trains moving them—would be completely out of position and moving in the wrong direction, interfering with the assembly and movement of other units.

The political reasons arguing against a partial mobilization were more complex and in some ways less justifiable. For all of its boastfulness and its arrogant presumption that as soldiers Frenchmen were inherently superior to Germans, the French Army, and along with it the French government, was secretly and utterly terrified that it would be as quickly overrun by the Germans in any future war as it had been in 1870. Consequently, from the beginning of the Franco-Russian alliance the whole of French military planning as well as French diplomacy was bent toward reducing the strength of the armies Germany could deploy against France. The reasons for the massive scale of French investment in Russian railways and industry in the first decade of the 20th century were not limited to those of mere capitalism. By making the availability of loans and technical assistance provided to Russia by French financiers and industrialists conditional on how and where they were employed, the French were able to assure that improvements in Russian railways and industries would be in the areas most beneficial to France's strategic needs. While the Russian rail network east of the Urals languished, the railroads of western Russia, though still considered sparse by western standards, grew in density and quality at a rate unequalled anywhere else in Europe. Likewise, the industries in which the French most heavily invested were those which either produced armaments and munitions for the Tsar's armies or could be quickly converted to the production of war materials.

Next the French sought to influence Russian strategy and deployment. Since 1906, when the French first began to suspect the nature of the Schlieffen Plan, the French General Staff had been urging its Russian counterpart, in the event of a war with Germany, to launch an attack against the Germans in East Prussia as early as possible, in order to reduce the strength of the German armies in the west, reducing the pressure on the French Army. Ultimately persuaded, in 1912 the Russian General Staff agreed to launch an offensive into East Prussia by the fifteenth day after mobilization, regardless of the actual state of Russia's army; out of this commitment would grow Russia's Plan 19. Here the Russians were subordinating their national strategy to their loyalty to their ally, risking increasing the peril to Russia in order to provide succor to France, who was in no position to reciprocate should the tables be turned. It would be a pledge that when redeemed the Russians would scrupulously, tragically honor, from which the French would benefit not one whit, but for which Russia would ultimately pay dearly.

When the crisis came the French were of little real help in resolving the situation. The signals coming out of Paris were, quite literally, mixed. Poincaré and Viviani had returned to the French capital on July 28 and immediately begun to grapple with the problem. Unfortunately France was not speaking with one voice. On one hand, Premier Viviani, acting in his secondary role as Foreign Minister, and his deputy, Jean-Baptiste Bienvenu-Martin, were urging Sazonov to continue negotiations with Austria-Hungary, while on the other the French General Staff was demanding that Russia's senior military commanders fully mobilize and launch a peremptory strike into East Prussia in the hope that it would disrupt the carefully calculated scheduling of the Schlieffen Plan.

These communications were arriving simultaneously with Sir Edward Grey's first proposal for arbitration through the Six Power Council in London, which added yet another degree of complication to the developing scenario. Sazonov promptly informed Ambassador Paléologue that he was determined to do everything within his power to keep the peace, and was prepared to agree to anything France or Great Britain might propose toward that end. It was at this moment that Paléologue showed his worst side. Instructed by Paris to inform Sazonov that France was willing to support any Russian initiative undertaken "in the interest of the general peace," the French ambassador instead communicated to the Foreign Minister that "he could officially declare the complete readiness of France to fulfill her obligations as an ally in case of necessity." In the language of international diplomacy, Paléologue's mild-sounding words were an affirmation that France was preparing for war. Thinking that the French government had come to believe that there could be no peaceful resolution, not realizing that Paléologue was expressing what he wished the French government to be saying, Sazonov became resigned to the need for at least a partial mobilization of the Russian Army. It was in this mood that he received word of Austria-Hungary's declaration of war on Serbia, and in this mood he went to his audience with the Tsar on the morning of July 28. By the time Sazonov left, the Tsar had signed the decree ordering the partial mobilization to begin at midnight on July 29.

With Russia's partial mobilization now underway and the looming possibility of a full mobilization behind it, the scope and nature of the crisis begun by the Sarajevo murders had now changed entirely. It had ceased to be the sort of small-scale diplomatic confrontation marked by bluster and empty belligerence which had characterized the relationship between Austria-Hungary and Serbia for decades. Instead it had become a fully fledged exercise in power politics in the hands of four of Europe's Great Powers. What was developing with each passing hour was a confrontation over whether or not the alliance of Germany and Austria-Hungary would continue to be the dominant political and military combination in Europe. Or would those two nations, who would soon become known as the Central Powers, be eclipsed by the Dual Entente and its fellow-traveler, Great Britain? The origin of the crisis—the fate of Serbia at stake—was being eclipsed by the larger question that would be decided by the looming war: the fate of the Continent.

It was the slow dawning that such a shift was underway which caused such consternation in Berlin and Vienna when it was learned that St. Petersburg had ordered a partial mobilization. Not unexpectedly the reaction was sharpest in Germany, for with the specter of a two-front war before her she was running the greatest risk. Why, Wilhelm demanded to know, had the Russians chosen to fight—and for the Serbs of all people! Von Bethmann-Hollweg had no explanation. He had always known that supporting Austria-Hungary in whatever action she chose to take against Serbia had been a risky policy, but the reward was, to the German Chancellor, worth the risk. It could all be solved by swift action, as he put it, "a quick *fait accompli*, then a friendly gesture to the Entente." What had never been anticipated was an equally swift response by Russia, which made both the *fait accompli* and the "friendly gesture" an impossibility.

In Vienna, Berchtold single-mindedly continued to pursue his policy of vengeance on Serbia. Not bound by any equivalent of the iron hand of the Schlieffen Plan, the Dual Monarchy had believed it could afford to take more time in reacting to Russia's unexpected announcement. However, the unexpected Russian response did make short shrift of all of Berchtold's political calculations; he now had to consider the distinct possibility that the German government might feel compelled, in the name of self-defense, to act against Russia before Austria-Hungary was ready to do so. He was compelled to develop a new equation, one which would allow Austria-Hungary to punish Serbia while at the same time avoiding the sort of confrontation with St. Petersburg that might provoke the neurotic monarch and overly sensitive politicians in Berlin into a pre-emptive declaration of war. Carefully, deliberately, Berchtold kept the lines of communication open with Sazonov, believing the longer that the Russians were kept talking rather than acting, the less likely the possibility of some precipitate and irrevocable action by Germany.

In Berlin Wilhelm knew better. It was at this point that, in Winston Churchill's unforgettable phrase, "the iron dice began to roll." The Russian mobilization could not be ignored, however limited it might be, and despite the fact the forces assembled would not be an immediate threat to German soil. The danger, as the men in Berlin understood it, was that the French might choose to act in the spirit of the alliance treaty with Russia, rather than according to the letter of its provisions. Strictly speaking, in any crisis involving Russia and Germany, should the Russian Army be the first to mobilize, the French Army was not obligated to follow suit. Nevertheless, as the Kaiser, the Chancellor, and the Great General Staff all saw it, the French, knowing as they did the broad strokes of the Schlieffen Plan and its inexorable scheduling, and fearful that the Germans might seize upon Russia's partial mobilization as a pretext for putting the Plan into motion, might begin their own mobilization, possibly even allowing the French Army to strike first. Wilhelm and company all too understood the inflexible nature of the Schlieffen Plan's timetable, and the rigidity it imposed on the deployment and movements of the German Army; they also understood that as long as the threat of war in the east loomed, there was an equal or even greater threat in the west.

That Wilhelm in particular did indeed understand all of this was an important point in the drama which would unfold over the next seven days, for he and he alone possessed the authority to put the German war machine into motion. He was not accountable to the Reichstag, no ministers' counter-signatures were required on the orders to begin the German Army's march to war. Constitutionally, the Kaiser was Germany's Supreme War Lord. Whatever advice or counsel his ministers, generals, and advisors might give him, the ultimate burden for deciding in favor of war or peace would lie with him. The responsibility borne by his subordinates would lie in the nature of the counsel that they provided for him. It was with this knowledge that, with typical bombast and lack of tact or subtlety Wilhelm chose this moment to personally intervene in the crisis. What followed was one of the most dramatic diplomatic exchanges in history, which would be remembered as the "Willy-Nicky" telegrams.

Chapter VII

"WILLY" AND "NICKY"

The Kaiser was simultaneously aghast and furious when he learned of Russia's partial mobilization: the entire grand design created by von Bethmann-Hollweg and von Jagow, which he had endorsed, was about to come crashing down about his ears. From the outset of the crisis following the Sarajevo assassinations he believed that any war between Austria-Hungary and Serbia could be localized and that the same disorganization and weakness which had kept Russia's army from intervening in the Balkans in 1908 and 1912 would continue to cripple the Tsar's regime. Knowing that without Russia's support the Serbian kingdom would ultimately be overwhelmed by the Austrian Army, the war would end with Serbia punished and reduced to vassalage, while Austria-Hungary's prestige would soar. At the same time, Russia's prestige would plummet, while her reliability as an ally would become questionable, her status as a Great Power jeopardized. The end result would be a dramatic redress of the balance of power in central and eastern Europe, shifting once more in Germany's favor.

The presumption which produced this whole chain of reasoning and the policy decisions which sprang from it was the belief shared by the Kaiser along with von Bethmann-Hollweg and von Jagow, along with Berchtold and Tisza in Vienna, that Russia would simply refuse to go to war to save Serbia: the kingdom's recent history was too bloody and it had been provoking Austria-Hungary for too long. In a way, they believed, Serbia had long been asking to be attacked by the

Dual Monarchy, and for the Serbs to now flee into Russia's protective shadow claiming that Austria-Hungary was suddenly acting the bully, was tantamount to announcing that Belgrade regarded St. Petersburg as being populated by credulous fools. Once word of Russia's partial mobilization reached Berlin, however, all such German and Austro-Hungarian assumptions were shredded like tissue paper.

The first inkling Wilhelm had that events might be taking a turn far different from that which he had planned or anticipated came in the early hours of July 29, before the Austrian artillery batteries opened fire on Belgrade. Desperately seeking a way to save the peace, the Tsar sent a personal telegram to the Kaiser, in which he declared that:

> An ignoble war has been declared to a weak country. . . . I foresee that very soon I shall be overwhelmed by the pressure forced upon me and be compelled to take extreme measures which will lead to war.

Nicholas then implored Wilhelm, "in the name of our old friendship to do what you can to stop your allies from going too far." He signed it "Nicky," the name by which Wilhelm had first known him as a young prince. The two sovereigns were first cousins—their mothers were both daughters of Queen Victoria—and it was Nicholas' hope that family ties might cut across the clutter and confusion of diplomatic formality to bring about a peaceful resolution to the crisis. (In the text to follow, where telegrams are quoted in full they appear exactly as transmitted, with any spelling or grammatical errors included. The complete texts of the ensuing exchange, which would become known to posterity as the "Willy-Nicky telegrams" can be found in the appendices.)

The Tsar's telegram crossed paths with one sent from Berlin to St. Petersburg, in which the Kaiser gave the initial impression that he was willing to cooperate with the Tsar in preventing any war from beginning. He began by declaring that "The unscrupulous agitation that has been going on in Serbia for years has resulted in the outrageous crime, to which Archduke Francis Ferdinand fell a victim." He then went on to lay out what he regarded as one of the paramount reasons which should compel the Tsar to refuse to intervene in the crisis:

You will doubtless agree with me that we both, you and me, have a common interest as well as all Sovereigns to insist that all the persons morally responsible for the dastardly murder should receive their deserved punishment.

Then, after acknowledging that Nicholas could not completely ignore the pro-Slav sentiments among his people and within his government, he assured the Tsar that:

I am exerting my utmost influence to induce the Austrians to deal straightly to arrive to a satisfactory understanding with you. I confidently hope that you will help me in my efforts to smooth over difficulties that may still arise.

He signed the telegram, "Your very sincere and devoted friend and cousin, Willy."

Here Wilhelm was dissembling, as he was waiting for Russia to provide the pretext for Germany to mobilize against her, convinced as he was that the hour of reckoning with Imperial Russia had come at last, and would swiftly pass if not seized at once. When he received the Tsar's first telegram, which he realized Nicholas had sent before he could have read Wilhelm's own initial communication, he composed a reply which was accusatory in tone and attempted to shift any question of blame for any widening of the war onto Russia. Simultaneously, he demanded that Nicholas halt Russia's mobilization, warning that should it continue, a German mobilization—and by implication a German attack—would be the inevitable result.

He began by contradicting the Tsar's position that Austria's declaration of war was unjustified, saying, ". . . as I told you in my first telegram, I cannot consider Austria's action against Serbia an 'ignoble' war. Austria knows by experience that Serbian promises on paper are wholly unreliable." He then went on to suggest that "it would be quite possible for Russia to remain a spectator of the Austro-Serbian conflict without involving Europe in the most horrible war she ever witnessed." He continued to dissemble, telling Nicholas that "my Government is continuing its exercises to promote" what he called "a direct understanding between your Government and Vienna. . . ."

Then his innate pomposity took over, as he declared that the:

> military measures on the part of Russia would be looked
> upon by Austria as a calamity we both wish to avoid and
> jeopardize my position as mediator which I readily accepted
> on your appeal to my friendship and my help.

Once again, he signed himself "Willy."

The truth was that the Kaiser had little or no intention of attempting to mediate between St. Petersburg and Vienna, even if the Austrians had been so inclined to accept him in such a role. Such efforts, in Wilhelm's opinion, were pointless: Sir Edward Grey's offer of arbitration had already been rejected outright by both Berlin and Vienna. At this moment Wilhelm's thinking was heavily influenced by a lengthy memorandum submitted to him by the Chief of Staff of the German Army, Field Marshal Helmuth von Moltke. As von Moltke was watching the confrontation between Austria-Hungary and Serbia develop, his thoughts harked back to the December 1912 conference where the outlines of a militant German foreign policy had been drawn. Seeing the scenario before him unfolding almost exactly as had been anticipated at that conference, he recalled his declaration that "The sooner war comes, the better," as well as the Kaiser's endorsement of this view. Believing that the time had come to force the issue, von Moltke prepared a missive outlining the reasons, rationale, and justifications for going to war with Russia, even if it also meant war with France. When he was finished, he submitted the document to the Chancellor, who in turn gave it his tacit endorsement by presenting it to the Kaiser on the afternoon of July 29.

The attitude von Moltke displayed throughout the memorandum reflected a growing conviction—almost a fatalism—within the German officer corps that Germany's strategic position and military supremacy had been in steady decline since the beginning of the century; it was in Germany's best interest then to bring about a war with France and Russia while there was still a chance it could be won. The document makes for depressing reading, for as an exercise in political self-justification it has few equals in history.

Von Moltke opened by declaring that:

no state in Europe would take more than a general human
interest in the conflict between Austria and Serbia if this
conflict did not carry the risk of a broader political
engagement that today threatens to unleash a world war. . .

This was a remarkable statement which established beyond question
that von Moltke and the rest of the General Staff understood the full
implications of the Schlieffen Plan—and by understanding them were
accepting responsibility for them. Referring to Serbia as "a tumor" to
which Austria was applying "a red-hot iron," he then opined that
"One would have thought that the whole of Europe would be
grateful, that it would have breathed a collective sigh of relief to see
. . . peace and order restored to the Balkans." However—and here the
influence of von Moltke's memorandum on the Kaiser's thinking
begins to become crystal clear—"Russia took sides with the rogue
state. This has turned the Austrian-Serbian affair into a storm cloud
that could break over Europe at any moment."

After repeating Austria-Hungary's reassurances of Serbia's
continued existence, he reiterated Vienna's position that:

the Austrian-Serbian affair is a purely private conflict in
which, had Russia not intervened, the European states would
have taken no deep interest-—and any interest shown by them
would not have threatened but rather strengthened European
peace. It was only Russia's intervention that gave this matter
its menacing character.

Then, in a twisted version of military logic, he recognized the limited
nature of Austria-Hungary's mobilization against Serbia as a demonstration of admirable restraint, but accused Russia of over-reaction
with her own partial mobilization against Austria-Hungary. Then von
Moltke resorted to deception, accusing Russia in a carefully worded
passage of ordering "similar preparatory measures to be taken in the
north, namely, opposite the German border and on the Baltic Sea,"
implying that an unannounced mobilization against Germany had
begun when in fact no such action had taken place.

Next, peering into his strategic crystal ball, von Moltke pontificated on what would happen should Austria-Hungary go forward with her planned attack on Serbia. She would "confront not only the Serbian Army but a vastly superior Russian force," and "not be in a position to wage a war against Serbia without first protecting itself from Russian intervention." The Austrians would naturally be compelled to mobilize the rest of her army, with the result that—and here von Moltke made a strategic pronouncement which had no basis in military or political fact—"the moment Austria mobilizes its entire army, a clash with Russia is inevitable, and this will be the *casus foederis* for Germany." The plain truth was that the mobilization plans of neither Russia nor Austria-Hungary automatically compelled either army to take the offensive: of all of the Great Powers, only Germany's mobilization committed her army to immediate, precipitate action.

Blithely ignoring the realities of the situation, von Moltke then went on, asserting that in any event Germany would then have no choice but to mobilize in turn, "if it does not want its ally to be crushed by superior Russian forces," giving Russia political victory by allowing her to claim that she was the victim of a German attack, the immediate consequence of which would be to bring France into the war as required by her treaty obligations to Russia. The final outcome, as von Moltke saw it, was that then "the mutual destruction of the civilized states of Europe can begin."

Von Moltke went on in an attempt to shift the onus of the blame for the current situation squarely on Russia, describing how she "cleverly orchestrated this affair" by positioning herself politically and militarily so that no matter what course of action she followed, in every conceivable contingency she could claim that she was acting in self-defense. He then repeated his claim that the coming war was inevitable: "The matter will and must proceed in this manner if there is no last-minute miracle to avert a war that is destined to destroy, for decades to come, almost all of European civilization." He closed by once more urging pre-emptive action on Germany's part, saying:

> As for our intended military measures, it is extremely important to clarify as soon as possible whether Russia and France are willing to risk a war with Germany. As our

neighbors proceed with their preparations, they will be in a position to carry out mobilization more quickly than us. As a result, the military situation is becoming less and less favorable by the day, which could have calamitous consequences for us if our probable opponents' preparations carry on unchecked.

This was the considered opinion of the man who was Germany's senior soldier, who led what was acknowledged to be the finest collection of military thinkers in the world, the German Great General Staff. Wilhelm knew that while he possessed the authority to dispute von Moltke, he lacked the experience, expertise, and training to do so effectively. He also lacked the will: he was always somewhat intimidated by the Field Marshal. In a curious episode which established von Moltke's moral ascendency over the Kaiser, when Wilhelm first offered the post of Chief of Staff to the old soldier, von Moltke had refused to accept the appointment unless the Kaiser agreed to put an end to his habit of insisting on always winning the war games which were the culmination of the annual army maneuvers. Wilhelm, accustomed to habitual subservence on the part of his officers, was stunned into acquiescence at this display of independence, and since that incident had continued to defer to his Chief of Staff on military questions.

Part of it may have been von Moltke's appearance: tall, bald, and heavily built, constantly surrounded by an air of forbidding melancholy (the Kaiser called him *der traurige Julius*—"sad Julius") the sixty-six year-old von Moltke was a near-caricature of the arrogant, overbearing Prussian general. In fact he was anything but: introspective and self-doubting, when offered the post of Chief of Staff in 1906, he asked the Kaiser—who in truth had been influenced by von Moltke's famous name—if he expected "to win the big prize twice in the same lottery," then bluntly went on to say, "I do not know how I shall get on in the event of a campaign. I am very critical of myself." Certainly part of his problem lay in inheriting the name and position of his uncle, the Prussian military genius who, together with Bismarck, had forged the German Empire in the years from 1865 to 1871. It was an uncomfortable legacy of which he was daily reminded, as his office in the General Staff building on Berlin's *Königplatz* overlooked a bronze equestrian statue of the elder von Moltke.

There were sides of the younger von Moltke's character which flew in the face of the stereotypical German officer. Unlike the vast majority of his colleagues he was neither a Lutheran nor a Catholic: a practicing Christian Scientist, he also had a curious interest in anthroposophism. Some of his fellow officers regarded his personal interests as "soft" and unbecoming to a German general: he played the cello, painted watercolors, was translating Maeterlinck's *Pelleas et Mellisande* into German, and habitually carried a copy of Goethe's *Faust* about with him. He was also an indifferent horseman who had the embarrassing habit of falling off his mount during staff rides and maneuvers.

For all of his peculiarities, von Moltke was neither effeminate nor particularly timid, personally or professionally. In 1900, when the Kaiser consulted him on the planned expedition being sent to Peking to crush the Boxer Rebellion, von Moltke, in his own words, told him "quite brutally" that the idea was a "crazy adventure" which would only leave Germany open to ridicule. In 1911, at the height of the Agadir crisis, when Germany was forced to back away from her attempt to annex Morocco, he wrote in disgust to his Austrian colleague, Conrad von Hötzendorf, that he was considering resignation, after which he would propose disbanding the army and placing Germany ". . . under the protection of Japan; then we can make money undisturbed and turn into imbeciles."

Yet for all of his personal courage and apparent technical competence—nephew of the first Field Marshal von Moltke or not, he would never have risen as high in the ranks of the German *offizier korps* as he did if his peers did not believe he possessed the requisite skills for his position—von Moltke was unequal to the moral burden of command. He was not a leader. The great American Confederate general Robert E. Lee is said to have once quantified the great dilemma of military command when he remarked, "To be a good officer, you must love the army; to be a good commander, you must be willing to order the death of the thing you love." Deep within Lee's words lay not the implication that a good commander must ultimately be soulless and indifferent, but that he has to have the capacity to make decisions requiring great moral courage. As the events of the next few days would demonstrate, this von Moltke could not do. He was secure in carrying out someone else's plans, but could never muster the will to alter or abolish them and impose his own imprimatur on the events to come.

In this case, the influence of von Moltke's memorandum was strengthened not only by his professional stature, but also because much of what it said only reinforced what Wilhelm already believed. What made the Field Marshal's document so unfortunate was its timing: it appeared before the Kaiser at the same time that the Tsar was asking for restraint on the part of both Germany and Austria-Hungary. The memorandum combined with the Tsar's pleas suddenly brought out Wilhelm's latent paranoia, and he began to suspect Nicholas of attempting to delay the Austrian mobilization as well as block Germany's, in order to gain time for Russia to complete her own. His suspicions were further fueled by the Tsar's response to his second telegram. Received in Berlin at 8:20 p.m. on July 29, it read:

> Thanks for your telegram conciliatory and friendly. Whereas official message presented today by your ambassador to my minister was conveyed in a very different tone. Beg you to explain this divergency! It would be right to give over the Austro-Serbian problem to the Hague conference. Trust in your wisdom and friendship.
> Your loving
> —Nicky

The "official message" to which Nicholas referred had been presented in a meeting which had taken place that morning between Ambassador von Pourtalès and Foreign Minister Sazonov. Though the two men had become quite friendly personally during von Pourtalès' seven-year tenure in St. Petersburg, their official relationship had been growing increasingly tempestuous over the preceding few days, as tensions increased between Austria-Hungary and Serbia while Russia's intentions remained unclear. Such tensions were in no small part due to the two-faced game which von Bethmann-Hollweg was playing with St. Petersburg and Vienna, and with the Kaiser as well.

When Wilhelm had returned from his abbreviated Norwegian holiday on July 27, he had declared that Serbia's reply to Austria-Hungary's ultimatum "removed every reason for war," and instructed the Chancellor to initiate arbitration by Germany between the two nations. As this was contrary to what von Bethmann-Hollweg, von Jagow, Berchtold and Tisza intended, no such initiatives ever took place; yet to placate the Kaiser should he make inquiries, von Bethmann-Hollweg had cabled Germany's ambassador to Vienna, Count von Tschirschky, with instructions to open talks between St. Petersburg and Vienna, knowing that Serbia would follow whatever lead Russia might offer. At the same time Tschirschky was to be mindful that he was "to very carefully avoid giving rise to the impression that we wish to hold Austria back. The case is solely to find a way to realize Austria's desired aim. . . ." Von Bethmann-Hollweg then outlined four conditions on which, so he maintained, a negotiated settlement could be reached which would allow the Austro-Hungarian Army to march on Serbia while at the same time avoiding hostilities with Russia.

First, Russia must accept an Austrian occupation of Belgrade; since the Serbian capital sat opposite the Danube from Austria-Hungary, such an occupation would be almost inevitable in any circumstance, and would be more of a symbolic gesture than a significant military victory. Second, Russia must persuade Serbia to accept the occupation; again, given Belgrade's strategic position, there was little Serbia could do to prevent the occupation from being a *fait accompli*, so that Serb acceptance was all but a formality. The third condition was that Austria-Hungary would negotiate a settlement with Serbia based on the Serb's reply to the ultimatum—no one seriously expected the Serbs to yield to the ultimatum entirely, which, of course, they did not do. Finally, hostilities would be suspended while negotiations were taking place. This became known as the "Stop-in-Belgrade" plan, and for several days the hopes of many of the capitals of Europe would rest on it. What was unknown outside German diplomatic circles was that even as the details of von Bethmann-Hollweg's proposal were being circulated, Foreign Minister von Jagow was, with the Chancellor's knowledge, reassuring Ambassador Szögyény that the German government was making these proposals as a sop to foreign opinion as well as the Kaiser's pride, but that it had no intention of actually supporting any proposal of negotiation or arbitration.

Consequently Sazonov believed that the "Stop-in-Belgrade" proposal was a legitimate initiative, and wholeheartedly embraced it. In his words, it offered "golden bridges" to Austria-Hungary by allowing her the full measure of restored prestige which such a political and military victory would bring her, while deservedly serving up to the Serbs "bitter pills" as recompense for their violent agitation over the preceding decades—all without risking a wider war which might eventually engulf the Continent. When at 9:30 a.m. on July 29 Ambassador von Pourtalés requested an appointment with Sazonov in order to deliver an "agreeable communication from Berlin" Sazonov was certain that he was going to present a formal proposal for arbitration.

What he got was something far different. While von Pourtalés took pains to praise Sazonov for offering his "golden bridges" to Austria-Hungary, all he could offer by way of arbitration was an assurance that Berlin was trying to convince Vienna to begin frank and open discussions with St. Petersburg in order to prove the "limited nature" of the Austro-Hungarian plans for an invasion of Serbia. In other words, it was little more than a thinly disguised request for Russia to stand aside while Austria-Hungary administered its punishment to Serbia. The only concession offered was an assurance that Vienna had no desire for territorial expansion at Serbia's expense.

Then von Pourtalés' tone became darker. Because Austria-Hungary had no designs on Serbian territory, the integrity of Serbian autonomy was not being threatened, therefore there was no need for Russia to mobilize any part of her army in support of Serbia. What von Pourtalés was implying was that if Russia did mobilize against Austria-Hungary, she was running the risk of having Germany mobilize against her. Sazonov, wondering where was the substance of von Pourtalés' communication, replied that he would be happy to enter into talks with Vienna, but Vienna had given no sign whatsoever of any willingness to talk to St. Petersburg. As for mobilization, Austria-Hungary had already begun her own, and in the interests of self-protection if nothing else, Russia would be compelled to mobilize the four military districts facing the Dual Monarchy—the orders were already drawn up and would be issued later that day.

Von Pourtalés later recalled that at this point he all but begged Sazonov to put off the Russian mobilization. Sazonov remembered the scene quite differently, saying that the German ambassador's tone turned threatening, and warning that in the case of a full Russian mobilization, "the danger of all military measures lies in the counter-measures of the other side." Which version of what transpired—if either is entirely true—remains open to debate, although unquestionably it was Sazonov's account which reached the Tsar's ears, leading to Nicholas' remark to Wilhelm about the "very different tone" of the "official message" delivered that morning.

Wilhelm bridled at the implication that the *Wilhelmstrasse* was speaking with two voices, and in his reply to Nicholas informed the Tsar of such:

> It is quite out of the question that my ambassador's language could have been in contradiction with the tenor of my telegram. Count Pourtalès was instructed to draw the attention of your government to the danger & grave consequences involved by a mobilisation; I said the same in my telegram to you.

Wilhelm then took his cue from von Moltke's memorandum, saying that:

> Austria has only mobilised against Serbia & only a part of her army. If, as it is now the case, according to the communication by you & your Government, Russia mobilises against Austria, my rôle as mediator you kindly intrusted me with, & which I accepted at you express prayer, will be endangered if not ruined.

The telegram ended with an unconvincing attempt to shift the total responsibility for the outcome of the crisis onto Nicholas and Russia: "The whole weight of the decision lies solely on your shoulders now, who have to bear the responsibility for Peace or War." Once more the cable was signed "Willy."

Yet again one of the Tsar's telegrams crossed paths with one of the Kaiser's. Just as this latest communication from Wilhelm was being sent, one from Nicholas arrived; by this time it was very early in the morning of July 30. The Tsar's cable was remarkable for the way in which it appeared to have anticipated the content of the communication with which it crossed. Continuing to adopt the same friendly, almost conversational tone which had thus far been characteristic of all his telegrams, Nicholas informed Wilhelm that:

> . . . The military measures which have now come into force were decided five days ago for reasons of defence on account of Austria's preparations. I hope from all my heart that these measures won't in any way interfere with your part as mediator which I greatly value. We need your strong pressure on Austria to come to an understanding with us.
> —Nicky

It is worth mentioning at this point that the Tsar spoke no German and the Kaiser spoke not a word of Russian, so that their telegraphic exchanges were conducted in English, the only tongue they had in common, and were transmitted "in the clear," that is, uncoded. This makes the contrast in tone between the two monarchs all the more remarkable, for it cannot be attributed to a translator's devices or prejudices. The Tsar, confident that his actions were morally as well as politically justified, was unmistakably sincere and clearly felt no need to either hector or plead in order to make his case to the Kaiser. Wilhelm, on the other hand, was far less confident, and adopted a superior tone which was at once bullying, condescending, and patronizing. Given that Nicholas' fluency in English was, if anything, better than Wilhelm's, it is doubtful that he was unaware of this, and it may well have played a role in the decision the Tsar was about to make.

Having come into being only a little more than forty years earlier, the German Empire was very much the *arriviste* among European monarchies. Still, that was no inhibition to Kaiser Wilhelm II, who was not above lecturing Tsar Nicholas II, who sat on a throne ten times older than Wilhelm's, on how to rule. At one state visit Wilhelm had counseled Nicholas to give "more speeches and more parades" as a means of demonstrating his authority. On another occasion, Wilhelm wrote his cousin with the advice to "occupy yourself with your fine Guard by inspecting them and speaking to them. It gives you pleasure and gratifies the troops." Nicholas had long ago resigned himself to his cousin's pomposity and bombast; when it manifested itself in the exchange of telegrams, however, it appears that Wilhelm finally went too far, and Nicholas decided that he had tolerated the Kaiser's condescension long enough. Late in the morning of July 30, he issued the order for the whole of the Russian Army to begin mobilization.

July 30 would prove to be an exceptionally busy day for both monarchs, and nearly twenty-four hours would pass before another exchange of telegrams between the two monarchs began. In the meantime, throughout July 29 and 30, the Kaiser and Field Marshal von Moltke notwithstanding, von Bethmann-Hollweg searched desperately for a way to avoid Germany going to war with Russia should the Austrians and Russians come to blows. This would not be, he decided, the war that he had wanted after all. At the same time he hoped to preserve the dignity and prestige of all three monarchies. One of the great mysteries of July 1914 is the German chancellor's ambivalence toward the aggressive policy he had helped create and then openly endorsed. For the critical week from July 25 to July 31, he continually vacillated between belligerence and caution. On one hand, von Bethmann-Hollweg accepted, even embraced, the looming war as inevitable, believing it was necessary, and would be the salvation of the German Empire and Hohenzollern monarchy. At the same time, knowing of the iron-bound constraints of the Schlieffen Plan and perhaps even having some inkling of its flaws, the Chancellor seemed genuinely frightened by the implications of such a strategy. The source of his unease was his knowledge that the one nation which alone possessed the power to make a shambles of all of Germany's ambitions was the one Great Power which thus far had played only a minor role in the crisis, Great Britain.

He did not fear war with France—he was certain that she would fall as swiftly and completely as she had in 1870—nor did he believe that the Tsar's army, however valiantly it might fight, could defeat the German war machine. However, the prospect of Great Britain entering the war at France's side as a consequence of a German attack was terrifying. It may have been true that Great Britain herself was a power that had already passed its peak: by the turn of the century Germany had already overtaken the island nation in every significant measure of economic strength and industrial capacity. However, powerful as it was, the German juggernaut was dwarfed by the resources and might of the British Empire.

Von Bethmann-Hollweg's fears of British intervention on the side of France had first been spawned by hints and whispers dropped in diplomatic exchanges across Europe, then had solidified when a report came to his desk in the evening of July 29. The British Foreign Minister, Sir Edward Grey, had summoned the German ambassador, Prince Lichnowsky, to the Foreign Office that afternoon for an urgent meeting. Rightly believing that with Austria-Hungary's declaration of war on Serbia events were rapidly getting out of hand, Grey presented Lichnowsky with a proposal remarkably similar to von Bethmann-Hollweg's "Stop-in-Belgrade" plan. Austria-Hungary would be permitted to occupy Belgrade, but once that was accomplished she would immediately submit the entire issue to a four-nation council of arbitration. There was nothing new or original in this—Grey had been pressing all parties concerned to turn to arbitration to settle the crisis. What set this proposal apart was Grey's warning that should Austria-Hungary refuse to accept the proposal, it would be taken as an indication that both Vienna and Berlin were seeking a wider, larger war, in which case the neutrality of Great Britain could not be guaranteed. To Lichnowsky, Grey's meaning was clear: if the four Great Powers, Austria-Hungary and Germany in one camp, and France and Russia in the other, finally came to blows, Britain was prepared to stand alongside France. Any possible solution to the crisis which could avoid such an outcome was, in Lichnowsky's opinion, worth exploring.

It was just on midnight on July 29 when von Bethmann-Hollweg, who was not getting much sleep during these days of crisis, summoned the British Ambassador, Sir Edward Goschen, to his office in the Reichskanzlerie. According to Goschen's report to London, the Chancellor said that he "fully understood that the British could not stand by and allow France to be crushed." However, would Great Britain be willing to remain neutral if Germany guaranteed that she would make no post-war territorial demands on France or Belgium? Goschen quickly noted that no mention was made of the security or integrity of the French or Belgian colonies, and deduced—correctly as it turned out—that Berlin was already casting a covetous eye on those overseas possessions. Already certain of London's reply, Goschen dutifully forwarded von Bethmann-Hollweg's proposal to the Foreign Office. Upon reading it the next morning Grey rejected it out of hand, calling the proposal both "disgusting" and "a disgrace." One unexpected consequence of von Bethmann-Hollweg's meeting with Goschen was that when the German Chancellor made mention of Belgium, which up to this point had appeared to be completely outside of the crisis, it became clear to Goschen that the eyes of the German High Command were firmly fixed on the little kingdom. Communicating this to London, Goschen made certain that Grey would begin to see that maintaining the integrity of Belgium's neutrality might exert an influence over Great Britain's own decision whether or not to stand aside when the storm broke.

While von Bethmann-Hollweg's personal drama was unfolding, the Tsar and the Kaiser were once again exchanging telegrams. The news of Russia's general mobilization had raised the tension in Berlin to a level it had not known since 1871. Yet it was not, as Wilhelm would later maintain, fear of the approaching war which fueled the tension, but rather anticipation. In his memoirs Wilhelm would attempt to paint a scene where the Chancellor and the Foreign Ministry, appearing as the very soul of European cosmopolitanism, were taken by surprise as Russia mobilized, while the General Staff, all Teutonic efficiency and preparedness, were muttering "I told you so" in the background.

> Upon my arrival at Potsdam I found the Chancellor and the Foreign Office in conflict with the Chief of the General Staff, since General von Moltke was of the opinion that war was sure to break out, whereas the other two stuck firmly to their view that

things would not get to such a bad pass, that there would be some way of avoiding war, provided I did not order mobilization.

This dispute kept up steadily. Not until General von Moltke announced that the Russians had set fire to their frontier posts, torn up the frontier railway tracks, and posted red mobilization notices did a light break upon the diplomats in the *Wilhelmstrasse* and bring about their own collapse and that of their powers of resistance. They had not wished to believe in the war.

Again Wilhelm was being disingenuous: the scenario which was being played out between Vienna, St. Petersburg and Berlin was exactly as the one that had been anticipated at the Potsdam conference in December 1912. That meeting had been convened to determine German strategy during another, earlier Balkan crisis involving Serbia and Austria-Hungary, as Admiral von Müller had recalled, the Kaiser, Foreign Minister von Jagow, the War Minister, the Navy Minister and the Army Chief of Staff all agreed that "If Russia were to support the Serbs, which she is apparently already doing (Sazonov's remark that Russia will go straight into Galicia if the Austrians march into Serbia), war would be inevitable for us," and accordingly decided on the shape of German strategy. Now the scenario was repeating itself: this was the war that the Kaiser, his generals, and his government had been anticipating for years.

Meanwhile, Wilhelm's natural bellicosity began to override his common sense, and his next communication with the Tsar, sent on the morning of July 31, was belligerent to the point of insult. It is highly unlikely that at this point the Kaiser could have avoided ordering the mobilization of the German Army, for as he pointed out in this telegram, as a sovereign he was responsible for the safety of his realm. Yet there is a provocative, almost taunting, tone of self-righteousness to the text, as if Wilhelm were attempting to goad Nicholas into some impulsively aggressive act which would exculpate Germany from any blame for the war which was now likely only days, even hours, away. As it is the Kaiser gave what would become for the rest of his life his justifications for his actions: Germany did not want the war but it was being forced upon her, she was only acting in self-defense, and the responsibility for starting the war would lie with everyone but Germany.

> On your appeal to my friendship and your call for assistance began to mediate between you and the Austro-Hungarian Government. While this action was proceeding your troops were mobilised against Austro-Hungary, my ally. Thereby, as I have already pointed out to you, my mediation has been made almost illusory.
>
> I have nevertheless continued my action. I now receive authentic news of serious preparations for war on my Eastern frontier. Responsibility for the safety of my empire forces preventive measures of defence upon me. In my endeavours to maintain the peace of the world I have gone to the utmost limit possible. The responsibility for the disaster which is now threatening the whole civilized world will not be laid at my door. In this moment it still lies in your power to avert it. Nobody is threatening the honour or power of Russia who can well afford to await the result of my mediation. My friendship for you and your empire, transmitted to me by my grandfather on his deathbed has always been sacred to me and I have honestly often backed up Russia when she was in serious trouble especially in her last war.
>
> The peace of Europe may still be maintained by you, if Russia will agree to stop the military measures which must threaten Germany and Austro-Hungary.
> —Willy

It is difficult to imagine precisely what, apart from self-justification, Wilhelm believed this communication would accomplish. There was no real chance of intimidating the Tsar: if anything the Kaiser's tone only served to harden the resolve in St. Petersburg to stand by the actions already undertaken and carry through with the mobilization. In any case, once more one of Nicholas' telegrams crossed with one of Wilhelm's, and in this latest message the Tsar demonstrated yet again that while he was prepared to react to any aggressive movements by Austria-Hungary or Germany, he had no intention of provoking any precipitate actions by either empire.

> I thank you heartily for your mediation which begins to give one hope that all may yet end peacefully.
> It is *technically* impossible to stop our military preparations which were obligatory owing to Austria's mobilisation. We are far from wishing war. As long as the negotiations with Austria on Serbia's account are taking place my troops shall not make any provocative action. I give you my solemn word for this. I put all my trust in Gods mercy and hope in your successful mediation in Vienna for the welfare of our countries and for the peace of Europe.
> Your affectionate
> —Nicky

Here the Tsar was laboring under a tragic misapprehension: he had no way of knowing that the "negotiations" between Austria-Hungary and Serbia were a sham, merely intended to lull Russia into a sense of false security. Vienna had no intention of coming to a settlement with Serbia until after the Serbian Army had been destroyed and the whole of the kingdom occupied. Count Szápáry had carefully duped Foreign Minister Sazonov, using elliptic phrases and imprecise terminology to lead the Russian to believe that Vienna had suddenly chosen to allow negotiation of the terms of the ultimatum to Serbia. In fact he was only authorized to explain the specifics of why Austria-Hungary had made particular demands and clarify their meaning: no substantial changes were to be allowed.

In Berlin it was mid-morning on July 31 when the Tsar's latest telegram arrived, and after reading it Wilhelm decided that he could wait no longer. Nicholas had said nothing about halting Russia's mobilization, instead he had categorically stated that it was impossible to stop at this point. For his part Wilhelm had no way of knowing that his most recent message had arrived hours after Nicholas had ordered the general mobilization to begin. However mercurial and immature he may have been, Wilhelm always understood that a monarch's first responsibility was the protection of his realm, and with the threat of Russian armies starting to gather on his eastern borders within a matter of days, he had to act. The previous day Wilhelm and von Bethmann-Hollweg had agreed that unless St. Petersburg halted the Russian mobilization by noon on July 31, the *Kriegesgefahr* (Period Preparatory to War) would be announced. When a cable from Ambassador von Pourtalés arrived at the *Wilhelmstrasse* at 11:40 a.m. confirming that the "first day of [Russia's] mobilization is July 31," the order went out. The *Kriegesgefahr* became official at 11:55 a.m.

It was not quite war, but it was perilously close to it; the enormity of what was now almost inevitable was sufficient to rein in, if only briefly, even the Kaiser's usually unchecked pomposity. That afternoon, as thousands of Berliners slowly coalesced into a crowd outside the *Neue Palas*, Wilhelm stepped out onto a balcony which overlooked his gathered subjects, standing before them in the *feldgrau* uniform of a *Feld Marschall*. For once he abandoned his characteristic bombast, addressing them in measured tones:

> A fateful hour has fallen upon Germany. Envious people on all sides are compelling us to resort to a just defense. The sword is being forced into our hands. . . . And now I command you all to go to church, kneel before God, and pray to Him to help our gallant army.

Von Bethmann-Hollweg still had one last diplomatic card to play with Russia, however, though it was a weak one under the circumstances: an ultimatum. Perhaps the "unofficial" warnings in Wilhelm's telegrams, however heavy-handed they may have been, failed to sufficiently impress upon the Russians the gravity of their actions and the potential consequences. There could be no such mistake made with an official communication in the form of an ultimatum. The Chancellor and Foreign Minister von Jagow huddled together in von Jagow's office in the *Wilhelmstrasse*, working out the details. Ambassador von Pourtalés would be instructed to inform Foreign Minister Sazonov that as of midnight, Russia would have twelve hours in which to order a halt to her general mobilization. Unless a "satisfactory answer" was received by noon on August 1, Germany would order a mobilization of her own, which would be followed in very short order by a declaration of war.

Self-serving cables went out to London and Paris at the same time as von Pourtalés instructions were telegraphed to St. Petersburg, announcing that:

> in spite of the still-pending and not apparently hopeless mediation, and although we ourselves had taken no mobilization measure of any kind, Russia has today ordered the mobilization of her entire army and navy, thus against us also. We have had to declare. . . a State of Imminent War, which must be followed by mobilization, in case Russia does not suspend all war measures against Austria and ourselves within twelve hours.

Once more von Moltke made himself the center of attention when he insisted that an ultimatum be sent to France at the same time that the one to Russia went out. To von Moltke and the General Staff it seemed inconceivable that, no matter what the fine print read in the terms of her treaty obligations to Russia, France would stand idly while Germany and Russia came to blows. It was more likely that the French would use the opportunity to attack a near-defenseless Germany from the rear while the bulk of the German Army was locked in mortal combat with the Russians. A French pledge of neutrality could only be guaranteed by surrendering key fortifications along the Franco-German border. Von Bethmann-Hollweg and von Jagow hurriedly drafted a note to Paris to that effect, and at 3:30 p.m. on July 31 both communications were sent out. Russia's deadline would expire at noon the next day, France's at 6:00 p.m.

Now there was little left for the diplomats to do until the ultimatums expired or some other Power introduced a new initiative. Meanwhile, Nicholas took the time to reply to Wilhelm's most recent telegram. This would be the last communication Wilhelm would ever receive from his cousin, the Tsar; it is the shortest and appropriately enough it is the most personal of the entire exchange. The tone is altered, with Nicholas no longer making any mention of mediation—

apparently he understood by this time that a war with Austria-Hungary was a sideshow in comparison to the one which would engulf Europe should some sort of eleventh-hour accommodation not be reached between Russia and Germany. This time the appeal is to friendship and the two men's shared faith in God.

> I received your telegram. Understand you are obliged to mobilise but wish to have the same guarantee from you as I gave you, that these measures do not mean war and that we shall continue negotiating for the benefit of our countries and universal peace deal to all our hearts. Our long proved friendship must succeed, with God's help, in avoiding bloodshed. Anxiously, full of confidence await your answer.
> Nicky

By the time Wilhelm replied to this final message from Nicholas, the German ultimatum had expired, the mobilization of the German Army begun, and the declaration of war on Russia was being drafted. Another cornerstone of the establishment had crumbled away—dynastic diplomacy. Gone were the days when one monarch could communicate with another and determine their nations' policies, decide issues of peace and war, and shape the future of the Continent among themselves. The old order was passing away before the eyes of the men and women who were its pillars. It would be a happy event to record that the Kaiser's final telegram to the Tsar was as gentle in tone as Nicholas' had been, but, Wilhelm being Wilhelm, that was impossible, and the same self-serving cant that had doomed this chapter of Europe's history wrote its closing passage.

> Thanks for your telegram. I yesterday pointed out to your government the way by which alone war may be avoided.
> Although I requested an answer for noon today, no telegram from my ambassador conveying an answer from your Government has reached me as yet. I therefore have been obliged to mobilise my army.

Immediate affirmative clear and unmistakable answer from your government is the only way to avoid endless misery. Until I have received this answer alas, I am unable to discuss the subject of your telegram. As a matter of fact I must request you to immediatly order your troops on no account to commit the slightest act of trespassing over our frontiers.
—Willy

Perhaps the tone of Wilhelm's last message can be explained by a new development in what was already a rapidly deteriorating situation, one that had the gravest possible consequences for Germany. For a week now, since Austria-Hungary had delivered her ultimatum to Serbia, the great unresolved variable in the diplomatic equation had been "What will Great Britain do?" As long as the crisis was localized between Serbia and the Dual Monarchy, or remained an issue between Austria-Hungary, Serbia and Russia, it appeared unlikely in the extreme that there could be a threat to any British interests. In that case the chances of Great Britain's involvement in anything outside of arbitration were slight to the point of non-existence. However, with war between Germany and Russia now all but an accomplished fact, and with it the near-certainty that France could be drawn into the conflict, the situation was far different. Any German attack which threatened to overwhelm France—and every military attaché in Europe was cognizant enough of the provisions of the Schlieffen Plan to know that it was predicated on a swift, crushing offensive against the French Army—would be regarded as a menace to British interests. If His Majesty's Government perceived the threat to be great enough, that could mean war between Great Britain and Germany; it would be a war Germany would have little hope of winning.

Chapter VIII

A WARNING IN LONDON

Apart from all of the terrible chaos on the Continent stood, figuratively and literally, Great Britain. In the summer of 1914, the focus of the British government—and the British people—was not on the Continent's troubles, but instead was on northern Ireland, which threatened to explode in civil war. Home Rule for Ireland, the issue which had been the hobgoblin of Britain's domestic politics for almost half a century, had finally become law. No sooner had it had done so than the six predominantly Protestant counties of northern Ireland announced that they would resist any attempt at rule from Catholic Dublin, and back up that refusal by force if necessary. The Irish Nationalists in turn refused to accept any form of Home Rule that did not include the whole of the island of Ireland.

When the Government contemplated using the Army to coerce the six counties of Ulster to accept Dublin's authority, a major crisis erupted within the ranks of the British officer corps. Many senior officers, including General Sir Henry Wilson, the Director of Military Operations, declared that they would resign their commissions *en masse* rather than lead troops against the men of Ulster. It was a sentiment shared by many of the other ranks, as the Government was warned that there would be "wholesale defections" among units deployed against the Ulstermen. An incipient mutiny was brewing within the British Army, and because so many of its officers were members of the aristocracy, an unbridgeable rift threatened to open up within Britain's ruling class.

157

It was this morass which occupied the Cabinet of Prime Minister Herbert Asquith during the month of July 1914, and was once again the primary topic of a Cabinet meeting on the afternoon of July 24. Struggling to find a compromise which was still eluding them, the assembled Ministers and Secretaries were just about to break up for the day when the Foreign Secretary, Sir Edward Grey, began reading from a document which had just been handed to him. It was the Austrian ultimatum to Serbia. At first the implications of the note failed to register with the men sitting around the table in the Cabinet Room; their minds were too focused on the problem in Ireland. It was Winston Churchill, then First Lord of the Admiralty, who later described the dawning of comprehension in a particularly memorable passage:

> [Grey] had been reading for several minutes before I could disengage my mind from the tedious and bewildering debate which had just closed. . . . Gradually as the phrases and sentences followed one another. . . the parishes of Fermanagh and Tyrone faded back into the mists and squalls of Ireland and a strange light began immediately, but by perceptible gradations, to fall and grow upon the map of Europe.

When comprehension dawned, the full gravity of the crisis that had erupted in Central Europe was quickly appreciated in London, but Asquith was convinced that there would be no cause for Britain to become involved as he believed that diplomacy would prevail as it had in 1905, 1908 and 1911.

Equally important to Asquith's reasoning was that the crisis appeared to threaten no British interests—diplomatic, political or economic—and it seemed likely to be confined to Austria, Serbia, and perhaps Russia. Should war come, and Germany and France become involved on behalf of their respective allies, Austria-Hungary and Russia, there was still nothing to compel Britain to become a belligerent due to her policy of "Splendid Isolation." The only binding agreements to which Great Britain was party were two five-power treaties which assured the neutrality of the kingdom of Belgium and the duchy of Luxembourg. Only in the last decade had

Britain felt the need for formal alliances, and only where those would safeguard British interests in the far reaches of the Empire: the 1902 alliance with Japan, for example, had come into being for such a reason. However, where the Continent was involved, the policy of Great Britain by tradition and necessity demanded the utmost flexibility, which in turn precluded binding alliances.

This requirement had been the blight of the efforts by the Conservative government, which had been in power until 1905, to conclude an alliance with Germany. There were sound political as well as sentimental reasons for such an alliance: Great Britain and Germany were respectively the strongest naval and military powers in the world, their economies were the most robust in Europe, and there were strong ties of kinship between the two nation's ruling families, not to mention common ethnic and racial roots. Together the two empires would have been a combination of unstoppable world power. Yet German diplomats, with a very Teutonic legalistic penchant for crossing "t"s and dotting "i"s could not comprehend why their British counterparts were utterly unwilling to work out a treaty of alliance which spelled out in detail the obligations and responsibilities of each country in every conceivable circumstance.

What German officialdom, from the Kaiser down, never understood was the British commitment to the doctrine of a "balance of power" in Europe. In simplest terms, it meant that in any combination of hostile states in Europe, Great Britain must inevitably take the part of the weaker of the two sides. This automatically prevented any one nation from ever gaining a preponderance of power on the Continent, which in turn meant that no viable, vital threat to the integrity of Great Britain could ever be mounted from a European shore. It was a doctrine drawn up out of brutal experience in the seemingly endless succession of wars against the Spanish, the Dutch, and especially the French, first under Louis XIV and XV, then later under Napoleon Bonaparte.

Such a balance of power existed in Europe in the summer of 1914, albeit somewhat precariously. The single most powerful military presence on the Continent was Germany, and once she allied with Austria-Hungary to form the Central Powers, this coalition was the strongest power bloc in Europe. (The third partner in the Central

Powers alliance, Italy, was very much a negligible quantity in the political equations of Europe, so much so that she was more of a liability than an asset, and throughout the July crisis was effectively ignored by both Berlin and Vienna.) However, the Central Powers were not overwhelmingly strong, and the Franco-Russian alliance served as an effective counter-balance; with each passing year the relative strengths of the two alliances grew ever closer to a true equilibrium.

As long as this state of affairs remained the *status quo*, there was no need for Great Britain to take a place in either camp. Only if some sudden stroke were to disrupt this balance would the necessity arise for Great Britain to intervene, and then it would be for the sake of British interests—and by definition "British interests" included British honor.

The Schlieffen Plan was just the sort of sudden stroke that might provoke British intervention, drawn up as it was to swiftly knock France out of any war, dramatically altering the balance of power on the Continent. Though the British Imperial General Staff lacked the detailed knowledge of the Schlieffen Plan that the French possessed, it had long suspected that the only way the German Army could bring an overwhelming weight of numbers against its French counterpart would be to fall on the French left flank *en masse*, which would require the German troops to march across the length of Flanders, grossly violating Belgium's neutrality. This made Belgium a cause for some concern: as far back as the 16th century the great plain of Flanders had served as a highway for armies marching to and fro between western and central Europe, and it remained some of the most easily traversed terrain on the Continent. Yet even as they contemplated the thought of Germany taking such a course of action, the British discarded it: as heir to Prussia's signatory obligations, Germany was bound to observe the treaty of 1839. To think that the meticulously legalistic Germans would flagrantly violate such a solemn agreement seemed absurd.

Absurd or not, it was a thought which was growing in importance in the mind of the Foreign Secretary, Sir Edward Grey, during the week following the delivery of the Austro-Hungarian ultimatum to Serbia. The course Great Britain would ultimately follow in the critical days from July 29 to August 3 would be decided in a very great measure by the personality and character of Sir Edward. Born in 1862 to Scottish parents, Grey was educated at Winchester and Balliol College, Oxford, and stood for Parliament for the first time as a Liberal in 1892, being elected to the seat of Berwick-on-Tweed. He immediately came to the attention of William Gladstone, and served as Foreign Secretary in the Grand Old Man's final administration, from 1892 to 1895. When the Liberals were returned to power in 1905, the new Prime Minister, Sir Henry Campbell-Bannerman, acknowledged his talents, although he disliked Grey personally, and returned him to the Cabinet as Foreign Secretary. When Herbert Henry Asquith succeeded Campbell-Bannerman, Grey retained his office. He would hold it until Asquith resigned in 1916.

Few men have ever been as suited to public office as was Grey to his. His hawk-like gaze, Roman nose and thin-lipped, straight mouth bespoke of his intelligence and integrity. Educated, conscientious, insightful, and perceptive, he was completely lacking in the sort of personal ambition that sometimes causes public officials to place personal agendas ahead of the general welfare. Grey was not an office-seeker, nor did he regard public service as a mere "privilege;" to him it was a duty, one which he took very seriously, but which he would have gladly laid aside had someone better qualified for the office than he appeared on the scene. He and his wife Charlotte were deeply in love with each other, and denied the joys of children were utterly devoted to one another. When Charlotte Grey died as result of injuries she suffered in a carriage accident in 1909, Sir Edward tried to fill the resulting emptiness in his life by throwing himself even more completely into his work. To Grey, his "work" consisted of protecting when necessary and advancing where possible Britain's interests and Britain's honor.

As the crisis in Central Europe began to spread outward, the French ambassador to London, Paul Cambon, had been pressing Grey to make a swift, clear declaration on behalf of the British government that Great Britain would stand solidly beside France. Cambon's hope was that such a declaration might give the Germans pause in any headlong rush they might be considering toward an attack on France. The basis for such an announcement would be the Entente Cordiale between France and Great Britain, which was the crowning achievement of Grey's career. By July 29, however, no such announcement had been forthcoming. Refusing to fall prey to flattery, Grey made it perfectly clear that the diplomatic terms of the Entente Cordiale with France, as well as the Anglo-French naval and military staff talks which had been held annually for several years, had in no way bound Great Britain to act on France's behalf in the event of a European war. Britain might choose to stand by France but she would not be compelled to do so.

Here Grey was playing a careful game. He and many other members of the Cabinet felt that while the Entente was not an explicit British pledge to stand beside the French should Germany attack France, it held a moral obligation to do so. Allowing France to be reduced to little more than vassalage to Germany would be disastrous for Britain as Germany's industrial and political supremacy would become unchallengeable, leaving Britain vulnerable economically as well as militarily. In fact Grey was convinced that Britain's interests demanded that she support France: so strong was his conviction on this that he was prepared to resign his office if the Government chose to remain neutral. Instinctively, he knew that events were on his side and that an overt act by Germany would force Great Britain's hand, but he could say nothing officially to Ambassador Cambon. What was more, these were not sentiments guaranteed to carry the House of Commons: Grey's own Liberal Party was traditionally pacifist, and Labour would almost certainly stand opposed to any intervention that appeared to be solely for the benefit of Britain's commercial interests.

In any case, as it became clear that the aftermath of the Sarajevo murders was escalating from a diplomatic confrontation into all-out war, Grey's first efforts were not to find an excuse for bringing Britain into the war alongside France, but rather to avert a war entirely. Hardly had word of Austria-Hungary's ultimatum to Serbia reached his desk than he set about seeking to have all the nations involved agree to an international arbitration of the crisis.

As Grey saw it, although the case for Serbia's complicity in the Sarajevo assassinations was far from conclusive, the consensus among the Great Powers was that Serbia deserved to be punished in some way, as the Serbs' belligerent attitude and provocative policies had made few friends for their little kingdom and they had been provoking Austria-Hungary for decades. As early as the morning of

July 28, Count Sazonov, wholeheartedly embracing the idea von Bethmann-Hollweg had put forward earlier that day, began suggesting that it would be sufficient punishment for Serbia if the Austrian Army be allowed to occupy Belgrade, after which a settlement could be negotiated between the Dual Monarchy and the Serbian kingdom.

It was a face-saving idea with a great deal of merit, for it allowed the Austrians, the Serbs, and the Russians to each avoid humiliation, and in particular permitted Vienna and St. Petersburg to emerge from the crisis with their prestige as Great Powers somewhat enhanced. For the Serbs the consequences of the "Stop-in-Belgrade" plan were simple and obvious: despite the loss of the capital, Serbia would continue to exist as a separate, independent nation. For Austria-Hungary, it permitted the Dual Monarchy to demonstrate to the rest of Europe that it was neither weak nor feeble. Russia could claim that by preserving Serbia's national identity, it had fulfilled its self-appointed role as the protector of southern Europe's Slavic peoples.

Grey whole-heartedly embraced the "Stop-in-Belgrade" concept, sensing that it was the best compromise available, not realizing that it was merely a ploy to distract foreign attention from Germany and Austria-Hungary's provocations of Russia, and brought to bear as much diplomatic pressure as he could to urgently press for some form of arbitration of the Serbian issue. In Berlin, Chancellor von Bethmann-Hollweg continued his diplomatic charade and appeared to endorse the idea, as did Kaiser Wilhelm, who at that moment was vacillating wildly between belligerence and conciliation and took the proposal seriously. Late on the night of July 28 the cable went out from the *Wilhelmstrasse* outlining the four points of the Chancellor's proposal.

For a brief, shining moment, it appeared as if common sense had reasserted itself and the peace of Europe was salvaged. To Grey, the most immediate and personal result was that there would be no need for His Majesty's Government to openly and decisively commit itself one way or the other on the question of whether or not to support France. However, unknown to Grey, despite the contents of von Bethmann-Hollweg's cable, the German Foreign Minister, von Jagow, had earlier assured the Austrian ambassador, Count Szögyény, that for the sake of appearances the German government was obligated to go through the motions of entertaining proposals of arbitration, but had no intention of allowing them to succeed. At the same time, General von Moltke was wiring Conrad von Hötzendorf to "stand firm against [the] Russian mobilization. . . mobilize at once against Russia. Germany will mobilize." Consequently, Grey was forced to watch helplessly as over July 29 and July 30, Germany, Russia, Austria-Hungary and France drove each other to the very brink of war.

Still, there was no reason for Britain to become involved. While many within and without the Government might agree that Britain had a moral obligation and a strategic interest in defending France, their case was far from compelling. Those who believed in the necessity of intervention did what they could, the most spectacular— and as events would have it, the most far reaching—act being a decision by Churchill, First Lord of the Admiralty. With marginal legal authority though with exceptional prescience, he issued what may have been the most critical order that would be given during the next four years.

Churchill, whose aggressive temperament sometimes got him into trouble, was, as Barbara Tuchman described him, much like "the war horse in Job who turned not back from the sword but 'paweth in the valley and saith among the trumpets, Ha, ha.'" There was no question in Churchill's mind where Britain's obligations and interests lay, and on July 26 he acted on his convictions. Learning that Austria-Hungary had rejected Serbia's reply to the ultimatum, on some instinctual level he foresaw where the coming confrontation might lead. The Royal Navy was the foundation of Britain's power and security. The island nation depended on it for its life, to establish and maintain the trade routes by which Britain was fed. The Navy protected the kingdom from invasion and it would be the instrument by which the German fleet might be destroyed when it sought battle. Keenly aware of all of this, on his own authority Churchill took a dramatic step, for which the nation, and the world, would later be forever grateful.

That afternoon the Grand Fleet, the amalgamation of all British warships stationed in and around the British Isles, and the greatest concentration of seapower yet assembled on the planet, had just completed a ten-day-long practice mobilization. This meant that every ship was fully crewed, equipped and armed as if it were going to war. The fleet was scheduled to disperse the next morning, two-thirds of the ships involved returning to distant stations, training schools or dockyards, the reservists in their crews being discharged to their homes. If events unfolded as Churchill foresaw them, Britain would soon be again in need of this fleet, and the chaos of trying to recall all the ships and crewmen who were in the process of dispersing to the corners of the Empire would be indescribable—and potentially catastrophic. To Churchill there was no choice: it would be far wiser to keep the fleet assembled and to hand until the crisis passed and it was no longer needed, than to suddenly need it and be unable to bring it together. The dispersal would have to be delayed; the fleet would remain in British waters, alert and ready on its wartime stations. Abandoning his vacation and leaving his wife and children by the seashore, he rushed to London, determined to arrive before the fleet dispersed.

In Whitehall, the First Sea Lord, Admiral Prince Louis Battenberg, had kept a close watch as the situation had developed on the Continent. Anticipating Churchill's reaction, Battenberg sent out a signal at 4:05 p.m.: "Admiralty to C in C Home Fleets. Decypher. No ships of First Fleet or Flotillas are to leave Portland without further orders. Acknowledge." If worse came to worst and Britain needed the Fleet, the Royal Navy would be ready.

Upon arriving at the Admiralty, Churchill promptly endorsed Battenberg's orders and thanked the Admiral for his foresight and action. Next he began to inform his colleagues in the Cabinet of just what the Admiralty had done. When Grey was informed, he whole-heartedly approved, and made certain that word of it reached Berlin and Vienna, in the hope that it might have "a sobering effect." While it would later be learned that Churchill's action had no effect on Berlin's decision to go to war, it would have an unanticipated strategic consequence: the Royal Navy would have absolute mastery of the English Channel and the North Sea should the decision be taken to send the British Army to France. There would be no opportunity for the Kaiser's navy to attack the troopships carrying the B.E.F. across the Channel: the German High Seas Fleet would be denied its one moment of glory to exert a decisive influence on the war.

(After the war, Churchill would take credit for the decision to
mobilize the fleet, something his critics would seize upon as typical of
what they saw as his inflated sense of self-importance. They were
wrong. True, it was Battenberg who made the original decision to
mobilize the Grand Fleet, based on what he believed Churchill would
want done, but in this sense the First Sea Lord was acting as the First
Lord's "executive officer," properly anticipating his superior's actions
and requirements. Also, it was still necessary for Churchill to endorse
the order: he could have easily countermanded it using the First
Lord's authority had he decided that the First Sea Lord had gone too
far. However, there is a larger sense to saying that Churchill
"ordered" the mobilization of the Grand Fleet. By confirming
Battenberg's decision, Churchill did two things: he took personal
responsibility for the order, thus protecting Battenberg from any
possible charges that the First Lord had exceeded his authority or
acted improperly, and also, as a consequence of his position as a
member of the Cabinet, Churchill made the decision to mobilize the
fleet a part of the Government's policy, rather than simply a
subordinate's implementation of a contingency plan. Therefore, in a
very real sense, both Battenberg and Churchill issued the mobilization
order, for rather different but equally valid purposes and reasons.)

Meanwhile, Grey, like Churchill, began taking indirect action
wherever he could. While he had no way of knowing that in Berlin
Field Marshal von Moltke, the German Army Chief of Staff, was
pressuring the Kaiser to order the mobilization of the German Army
and unleash the attack on France, from the reports sent by Sir Edward
Goschen, the British Ambassador in Berlin, he gathered a sense of the
rising tension in the *Wilhelmstrasse* and decided that the time had
come to give the German government a warning. If it were true, as
everyone believed, that the German war plan was based on an
invasion of Belgium in order to accomplish its strategic objectives,
Germany must be made aware that such a violation of Belgium's
neutrality would almost certainly provoke Britain's intervention.
Unlike the question of support for France, intervention on behalf of
Belgium was a far less divisive issue within the Cabinet, the Liberal
Party, and Parliament as a whole.

The rift over when and where Britain should become involved in the Continent's predicament did not follow simple party lines, but rather was a legacy of a long-standing debate over the role and responsibility of Great Britain and the British Empire in world affairs. The deepest division over the issue actually existed within the ranks of the ruling Liberal Party, and extended into the Cabinet itself. It was a schism which had its origins in the Boer War, when "Liberal Imperialists" sided with the then-ruling Conservative Party in support of the war. "Liberal Imperialism" believed that Great Britain had an obligation to take an active role in world affairs, intervening where and when necessary for reasons which were as much moral as they were commercial or political. The leading lights of the Asquith government were all "Liberal Imperialists" and included Asquith himself, as well as Grey, Sir Richard Haldane, and Churchill. As this quartet understood the situation, and this was a perspective shared by the Conservatives, it was in Britain's national interest to defend France, for, as Grey dryly put it, "If Germany dominated the Continent it would be disagreeable to us as well as to others, for we should be isolated."

Those Liberals within the Cabinet and Parliament who disagreed with the Liberal Imperialists were not in their turn small, timid, narrow-minded men. They were the ideological heirs of William Gladstone, and shared his belief that the only involvement in foreign affairs which Great Britain should undertake was to assist oppressed peoples who were struggling for their freedom. Under any other circumstance, foreign alliances and commitments were viewed with deepest suspicion, believed (not without some past justification) to be the instruments by which unscrupulous businessmen and commercial interests exploited other nations and peoples. The Holy Trinity of these Liberals were Free Trade, Retrenchment (disarmament) and Reform; anything else was irrelevant. They regarded France with the deepest suspicion and Germany was simply one more trading partner, albeit one ruled by a pompous windbag. War, any war, was always evil and usually unnecessary: going to war to defend France was unthinkable, and it could even be argued that a seventy-five-year-old treaty assuring the safety of a small European kingdom was no longer relevant in the modern world.

It was the responsibility of the Prime Minister to keep his party in line if he were to remain in office, and clearly Asquith had his work cut out for him bridging the rift between the Liberal Imperialists and their opponents. It would require the skills of a consummate politician, and that is the description of Herbert Henry Asquith in a nutshell, although it is worth bearing in mind that "politician" and "political leader" are not synonymous.

H. H. Asquith (he began styling himself thus at the age of nine and did so for the rest of his life) was a Yorkshireman, born into the middle class in 1852. Like Grey he attended Balliol College, Oxford, and then set up a successful legal practice in London in 1876. It was not until ten years later that he was elected to Parliament, a Liberal representing East Fife in Scotland. He and Grey served together in Gladstone's last Cabinet, from 1892 to 1895, and like Grey he supported the Conservative government during the Boer War, becoming one of the first Liberal Imperialists. Asquith became a somewhat controversial figure by being a vocal opponent of women's suffrage, while his outspoken views on Free Trade helped return the Liberals to power in 1905, and he was rewarded with the post of Chancellor of the Exchequer under Henry Campbell-Bannerman, whom he succeeded as Prime Minister in 1908. It was also during Asquith's time in office that the veto power of the House of Lords was permanently broken, which in turn led to 0000sweeping social reforms that began to slowly reshape British society.

All of this could lead to the impression being formed that Asquith was a dynamic and courageous leader; he was not. Truly the consummate politician, his style of governing more closely resembled that of a bank manager than the head of a government. The various offices of the Cabinet were more or less free to formulate and develop their own policies under a broad guideline provided by the Prime Minister rather than work to fulfill any specific vision or goal he might possess. Cabinet meetings were held more to report on progress made than to develop unified policy; they were used to build consensus rather than hold debate. (Asquith himself would frequently write love letters to his mistress during such meetings.) The reins of power were held very loosely in Asquith's hands, and he seemed to give a higher priority to retaining office than actually doing something effectual with it.

Asquith allowed Grey considerable latitude in carrying out his duties as Foreign Secretary, and in the hands of a less conscientious man Great Britain's foreign policy could have been hopelessly compromised. However, Grey was no opportunist. He pursued the maintenance of the balance of power with an admirable single-mindedness, twice thwarting German attempts to embarrass France and provoke a war with her, first in Morocco in 1905 and then in Algiers in 1911. The Algerian triumph had apparently cemented the diplomatic strength of the Entente Cordiale, perhaps too much so, for France began to regard British support as a given when formulating policy and strategy toward Germany. Now, as the July crisis was approaching its climax the French were asking the British to help them defend *la belle France* against the expected German onslaught.

The question that Great Britain might well ask was, with what? When contemplating the instrument of his own downfall, Napoleon Bonaparte had opined that "British infantry are the finest infantry in the world. Fortunately they are not numerous." Now, a century later, the whole of his statement still held true. Man for man, the soldiers of the British Army were without peer in the world, long-term professionals for whom soldiering was an honorable career. Their discipline unshakable, their morale indomitable, their musketry deadly beyond belief, the regiments of the British Army would prove time and again that they were easily the equal of forces four, five, sometimes six times their strength. However, that quality came with a price. The British Army was made up entirely of volunteers; there was no conscription. Consequently, the British Army could never hope to muster the massive numbers which could be mobilized by Continental conscript armies. The entire British Expeditionary Force (the B.E.F.) stationed in Great Britain consisted of no more than six infantry and two cavalry divisions, just over 160,000 officers and other ranks. There was a Territorial Force which acted as a ready reserve, but the British Army was thinly spread by responsibilities that literally spanned the globe. While between the Regulars, the Territorials, and the Indian Army more than a million men could theoretically be put into the field, the demands of the Empire dictated that barely half that number could actually be released for service—and most of them would require weeks or months to be transported to France.

At that moment, however, politics were more important than manpower. While lacking the depth of Grey's conviction, Asquith believed that Great Britain had a moral obligation to stand by France in the coming war. He made it clear to the Cabinet that he would not sanction a blanket statement of neutrality for Great Britain: such a declaration would repudiate Secretary Grey, who would be forced to resign. Asquith bluntly told the Cabinet that if Grey resigned, he would as well, bringing down the Government. At the same time, he was far from certain that the British people would accept such a clear commitment by Britain to support France, and knew that if his own Cabinet appeared divided on the issue, he had no hope of uniting the nation behind it. His first task, then, was to bring the whole of the Cabinet—or at least its most influential members—around to his point of view.

It was not going to be easy: the faction of the Cabinet opposed to intervention was led by Lord Morley, a classic Gladstone Liberal (he had, in fact, written a popular biography of Gladstone) of considerable political and moral stature. It was Morley who first raised what would become the thorniest issue for Asquith's government as well as for any Liberals in Parliament who supported intervention. By aiding France, Morley pointed out, Great Britain would also be supporting Russia. "Have you ever thought what will happen if Russia wins?" he asked at one Cabinet meeting.

> If Germany is beaten and Austria is beaten, it is not England and France who will emerge preeminent in Europe. It will be Russia. . . People will rub their eyes when they realize that cossacks are their victorious fellow-champions for Freedom, Equality of man. . . and respect for treaties.

Here Morley was not simply playing on an old British prejudice but was also drawing attention to political realities; it was an argument not easily refuted. Morley made it clear to his colleagues that every other question, including the integrity of Belgian neutrality, was "secondary to the question of our neutrality in the struggle between Germany and France." By Morley's count there were at least nine Cabinet members who would vote against intervention, and if the Chancellor of the Exchequer joined them, it would almost certainly assure that Britain would remain neutral no matter what might transpire on the Continent.

The Chancellor was, of course, David Lloyd George. Both camps were courting him, for he was already a key figure in the British government. Lloyd George was ambitious and cunning, and his Welsh roots had blessed him with a capacity for spellbinding eloquence. Already something of a demagogue, careful observers might have detected within him a craving for power for its own sake which would one day propel him to the office of Prime Minister, but would subsequently leave his reputation and legacy tarnished. Yet at this time, at least, he could still be the fiery radical free-thinker, unbeholden to any ideology but determined to do what was right and best for Britain. Whichever way Lloyd George went he would take with him a large portion of the Cabinet, and with it Parliament and the country.

A point which must be made most emphatically here is that the division within the Cabinet over whether or not to intervene on the Continent should Germany attack France was not simply an exercise in party politics. It reflected an equally deep rift in the mood of the country. Earlier that week the magazine *Punch* published a bit of verse that despite its tongue-in-cheek tone—or perhaps because of it—summed up the attitude of a great many Britons:

> *Lines designed to represent the views of an*
> *average British patriot:*
> *Why should I follow your fighting line*
> *For a matter that's no concern of mine? . . .*
> *I shall be asked to a general scrap*
> *All over the European map,*
> *Dragged into somebody else's war*
> *For that's what a double entente is for.*

For most of Great Britain, the real crisis of the day was the rising turmoil in Ireland. It was significantly closer to home than any dispute in Central Europe, and in plain fact it threatened to rend the very fabric of British society. In the spring of 1914, Home Rule for Ireland finally passed through Parliament, set to take effect in September. The citizens of Protestant-dominated Ulster declared that they would never accept Home Rule for Ireland as administered by

Catholic-dominated Dublin; their rallying cry was "Ulster is right and Ulster will fight." Their words were more than mere rhetoric—they were prepared to back up their defiance with arms, and they had the means to do so: earlier that month a German arms manufacturer, aided by the German government, had smuggled 25,000 Mauser rifles and three million cartridges into Belfast, adding to an already existing arsenal of at least 15,000 rifles.

The Ulstermen's determination created a terrible quandary for the British Army, for it placed the officers and other ranks of the Ulster garrison in an impossible situation: it was entirely possible that the Army would be ordered to open fire on people whose "crime" was loyalty to the same Crown the soldiers served. (At one point the King asked Prime Minister Asquith point-blank: "Will it be wise, will it be fair to the sovereign, as head of the army, to subject the discipline and indeed loyalty of his troops to such a strain?") If the government chose to resort to force in order to get the six counties to submit to rule from Dublin, officers of the Ulster garrison based in the Curragh announced that they would resign their commissions *en masse* rather than take up arms against their own countrymen. This was the beginning of the "Curragh Mutiny."

By early summer the situation had reached a critical point. Eight hundred additional troops who were not part of the Ulster garrison were ordered to secure the Army's supply depots in the six counties. Brigadier General Herbert Gough, commander of the 3rd Cavalry Brigade, which was part of the Curragh garrison, believed that this was the first move of a military occupation of Ulster, and formally tendered the resignation of his commission in protest, along with fifty-eight other officers. Gough was immediately summoned to the War Office in London to "give an account of himself"—in fact the inquiry he would face would be a thinly disguised court-martial. It was during this inquest that the Commander-in-Chief of the Army's main military encampment at Aldershot, General Sir Douglas Haig, came to London with a warning for the War Office. He reported, quite truthfully, that there was a strong undercurrent of support for Gough among the officers of the army, many of whom would resign if Gough were punished. Among them were the Chief of the Imperial General Staff, Field Marshal Sir John French; General Sir Henry

Wilson, the Director of Military Operations; and the Secretary of State for War, Colonel John Selly.

It was a situation without parallel in British history, although Lloyd George was not far off the mark when he declared it to be the "gravest issue raised in this country since the days of the Stuarts." The words "civil war" and "rebellion" were heard in the halls of the Houses of Parliament. Officers looked at rankers and rankers at officers, each wondering what the other would do: what was at issue was whether or not the Army possessed the right to refuse to carry out Government policy. There was a long-standing tradition in the British Army that a soldier had the right to refuse to obey an unlawful order—but what if the order came from the very body responsible for making the laws? A series of high-level conferences were held in a search for a solution, including a Royal Commission, but resolution eluded them. In the end, in order to prevent the threatened mass resignations, Brigadier Gough was reinstated and allowed to return to Ireland with a written guarantee that his troops at the Curragh would not be used to enforce a Home Rule Act on Ulster. While Field Marshal French and General Wilson were also reinstated at the same time as Gough, the underlying issue remained unresolved, and this was part of the Irish problems being discussed at the Cabinet meeting where Grey broke the news of Austria-Hungary's ultimatum to Serbia.

By July 29, as Russia prepared to mobilize her army, the question of what Great Britain would do was still unanswered. Asquith was determined to be prepared for every eventuality, which explains how Churchill was able to persuade him to send the "Warning Telegram" that afternoon. While not quite as drastic a step as Russia's "Period Preparatory to War" or Germany's *Kriegesgefahr*, sending the Warning Telegram under any circumstances was fraught with significance, for it was a tacit admission that diplomacy might fail. The Warning Telegram initiated the "Precautionary Period," in which officers commanding the naval stations and military posts of the Empire were expected to dispense with any extraneous activities and ensure that their commands were ready to execute a mobilization. Supplies would be inventoried, weapons and equipment checked, and mobilization schedules and requirements updated as needed.

At almost the same moment the Warning Telegram was going out to the military and naval posts of the Empire, Foreign Secretary Grey summoned Ambassador Lichnowsky to an urgent meeting at the Foreign Office. Grey had earlier met that day with the Austro-Hungarian ambassador, Count Albert Mensdorff, as well as the French ambassador, Paul Cambon. The meeting with Mensdorff had been rocky, the Ambassador insisting that Austria-Hungary's quarrel with Serbia was a purely local affair which did not involve any British interests. Therefore British attention, and by implication British involvement and interference, were unwelcome. Grey was blunt in telling Mensdorff that as Austria's quarrel was threatening to draw Germany, Russia, and France into it, it certainly did involve Great Britain's interests. As Mensdorff was leaving the Foreign Office, Grey's private secretary, William Tyrrell, took him aside for a last word, telling the ambassador that:

> Russian interests leave England cold but if French vital interests or the power position of France is at stake, no English government will be in a position to hold England back from taking part on the side of France.

While Tyrrell was not speaking officially, the warning had almost certainly been given with Grey's knowledge if not actually at his instigation, in the certainty that it would soon find its way to Germany.

Paradoxically, when Grey met with Cambon, he went to some pains to make it clear that Britain had no reason to become involved in any conflict involving any combination of Austria-Hungary, Serbia, and Russia, which was hardly surprising. He then went on to say that if France found herself caught up in a war with Germany because of the terms and conditions of her alliance with Russia, that would be a situation entirely of France's creation, which would also not offer any certain reason for Britain to become involved.

Cambon was furious: this was "perfidious Albion" at its worst.

> All our plans are arranged in common! Our General Staffs have consulted! You have seen all our schemes and preparations!

Look at our fleet! Our whole fleet is in the Mediterranean in consequence of our arrangements with you and our coasts are open to the enemy. You have laid us wide open!

He then declared that if Great Britain failed to stand by France, she would never be forgiven, ending his angry outburst by saying, "*Et l'honneur? Est-ce-que l'Angleterre comprend ce que c'est honneur?*"

That was hardly fair—or honorable—of Cambon. He and Grey had worked together for too many years and had honorably resolved too many Anglo-French disagreements for him to question whether or not England understood the meaning of honor. The Entente itself had come into existence because the two men, early in their professional relationship, had realized that they shared a common vision of ending the interminable antagonism between France and Great Britain, which no longer served a purpose for either nation but seemed to perpetuate itself simply because it had always been so. However, at this moment Cambon was a Frenchman thinking of France and Grey an Englishman thinking of England, just as their offices required, so perhaps Cambon's outburst was understandable.

Here an insight into Grey's feelings and beliefs are essential to understanding his efforts to bring Great Britain into the war alongside France. Grey was not at heart a passionate Francophile, although he greatly admired the French, their language, and their culture; in fact during his eleven-year tenure in office he never left British soil. Instead he was a man with a keenly developed sense of the realities within international politics. Grey fundamentally understood that France had long since ceased to have expansionist ambitions on the Continent: the last war she had fought on European soil, the Franco-Prussian War, was one into which she had been goaded as an affair of national honor. Partly as a result of Bismarck's encouragement, partly because there was no alternative, after the war France turned her aggressive energies toward building a colonial empire, a task Frenchmen found as challenging and exhilarating as any Continental warfare had been.

The sole extent of French territorial ambition in Europe was to reclaim the "lost provinces" of Alsace and Lorraine, forcibly separated from France after her defeat by Prussia and incorporated into the newborn German Empire. While it could be argued, and it was, that Lorraine—Lothringen to the Germans—was ethnically and culturally far more Teutonic than Gallic, no one ever suggested that Alsace was anything but to her heart and soul the very essence of France. But while the French might dream of *revanche* against the hated *Boche*, that streak of hard-headed realism which always managed a curious and inexplicable coexistence along the stream of romantic fantasy which ran through every Frenchman's heart kept them from single-handedly attempting to retake the two provinces by force of arms.

It was Germany who in Grey's mind was the expansionist threat on the Continent. While after the Franco-Prussian War Bismarck declared that Germany had no further territorial ambitions in Europe, his successors were never quite as convincing as he. With each passing year Germany's army, already second in size only to Russia's, grew larger, while the High Seas Fleet had been built with the explicit purpose of challenging the Royal Navy. Germany coveted Belgium's coalfields, while the Russian provinces of Lithuania and Estonia, already predominantly Germanic in population, seemed like natural additions to the Reich. To Grey the question was not if Germany's army would suddenly lunge across her borders at one of her neighbors, but rather when.

As a consequence, Grey was sympathetic to Cambon and his representation of France's plight. All the same, he would not compromise the stance he had taken nine years earlier and had steadfastly maintained ever since. The Entente was not, and was never intended to be, an alliance; the British government, regardless of which party was in power at the moment, always retained the freedom to act as the dictates of circumstance and public opinion required. Whatever his personal sympathies and convictions, Grey would not let them get in the way of the responsibility of his office, which was to carry out Britain's foreign policy in the best interests of the nation and the Empire.

The "plans arranged in common" to which Cambon had referred were the joint General Staff "conversations" which had been held annually between the French and British since the establishment of the Entente nine years earlier. It has been argued that these talks, which were responsible for developing a joint strategy for the French

Army and the B.E.F., were in substance little different from the military terms of France's alliance with Russia or Germany's with Austria. This was not the case, although in July 1914 the French seem to have lost sight of that fact. The staff talks were not merely paper exercises or a set of overly elaborate war games conducted simply to develop expertise in staff work, but neither were they were an unqualified commitment on the part of Great Britain to join France in a war with Germany. They were simply contingency plans, drawn up so that in the event that the French and British armies should find themselves fighting side-by-side, they would be acting together in a common strategy. However, such planning did not automatically commit the British Army to action.

The principle of "no commitment" had been established jointly by Secretary Grey and Sir Richard Haldane, who was the Secretary of War when the Entente with France had been formalized and the staff talks began. It had been accepted by the then-Prime Minister, Campbell-Bannerman, and maintained by his successor, Asquith, as well as by Grey. It was not, as some historians have maintained, "a fiction." It was a frank admission to France that while the British government could envision circumstances where standing with France in a war against Germany would be in Great Britain's best interest, it would be entirely up to the British to decide what those circumstances were. It was the responsibility of the French General Staff to develop plans and strategies which did not presume the assistance of the B.E.F. as well as plans which did: if the French Army failed to do so, it was not Great Britain's fault.

Yet there was, as Grey (and to a lesser extent Asquith) saw it, a degree of moral obligation on the part of Great Britain toward France as a consequence of the Entente. With her smaller population, more limited resources and inferior industrial base, France was and would continue to be the weaker power in comparison with Germany; this invited a natural combination with Britain. Twice in the previous decade Great Britain had provided the diplomatic support which allowed France to defy blatant attempts at bullying by Germany, first in Morocco in 1905 and then in Algiers in 1911. What gave Britain's diplomatic support legitimacy was the implication that it would be backed by military action. Germany did not fear Great Britain but she did fear the British Empire. To Grey, Asquith, and their supporters in the Cabinet and in Parliament, these two incidents had established a pattern and a precedent, one which Britain would ignore at peril to her prestige and reputation: to them, Britain's word was not something to be solemnly given then lightly withdrawn.

Making this point clear to Germany—to the Kaiser and Bethmann-Hollweg—was the reason Grey had summoned Ambassador Lichnowsky to his office on the afternoon of July 29. Knowing that the warning Ambassador Mensdorff had received earlier that day would duly find its way to Vienna and thence to Berlin, Grey decided to further reinforce it. To all appearances he was being extremely concil-iatory, telling Lichnowsky that if Berlin was unwilling to follow London's lead in arbitration, London would be willing to follow Berlin's, as long as the process produced genuine results. Grey acknowl-edged the legitimacy of Austria-Hungary's grievances against Serbia, but once more voiced the concern that their dispute was threatening to engulf other Powers, and should Germany and France become embroiled, vital British interests would become involved. All of this Lichnowsky had heard before. Then Grey dropped his bombshell: any action by Germany which would threaten France's status as a Great Power, and by extension upset the balance of power on the Continent, would cause any British government, Liberal or Conservative, to go to war. Now the issue was out in the open, Germany was risking not only war with Russia and France, but with the British Empire as well. Grey's statement was neither a threat nor an ultimatum. Germany had as yet taken no action overtly hostile toward France; she had not even begun to mobilize at this point. However, Grey, who knew full well that the Government had made no decision whether or not to actually side with France in the event of open hostilities, was hoping that by warning Germany off, no such decision would have to be made.

Lichnowsky understood Grey with perfect clarity. He had been an ideal choice as ambassador to the Court of St. James, for he was one of those rare Germans who truly understood the British. Speaking English, copying British manners and mannerisms, adopting British styles of dress (tweeds were almost as popular in Berlin as in London), and playing British sports were almost a mania among German aristocrats. When Admiral Sir John Fisher was being honored at a dinner in Berlin in 1911, he discovered that each of the forty German guests, who included Chancellor von Bethmann-Hollweg and Admiral von Tirpitz, the Naval Secretary, were fluent English-speakers. What set Lichnowsky apart from them was that he took this mania one step farther: he did not merely mimic British behavior and tastes, he adopted them, so that he was able to think like a Briton. This made the insights he offered in his reports to Berlin particularly valuable, although that value frequently went to waste as he was ignored or overruled. Lichnowsky and his wife were immensely popular with British society, and the two of them had taken Britain to heart. Lichnowsky was prepared to do anything within his power to prevent a war between the Fatherland of his birth and his adopted home of Great Britain. Accordingly, he reported the contents of his conversation with Grey to Berlin with the greatest accuracy, so that there would be no misunderstanding by the Kaiser or von Bethmann-Hollweg. Great Britain's neutrality, taken for granted when the crisis began brewing a month earlier, now was far from certain, and no one could say which way the British would decide. Nevertheless, some decision by Great Britain had to come soon. As one after the other Russia, Austria-Hungary and Germany began or threatened to begin mobilization, it was clear that events on the Continent were approaching some sort of climax. Asquith, faced with the prospect of a division within his Cabinet which would bring down his Government, was loath to make any decision which might force the hand of those Cabinet members who were still undecided or were unquestionably opposed to intervention. The bland entry in his diary for July 31 reflected this passivity: the question still waiting to be settled was "Are we to go in or stand aside. Of course everybody longs to stand aside." This passage is all the more remarkable for its omission of any reference to the thunderbolt Sir Edward Grey had hurled down at that afternoon's Cabinet meeting.

By this time Grey was making no effort to disguise his feelings about Germany. The Reich was, in his considered opinion, pursuing a policy as a "European aggressor as bad as Napoleon." The Cabinet was shocked: in the idiom of the day, invoking the Corsican's name had only one meaning—Germany represented a clear and present danger to the safety and integrity of the British Isles. The time had come, he said, when the Government must decide whether to declare its support for the Entente, which would mean that Great Britain would go to war alongside France, or announce its neutrality. If the choice was to be neutrality, it would be a policy which he would be unable to carry out. The unspoken threat of resignation hung like a cloud over the table at which the Cabinet members were seated. Such was Grey's stature within Parliament and the country, as well as abroad, that if he chose to resign it would bring down the Government. The Cabinet, shaken by this jolt of political reality, adjourned shortly thereafter, Grey's words still echoing in their ears.

Immediately after the meeting Grey took a bold step on his own initiative, hoping to reinforce the gravity of his earlier pronouncement regarding Germany. Two telegrams were dispatched, one to France, the other to Germany, each asking the respective governments for a formal assurance that they were prepared to respect Belgian neutrality "so long as no other power violates it." The results were everything Grey had hoped and dreaded. The *Quai d'Orsay* responded in less than an hour with an unequivocal reaffirmation of France's commitment to the 1839 treaty and the sanctity of Belgium's neutrality. From the *Wilhelmstrasse* came only silence.

Grey was now convinced of what was coming. Together with Sir Edward Goschen's report of von Bethmann-Hollweg's offer made on July 29 to respect the territorial integrity of France and Belgium in any post-war settlement, the refusal of the German Foreign Ministry to give a simple reassurance of Belgian neutrality could mean only one thing: Germany was planning an invasion of Belgium as part of her strategy to invade France. The Schlieffen Plan was real.

That this was not a given is one of the great curiosities of the years leading up to the Great War. As early as 1907, a French spy, who remains unidentified to this day, was providing the French General Staff with the details of the Schlieffen Plan. How this agent, who was apparently posted to the German Great General Staff, gained access to the Plan was, and is, unexplained yet after the war it was determined that his information was astonishingly accurate. Unfortunately, that very accuracy may have undone all the effort and risk the agent had undertaken, for the French simply refused to believe the information which was being sent to them.

The agent's reports had, to their eyes, all the hallmarks of the work of an *agent provocateur*: the information was so detailed that it seemed improbable that it had been obtained clandestinely. Might it not be, French intelligence officials argued, an ingenious ruse on the part of the Germans? It might be an attempt to cause the French Army to alter its plans and dispositions—and possibly even contemplate its own violation of Belgian neutrality in an effort to counter the predicted German attack. This would have presented the Germans with a *fait accompli,* allowing them complete freedom of movement across Belgium with none of the international political complications which would have resulted from their own flagrant violation of Belgian neutrality. Therefore, rather than being accepted as genuine, the spy's reports were disbelieved and discarded.

There is no way of knowing, of course, how influential the spy's reports might have been in London had the French chosen to share them with the British. It is entirely possible that the opponents of intervention would have argued that they were the instruments of French provocation. They certainly would have struck a nerve in any case, for the sanctity of Belgium's neutrality was a far different issue from choosing to join France in a fight which may or may not have genuinely been Britain's as well.

It was here that both Asquith and Grey saw an opportunity to fulfill what they regarded as the moral obligation to France, by linking it to Britain's treaty obligations to Belgium. Non-intervention-ists such as Lord Morley might argue that the 1839 Five-Power Treaty was outdated, but to much of Parliament and the British public it was still a vital, viable document. While France and Russia could almost certainly take care of themselves unaided if they were attacked by Germany, to many Britons the idea of a small country like Belgium being trampled by the German juggernaut, while Britain stood thoughtfully to one side, was repugnant.

The actual terms of the treaty also had a considerable bearing on the nature of any potential reaction by Great Britain. The document had been carefully crafted so that while it would be an all but iron-clad guarantee of Belgium's security, it would also restrict Belgium's autonomy as little as possible. An encroachment upon Belgian territory was not automatically a violation of Belgian neutrality: it was a violation only if the Belgian government declared it to be so. Any of the five signatory Powers to the treaty had the right to ask for free passage of its armies across Belgian territory, which Belgium in turn had the right to grant or deny. If a foreign army should trespass on Belgian soil, the government in Brussels had a variety of responses available to it. They ranged from permitting free passage, to allowing the advancing army to pass under protest, to offering token resistance (such as lining the roads with soldiers posted at port arms but not firing upon or hindering the invaders), to open and total resistance by the Belgian Army. Even if the last option were chosen, the guaranteeing powers were still only allowed to intervene if the Belgian government formally asked for assistance.

Accordingly, both London and Paris began making discreet inquiries in Brussels as to the Belgian government's plans should Germany demand free passage across the country. The Belgian king, Albert, although no doubt sensing what was coming, did his best to avoid provoking Germany, and so refused to detail in advance what were his intentions. This was particularly frustrating for Grey, who believed that a clear statement from Brussels that the Belgians planned to resist any German incursion would strengthen the position of those in the Cabinet and Parliament who favored intervention. However, it seemed to give support to the anti-interventionists, particularly Lord Morley, who argued that because there were so many options open to the Belgians, what mattered was not the fact of a German incursion onto Belgian soil, but rather the extent of any incursion.

By now almost no one believed that the Germans would stay out of Belgium entirely, but the most widely held view was that they would only traverse a small corner of that country, down in the southeast by the Meuse and Sambre Rivers where the German forces could fall on the French left flank. No one imagined that the German strategy was not to move against the French left, but rather to move behind it. It was unthinkable that the Germans would want or need to occupy the whole of Belgium, and if as predicted it was only a corner of the country that was violated, the Belgians themselves might not do more than make a token protest or show of force. Because of King Albert's caution, however, no one was sure exactly what Belgium would do.

Uncertainty was beginning to cause things to start to unravel. A wave of financial panic which had started when Austria declared war on Serbia was closing Exchanges all over Europe. Austria-Hungary, Germany, and Russia, concerned with how to pay for the war toward which they were rushing, were all hurriedly recalling the gold reserves they had invested overseas. Friday, July 31, was the eve of the August Bank Holiday weekend in Britain, and as bankers and brokers in the City worried about the collapse of foreign exchange the Stock Exchange closed down at 10:00 a.m. The business world's worst nightmare seemed to be about to become reality, as a war approached which would, in the words of Lloyd George, "break down the whole system of credit with London at its center." It had been an article of faith among the banking and business communities in Great Britain as well as the Continent that any war which involved all of the Great Powers would be so costly that it would utterly ruin the international credit structure and ruin the world's banking system. It was this belief which prompted the Governor of the Bank of England to telephone Lloyd George on Saturday, August 1, in order to inform him that the City—the network of banks, lending houses, and exchanges clustered in the heart of London—was "totally opposed to [Britain] intervening" in a war.

What weight the Governor's warning might have carried had it come a few days earlier will never be known. By the time Lloyd George was able to communicate it to his colleagues within the Cabinet on August 1, events had gained a further momentum; by now they were almost unstoppable. The division within the Cabinet and Parliament was growing by the hour: at that morning's meeting twelve out of eighteen Cabinet members voted against giving France any assurance of British support should Germany attack her. In a lobby of the House of Commons that afternoon, a caucus of powerful Liberal members met to take a vote on the question of whether Great Britain should remain neutral "whatever happened in Belgium or elsewhere." The motion passed, nineteen members voting "aye" and only four voting "nay." It was an ominous moment for the Asquith Government, and in particular for Sir Edward Grey, for even as the Liberal caucus was voting, the announcement was being made in Berlin that the German Army would begin mobilizing, with a declaration of war to be delivered to Russia that same evening.

Chapter IX

DECISIONS IN BERLIN

High noon, Saturday, August 1. As the bells of the clocktowers struck their last note, the German ultimatum to Russia expired—Berlin and St. Petersburg were now officially at war. Crowds numbering in the thousands, tense and anxious, milled about along the *Wilhelmstrasse*, in the *Königplatz*, and in front of the palace, waiting for official confirmation of what they knew must come next. Although the Kaiser had told his people, speaking the evening before in his address announcing the *Kriegesgefahr*, that "the sword has been forced into our hand," there was still the faint hope of a favorable Russian reply, and that war would not come.

The afternoon passed with no further word, and the atmosphere grew more tense, in the words of a journalist present in the crowd, "electric with rumor. People told each other Russia had asked for an extension of time. The Bourse [the German stock exchange] writhed in panic. The afternoon passed in almost insufferable anxiety." The Chancellor was little help. For some reason von Bethmann-Hollweg chose this moment to issue a statement which concluded: "If the iron dice roll, may God help us." Finally, at 5:00 p.m., a policeman appeared at the palace gate and announced that the decree for mobilization had been issued. Even as he spoke the motorcar carrying General von Moltke to the War Ministry passed through the gate behind him. In a scene which would find parallels in all of the capitals of the Great Powers over the next few days, after a brief outburst of cheering, a wave of song quickly spread over the crowd. It began with just a few voices at first, but quickly grew in a rising swell of patriotism until tens of thousands of throats sounded together. Curiously, movingly, it was not the brash and arrogant *"Deutschland über Alles,"* instead it was the humble yet dignified *"Nun Danket alles Gott"* (*"Now Thank We All Our God"*), the traditional German hymn of prayer and thanksgiving sung before and after battle.

Automobiles raced up and down Berlin's major thoroughfares, with horns sounding and officers standing on the running boards, waving handkerchiefs and shouting, "Mobilization!" In another scene which would also play itself out in Paris, St. Petersburg and London, a wave of patriotic feeling surged over the gathered crowds, suddenly manifesting itself in a venting of anger against foreigners. Russians, or even anyone who "appeared" Russian, were instantly suspected of being spies, saboteurs or subversives, and several of them were assaulted in the streets. Berlin would see numerous such violent outbursts for the next week, as foreigners were subjected to sudden attacks, some of them beaten or trampled to death, before they could flee the country or seek the asylum of a friendly embassy or consulate. As von Bethmann-Hollweg had hoped, fear and hatred of the Gallic and Slavic hordes supposedly massing on Germany's borders ran deeper than the pacifistic bonds of Socialism.

In the meantime, by 1:00 p.m. a telegram had been sent to Ambassador von Pourtalés in St. Petersburg, containing instructions that he formally submit Germany's declaration of war to Foreign Minister Sazonov by 5:00 p.m. Berlin time, the same moment the Kaiser would issue the orders for a general mobilization of the German Army. As was the case with Russia's "Period Preparatory to War," much of the administrative detail required by the mobilization had already begun when the *Kriegesgefahr* (Danger of War) had been announced the day before. Now, with the mobilization decree in his hand, General von Moltke was being driven from the *Neue Palas* at Potsdam to the *Kriegesministerium* on the *Königplatz*, where the appropriate orders would be issued.

Just moments after von Moltke departed, however, the Chancellor and the Foreign Minister, von Bethmann-Hollweg and von Jagow, alighted from an ordinary taxi at the steps of the palace and hurried

Archduke Franz Ferdinand, his wife Sophie, and their children. Breaking with Hapsburg tradition, Franz Ferdinand married for love, not for dynastic reasons, provoking a crisis with the Emperor that threatened his position as heir-apparent to Franz Josef's throne.

A few minutes after 11:00 a.m. on June 28, 1914, Franz Ferdinand and Sophie descend the steps of City Hall in Sarajevo. One of history's great "what ifs," Franz Ferdinand may well have been a better man than his detractors–and much of posterity–believed him to be.

As the Imperial couple smile at bystanders, the Archduke's motorcar is about to pull away from Sarajevo City Hall. Franz Ferdinand and Sophie are less than five minutes away from their fatal rendezvous with Gavrillo Prinzip.

Franz Josef, Kaiser and König (Emperor and King) of the Dual Monarchy of Austria and Hungary. Despite his advanced years (he was 84 in 1914) he was the hardest working monarch in Europe.

Count Leopold von Berchtold, the Dual Monarchy's Foreign Minister, and the driving force behind Austria-Hungary's decision to go to war with Serbia.

Chancellor Theobald von Bethmann-Holweg–politically amoral, he regarded the possibility of a European war as an opportunity to divert the German people's attention from domestic problems.

General Helmuth von Moltke ("Von Moltke the Younger"), Chief of the General Staff of the German Army. Indecisive and insecure, he lacked his famous uncle's moral courage as well as his martial abilities.

Kaiser Wilhelm II of Germany. Vain, neurotic, pompous, blustering, and more than a little unstable, he was "always playing at war."

Tsar Nicholas II of Russia. Nicholas faced a complex task: he believed he had a moral obligation to protect the Serbs while at the same time allowing for Austria-Hungary's right to punish the regicidal regime in Belgrade, all the while preventing the Serbian crisis from escalating into a confrontation with Austria-Hungary's ally, Germany. He might have succeeded had it not been for Kaiser Wilhelm II's duplicity.

Above: *Á Berlin!* Cheered on by young Frenchwomen, French *poilus* begin their march to the front.

Above left: August 1, 1914. A German officer reads the proclamation announcing the mobilization of the German Army to a clearly anxious crowd in Berlin.

Below left: *Nach Paris!* With garlands of flowers hanging from the muzzles of their rifles, fully kitted-out German reservists march to their assembly depot.

President Raymond Poincaré of France. Never a dynamic or inspiring leader, he nevertheless found in August 1914 a dignity commensurate with the courage of the French people as he and his countrymen prepared to face the onslaught of the Schlieffen Plan.

Vive le France! Looking like something out of a Phillipoteaux painting, a regiment of freshly mobilized French cuirassiers passes through a French town.

Albert I, King of Belgium. Young (37) but courageous, Albert, with the full support of his people, refused to turn Belgian sovereignty, or Belgian honor, into a bargaining chip with the Germans.

Great Britain's Prime Minister in August 1914, Herbert H. Asquith. However strongly he believed that Britain had a moral obligation to stand by France in the event of a German attack, he knew that the majority of the British people had no interest in getting involved in what they saw as just the latest episode in France's ongoing quarrel with Germany.

Sir Edward Grey, Great Britain's Foreign Minister in August 1914, and the most widely respected diplomat in Europe. His speech in the House of Commons on August 3, 1914, would persuade the nation that what the Germans dismissed as "a scrap of paper" (the 1839 Five Power Treaty) placed Britain's national honor at stake when Germany invaded Belgium.

First Lord of the Admiralty Winston Churchill, shown here inspecting Royal Navy cadets in 1912. Churchill's decision to mobilize the Royal Navy before Germany and Great Britain were actually at war would prove to be one of the most decisive acts of the entire conflict.

The German Army at flood tide. This photograph, taken during summer maneuvers in 1912, gives a very real sense of what the German advance across Belgium in August 1914 would have looked like.

Tommy Atkins. Scottish soldiers of the BEF ("The Old Contemptibles") stopped to rest in the Belgian village of Flameries on the march to meet the advancing German Army.

Left: The German Army's victory parade in Brussels, August 22, 1914. More than four years would pass, and over ten million soldiers on all sides would die, before they left.

A British recruiting poster from early 1915.

inside. Within minutes a uniformed officer of the Imperial household came dashing down those same steps, threw himself into a waiting automobile, and scurried off into Berlin, looking for the General. Just short of the War Ministry, the officer overtook von Moltke, and pulled him up short, breathlessly repeating the instructions for the Chief of Staff to return to Potsdam as quickly as possible. A last-minute proposal had come from Great Britain which seemed to hold out a hope that Germany would not have to go to war with France—or might avoid a war altogether. Disbelieving, von Moltke nevertheless returned to the New Palace, where a jubilant Kaiser explained this sudden change in the political situation.

Inside the *Neue Palas*, the Kaiser had come to the sticking point. Face to face at last with the specter of a two-front war, the Kaiser had for the first time in his reign reached a moment where bluster and bombast would avail nothing. The monarch who was "always playing at war" now was confronted with the very war which he had encouraged, promoted, and fostered, but never really wanted. Like all ambitious monarchs, Wilhelm had sought more power, increased prestige, a larger role in world affairs, and always greater authority over Germany's neighbors, but like a common bully he tried to achieve them by intimidation. Confronted by a monarch more courageous than he—Tsar Nicholas—Wilhelm was at last trapped by his own militaristic pretenses. "War" was no longer "play"—the martial fantasies had now turned to bitter reality, dreams of glory becoming nightmares of carnage. Yet to back down now on his threats and promises would shatter the Austro-German alliance, do near-irreparable damage to Germany's reputation abroad, and make both the Empire and its Emperor the objects of international ridicule. It was a trap of his own devising with only one way out—war.

It was at this moment that no small measure of the burden of guilt settled on Wilhelm's splendidly epauletted shoulders. He had given a near-irresistible impetus to events by issuing the "blank check" of unqualified support for Austria-Hungary following the Sarajevo murders. He had further propelled them by refusing any attempt to rein in the Dual Monarchy once the ultimatum to Serbia had expired. Then he bullied and threatened the Tsar at the very moment when Nicholas was hoping to draw Austria's fangs with nothing more aggressive than a show of force. There had never been any hope of reconciliation with France, of course, but the question of what Great Britain would do if war actually came was still unsettled because for two decades Wilhelm had methodically if unwittingly antagonized the British with his aggressive naval policies and heavy-handed diplomacy. This was a war which would bear unmistakably the stamp of Wilhelm's will and personality.

At the same time he seemed to seek solace in self-pity and delusion, declaring:

> The world will be engulfed in the most terrible of wars, the ultimate aim of which is the ruin of Germany. England, France and Russia have conspired for our annihilation. . . . The encirclement of Germany is at last an accomplished fact. . . .

And yet, in fairness to Wilhelm, it must be said that there was also an element of genuine regret over the decision he was about to make. Confiding in an Austrian liaison officer, he murmured, "I hate the Slavs. I know it is a sin to do so. We ought not to hate anyone. . . ."

He took heart reading reports coming from St. Petersburg that the announcement of Russia's mobilization had been met with widespread strikes, rioting, and looting. (Though Wilhelm didn't know it, the reports were untrue.) He also read an assessment—which also had no actual basis in fact—by Captain von Eggeling, the German military attaché, that when Russia mobilized, she planned "no tenacious offensive but a slow retreat as in 1812." Wilhelm took all this to mean that the Russian Army would go to war already seriously demoralized, which, if it were true, would mean that his own rapidly assembling juggernaut would face little if any serious opposition when it was unleashed in the east. It would, just as with so many of Wilhelm's other beliefs, prove to be a false hope.

Meanwhile, the telegraph keys at the *Kriegesministerium* clattered away as the ponderous, but smoothly functioning, mechanism of mobilization went into motion. Orders began going out to two million men, reservists who were being directed to report to their designated regimental depots. There they were issued uniforms, shoulder harnesses, belts and cartridge pouches, rifles and ammunition, backpacks, boots, bayonets, canteens and entrenching tools. Infantrymen were formed into platoons, platoons into companies, companies into battalions, and battalions into regiments. Cavalry drew up into sections, squadrons, troops, and regiments. The regiments were marched to the nearest railway depot, where they entrained for their assembly points, at which time they would meet up with the artillery, signalers, medical units, bicyclists, cook-wagons (called *gulaschkanonen*, "goulash guns," because of the peculiar shape of the chimney on the wagons' cookstoves), and blacksmith units who would combine with them to form divisions and corps.

It was an incredible feat of organization. To move a single army corps—and there were fifty-six of them in the German Army—required 6,010 railway cars: 170 for the officers, 965 for the infantry, 2,960 for cavalry (troopers and mounts), and 1,915 for the artillery and support troops. They would be organized into 280 trains, all moving at precisely fixed times at exact intervals. So detailed were the German Army's mobilization plans that the number of railroad cars which could pass over any given bridge within a given time were, for safety's sake, determined in advance.

While the mobilization was only hours old, however, the Kaiser was still hoping that by some miracle it could be called off before the trains began rolling, and a two-front war with France and Russia avoided—and at the last moment one seemed to appear. Precisely how it transpired and from whence came this *deus ex machina* to this day remains a mystery, but accounts of it do appear in reliable sources. Someone—exactly who has never been determined—approached von Bethmann-Hollweg sometime during the afternoon of August 1, and suggested a way to defuse France's true *casus belli*—the provinces of Alsace and Lorraine. For years the idea had been mooted of granting the two provinces autonomy as Federal States within the German Empire. If offered and accepted by the residents of the region, such an announcement would deprive France of the basis for her belligerence: as recently as July 16, the French Socialist Congress had gone on record as favoring such a proposal. The obstacle to implementing it had always been the German Army, which insisted that "military necessity" required the provinces to be permanently garrisoned by an army of occupation.

Von Bethmann-Hollweg's anonymous colleague suggested that now was the time to make an offer of autonomy, for at least the province of Alsace. An arbitration conference would be required, forcing France to remain neutral while negotiating the terms of the offer, and those negotiations could be prolonged indefinitely, certainly long enough to allow the German Army to defeat the Russian hordes in the east. An added benefit was that with France neutral, or at least non-belligerent, Great Britain would have no reason to enter the war.

The problem was that the offer would have to be made by the Chancellor, and it would have required a brave, even bold man to make it. Von Bethmann-Hollweg, with his long years of experience in fence-sitting, had never been bold and had long since forgotten how to be brave. Just as with Wilhelm, a burden of guilt was settling on von Bethmann-Hollweg: the storm which was about to break over Europe would have never coalesced if he had not permitted it to do so. Perhaps his single greatest failure came when the crisis began, though there were many to follow. The Chancellor's explicit endorsement of the Kaiser's unqualified support for whatever punitive action Austria-Hungary chose to take against Serbia was a political blunder of catastrophic proportions. As Chancellor, von Bethmann-Hollweg was not expected to be a mere rubber stamp for the Kaiser's decisions; indeed, he had a constitutional duty to his monarch and the German Reich to be anything but. His duty as Chancellor required him to make clear to the Kaiser the possible consequences of such a sweeping declaration, and then attempt to gain control over any awkward or unpleasant situations which might result from it. Given the nature of Wilhelm's ego, it probably would have been impossible to persuade him to make any sort of public restatement or clarification of Germany's support for the Dual Monarchy. However, von Bethmann-Hollweg was a skilled politician perfectly capable of working quietly behind the scenes, through diplomatic channels, tempering, modifying, or moderating the Kaiser's public pronouncements.

However, the Chancellor's own ambitions and expectations for the coming war were hopelessly muddled. While on one hand he repeatedly urged Berchtold and Tisza in Vienna to act with moderation, on the other he was encouraging them through von

Jagow and Zimmermann at the Foreign Ministry to continue with their aggressive plans for Serbia while merely going through the motions of negotiating with St. Petersburg. The Chancellor knew that the Kaiser's original declaration, the "blank check," had been made to be a typically Wilhelmine spectacle—a loud and public show of solidarity with Germany's ally—but that Wilhelm had never wanted events to reach such a fever pitch. The Kaiser genuinely expected him to press Austria-Hungary to accept some form of arbitration, and it should be pointed out that Wilhelm's motives in this were far from altruistic, for a successful resolution of the Serbian crisis resulting from the Kaiser's arbitration would have increased Germany's prestige and authority almost as much as a war. Von Bethmann-Hollweg could have brought the entire crisis to a screeching halt simply by declaring that the Dual Monarchy had exceeded the bounds of the support the Imperial German government had offered. He chose to say nothing.

As the time limit on the ultimatum to St. Petersburg ran out and it became clear that war with Russia at least was unavoidable, another aspect of von Bethmann-Hollweg's responsibility for the war appeared. Thus far France had initiated no actions which could in any way be interpreted as hostile or threatening to Germany; under the most recent revision of the Franco-Russian alliance, because the Tsar had mobilized the Russian Army without first consulting the French government, France was perfectly free to remain neutral in any war between Russia and Germany. There was no need for a German attack on France, and yet the iron-bound requirements of the Schlieffen Plan demanded that the German Army first take the offensive against France before turning on Russia. At almost the last minute, a solution presented itself, an opportunity to avoid attacking France and so eliminate the specter of British intervention which so haunted von Bethmann-Hollweg—the solution was proposing autonomy for Alsace—but the Chancellor, whether from ignorance or stupidity is immaterial, let it slip through his fingers.

While the Chancellor would later argue that he was never privy to the full details of the Schlieffen Plan, and so was unaware of the extent as well as the blatant manner in which Germany would violate Belgian neutrality, it is an excuse which is so insubstantial that it barely qualifies as flimsy. It cannot be argued that as a politician the Chancellor played no role in determining military strategy, for the means by which the Reich had been formed made that responsibility an essential function of the Chancellor's office. Bismarck himself set the precedent throughout the German wars of unification, using military strategy as a political tool, refusing to allow strategic opportunities to take priority over, or be developed apart from, political considerations.

Only once was Bismarck overruled in this by then-Kaiser Wilhelm I, grandfather of the present Kaiser. In 1871, in negotiating the settlement of the Franco-Prussian War, Bismarck declined to make any claims on French territory, believing that to do so would only create a bitter and lasting antagonism between France and Germany. Field Marshal von Moltke, the architect of Prussia's triumph over France, disagreed, and demanded that for strategic reasons the provinces of Alsace and Lorraine be forcibly incorporated into the new-formed Reich. The Kaiser agreed with von Moltke, the deed was done, and the enmity which Bismarck had feared quickly became a reality. Bismarck regarded it as the greatest failure of his entire career.

In his turn, even if von Bethmann-Hollweg was not familiar with the details of the Schlieffen Plan, it was his business to learn them. That the world's greatest military power should be committed to a war without recourse to any diplomatic solution was a situation that bordered on the absurd, that such a commitment would be made without the explicit consent of her Chancellor was ridiculous, yet that was precisely the situation in which Germany found herself on the evening of August 1, 1914. Von Bethmann-Hollweg had been Chancellor for five years, during which time the only strategic plan developed and employed by the German Army was the Schlieffen Plan: there had been ample opportunity for him to become familiar with its provisions and its implications. Whatever excuses he might later offer for failing to stop the German offensive into Belgium and France—and they would be many—ignorance could not be one of them. Knowing as he did the shape of the war to come, terrified that Great Britain would be drawn into it as yet another enemy, von Bethmann-Hollweg fretted, flustered, and fluttered, but in the end did nothing.

The offer to France was never made; instead, taking his cue from

General von Moltke, the Chancellor ordered that an ultimatum be sent to Paris at the same time as the one sent to Russia, giving the French government eighteen hours to decide if she would stay neutral in a war between Russia and Germany. If France chose to stand aside, she would be required "as a guarantee of neutrality" to hand over to Germany "the fortresses of Toul and Verdun which we shall occupy and restore after the war is over." In other words, the French were being asked to surrender the key defensive positions which protected the heart of France. When Baron von Schoen, the German ambassador in Paris, requested the formal French reply at 1:00 p.m. on August 1, he was informed that rather than submit to such a humiliation, France "would act in accordance with her interests." The opportunities for stepping back from the abyss were rapidly dwindling in number.

One more such opportunity presented itself that day—or at least appeared to. It was just after 5:00 p.m. when a telegram from Ambassador Lichnowsky in London arrived at the Foreign Ministry, where it was quickly deciphered then read by the Chancellor. Von Bethmann-Hollweg was stunned by its contents: it was Lichnowsky's understanding that, if it was possible to halt the German Army before it crossed the frontier of either Belgium or France, a war on two fronts might be avoided after all. As a result of a meeting between Lichnowsky and Sir Edward Grey that afternoon, the British were prepared to make a most extraordinary offer: ". . . in the case [Germany] did not attack France, England would remain neutral and would guarantee France's neutrality." Electrified by this seeming last-minute reprieve, von Bethmann-Hollweg and von Jagow rushed out of the Foreign Ministry, and rather than wait for an official car to be brought around, hailed the first taxi they saw and dashed off to Potsdam to inform the Kaiser.

When Wilhelm read Lichnowsky's report, he was galvanized into action: here was the miracle for which everyone in Berlin had hoped and prayed. With the neutrality of France and Great Britain assured, there was no need for an attack in the west, no call to invade Belgium, no reason for the Schlieffen Plan to go forward at all. The entire premise of the plan had been to secure Germany's western flank so that the entire might of the German Army could be turned against the

Russians. Now that security was being offered without the need to fire a single shot in the west! *Wunderbar!*

The question in everyone's mind but which no one dared articulate was whether or not it was too late. Mobilization, of course, had already begun, setting the mechanism into motion which would ultimately propel seven German armies across the French and Belgian frontiers. Such was the care with which the details of the Schlieffen Plan had been worked out that the first military action, the seizure of a railway junction in the independent duchy of Luxembourg, was set to take place within two hours. (Like Belgium, Luxembourg's neutrality had been guaranteed by a treaty signed by all of Europe's Great Powers, including Germany.) It had to be stopped, and immediately, but only von Moltke had the authority to issue the necessary orders as to prevent further confusing what was sure to be an already chaotic situation, German law provided that, once mobilization was announced, the only person authorized to modify or rescind mobilization orders was the Army Chief of Staff. At a sharp bark of command from the Kaiser, an officer dashed down to a waiting motorcar which rushed off into Berlin, siren screaming, in search of the missing general.

There were two ironies at work at this moment. The first was that if Wilhelm and his officers and officials had actually acted on this "initiative" which they believed Great Britain was offering them, they would have achieved exactly what they had hoped to accomplish all along: fighting Russia alone, without the need to go to war with France and risk war with Great Britain. The French government, having absolutely no desire to go to war with Germany at this moment, was carefully avoiding any action which might be considered provocative, even going so far as to order the French Army's border patrols to withdraw several kilometers from the Franco-German frontier in order to avoid possible "incidents." Tragically, when the moment came for decisive leadership, neither the Kaiser, Chancellor von Bethmann-Hollweg, or General von Moltke were capable of providing it, and the moment passed beyond hope of recovery. What took place in London and Berlin that afternoon and evening would always be remembered as one of History's great "might-have-beens;" it would also become History's greatest tragedy.

The second irony was that what had actually happened in London and what was perceived at the German Embassy in London and at the *Neue Palas* in Berlin to have happened were two different things, although for a few hours that really did not matter. The meeting which Lichnowsky reported to Berlin was actually a telephone conversation which had taken place that morning. The British Foreign Secretary, Sir Edward Grey, had called Lichnowsky at the embassy, and as the Ambassador understood him, said that he was prepared to formally offer Great Britain's neutrality, as well as guarantee the neutrality of France in a war between Germany and Russia if, in return, Germany formally pledge not to attack France. It was not an impossible situation, since, because Russia had begun mobilizing against Germany without consulting or notifying the French government in advance, France was not bound by her treaty obligations to go to war with Germany as well. Great Britain had no interests directly involved in an eastern European war involving Germany, Austria-Hungary, and Russia, and with France neutral there would be no potential for *casus belli* with the British in the west. At least, this is what Lichnowsky believed that Grey had said.

It was not quite that simple: in his anxiety to prevent Germany and Great Britain going to war with each other, Lichnowsky had misunderstood the Foreign Secretary. Grey had not made a formal diplomatic overture, he had been making inquiries. Grey had not assured Lichnowsky that Britain was prepared to guarantee her own neutrality along with that of France if Germany confined her quarrel to Russia alone. What he had done was ask the ambassador if Berlin was prepared to limit the war to the eastern front if both London and Paris pledged to remain neutral.

Given Grey's diplomatic mannerisms, and his elliptical way of talking all the way around a subject, it was an understandable mistake. In his eight years' experience as Foreign Secretary dealing with legalistic, pettifogging German diplomats, Grey had learned the value of avoiding point-blank, categorical statements and declarations. The Anglo-German alliance negotiations which had occupied much of the first decade of the 20th century finally failed because the Germans demanded a treaty in which the terms of every conceivable scenario were laid out in detail, while the British required a document which was far more flexible in content and interpretation. Those same constraints still applied to Anglo-German diplomacy. As a result of Lichnowsky's Anglophilia their interference was usually reduced to a minimum, but in this case old habits died hard, and Grey, in order to avoid being pinned to legalistic minutiae, had put his questions in a way which Lichnowsky, whose frame of mind in this situation was already predisposed to clutch at straws, promptly misunderstood.

The misunderstanding was not immediately obvious to Berlin, so when Field Marshal von Moltke was intercepted just a few blocks from the War Ministry by the officer dispatched by the Kaiser, he returned to Potsdam to find an unexpectedly optimistic atmosphere had overtaken everyone. When von Moltke was presented to Wilhelm, the new situation, its potential and the immediate action required were all quickly explained to the Chief of Staff. Holding up Lichnowsky's telegram triumphantly, the Kaiser declared, "Now we can go to war against Russia only. We simply march the whole of our Army to the East!"

Von Moltke was stunned. He had devoted ten years of his life, and the whole of his professional reputation, to the Schlieffen Plan. Beginning with his tenure as von Schlieffen's assistant, then succeeding the old man himself as Chief of Staff, von Moltke had never allowed himself even the briefest flirtation with another strategic plan. So total was von Moltke's devotion to the Plan that to him, von Schlieffen's strategic legacy was tantamount to holy writ, as immutably carved in stone as the two tablets Moses had carried down from Mt. Sinai. It was martial perfection, to be slightly revised or gently adjusted according to changing circumstances, but never, never to be rejected or abandoned as unnecessary or unwanted. This was it, *Der Tag*, Judgement Day, in which Germany would invoke the Plan to begin smiting her enemies so that she might accomplish the domination of Europe which was clearly the manifest destiny of the German people. To von Moltke, hearing the Kaiser announce that the sum total of the effort, the implementation, and the promise of the Schlieffen Plan was no longer needed was something approaching blasphemy.

Part of von Moltke's mind also reacted on a purely intellectual level. Redeploying over a million troops, turning around the 11,000 troop trains which carried them, rerouting their supply columns, transporting the tens of thousands of tons of guns, ammunition, equipment and materiel required to maintain a modern army in the field across Germany and into East Prussia, was a task which to von Moltke's mind was quite impossible. The railway schedules and timetables, worked out and developed over years, annually revised and updated with exquisite precision, could not be improvised in a matter of hours or days. All von Moltke could see was the abandonment of the Schlieffen Plan, and to his mind anything but the Plan was synonymous with chaos. In order to prevent such a calamity, von Moltke did the only thing he could think to do.

He lied and said:

> Your Majesty, it cannot be done. The deployment of millions cannot be improvised. If Your Majesty insists on leading the whole army to the East it will not be an army ready for battle but a disorganized mob of armed men with no arrangements for supply. Those arrangements took a whole year of intricate labor to complete and once settled, it cannot be altered.

Wilhelm, staring, could not believe his ears. There was a long moment of strained silence. "Your uncle" the Kaiser finally said bitterly, "would have given me a different answer."

The Kaiser was right. The plain truth was that the deployment could have been altered, and von Moltke knew it. Not for naught was the German General Staff regarded as the finest body of military planners and thinkers in the world. Although von Schlieffen's plan, and with it a pre-emptive attack on France, had been Germany's official military policy from its inception in 1905, an alternate plan for a campaign against Russia alone had always been drawn up, and its schedules and timetables were revised with the same care and attention to detail that was lavished on the more glamorous attack in the west.

Again, railways were the key. One fundamental part of the elder von Moltke's success was his careful, methodical, and detailed study of railroads. In 1914 Germany possessed the densest, best-organized rail network in the world. Owned by an arm of the Imperial government, Prussian State Railways, each major line had a staff officer assigned to it, responsible for overseeing its maintenance and improvement. The General Staff had the power of veto over the placement or alteration of every mile of track within Germany. Exercises were held annually to ensure that railway employees at every level, and the responsible army officers, were all capable of performing their assigned duties, as well as spotting potential problems. One aspect of the annual exercises which always received particular attention were those involving rerouting and rescheduling trains to accommodate interruptions in the rail network as well as changing strategic situations.

Upon hearing von Moltke's declaration that "It cannot be done," Wilhelm would have been quite justified in asking for what reason were tens of thousands of German officers assigned to the Railway Department of the army? Why were hundreds of thousands of *deutschmarks* spent annually on exercises? Why were hundreds of railway cars kept in reserve against the possibility they might be needed for mobilization? In short, what purpose did the whole of the Army's railway *apparat* serve if not to move the troops where they were needed when they were needed? The Kaiser could have just as easily asked von Moltke why, if the troop movements were immutable, had he demanded the ultimatum sent to Paris requiring the surrender of the French frontier fortresses as pledges of France's neutrality while he turned the German Army to the east to face the Russians? No one caught von Moltke's inconsistency then, but his deception would be laid bare after the war when Matthias Erzberger, a Reichstag deputy, revealed that six months after the war began (and barely more than a year before von Moltke's death) the Chief of Staff, who had since resigned in disgrace, confessed that "the larger part of our army ought first to have been sent East to smash the Russian steam roller, limiting operations in the West to beating off the enemy's attack on our frontier." The technical details were later provided by General von Staab, Chief of the Railway Department, who, furious that von Moltke's lie was beginning to gain wide acceptance as truth, produced a memoir in which he showed how, if the orders had been given on August 1, four out of the seven armies deployed on Germany's western frontier could have been transferred to East Prussia by August 15.

But no one was present at the New Palace that evening who possessed the professional expertise necessary to call von Moltke into question, and the General stood firm in his refusal to cancel the deployments required for implementing the Schlieffen Plan. Finally, after a number of loud arguments, von Moltke convinced the Kaiser that the mobilization plan could not be changed. At that, von Bethmann-Hollweg and von Jagow began drafting a reply to Lichnowsky, instructing him to inform the Foreign Secretary that "regrettably" the movements of German troops already underway "can no longer be altered." In a gesture meant to suggest that there was still time to negotiate but which was essentially meaningless, assurances were given that no units would cross the German border before 7:00 p.m. on August 3—which had already been set as the time at which the attack would begin.

Then the Kaiser took a hand, drafting a personal telegram to King George V. He began by explaining that for "technical reasons" the mobilization, once begun, could not simply be halted at a word, but went on to suggest that, ". . . if France offers me neutrality which must be guaranteed by the British fleet and army, I shall of course refrain from attacking France and employ my troops elsewhere. I hope France will not become nervous." It is unclear what Wilhelm meant by having Britain's army and navy "guarantee" France's neutrality, but it is clear that he was acting on his understanding of the British "offer" as presented by Lichnowsky. A tantalizing opportunity was flickering past, for it seems that Wilhelm was considering overruling von Moltke after all and would have done so if the proper conditions had come about; if the opportunity was to be seized, it would have to happen soon.

Time was in increasingly short supply, however, including time for arranging diplomatic preconditions. The hour was approaching 7:00 p.m. and as everyone there knew, that was the time set for the German Army's 16th Infantry Division to advance into Luxembourg and seize the railway facilities there. Von Bethmann-Hollweg, still believing that Grey's "offer" was valid, demanded that the 16th be recalled before it crossed the frontier lest it give the British reason to withdraw the offer. (This observation also gave the lie to the Chancellor's later assertion that he was ignorant of the details of the

Schlieffen Plan.) Without so much as a look in von Moltke's direction, the Kaiser ordered one of his aides-de-camp to send fresh orders by both telephone and telegraph to the 16th Division's headquarters at Trier, halting the division in place. Turning back to his telegram to King George, he added a closing sentence: "The troops on my frontier are in the act of being stopped by telephone and telegraph from crossing into France."

Though neither the Kaiser nor von Moltke were aware of it, Wilhelm's orders to Trier halting the 16th Division in place would not arrive in time. At 7:00 p.m. the first offensive action of the war took place, though it was hardly spectacular. A company of the 69th Infantry Regiment, some two hundred strong under the command of one Leutnant Feldmann, crossed the Luxembourg border some twelve miles south of a sleepy Belgian town called Bastogne. There stood the village of Ulflingen: surrounded by farmland and pasture, its only significance lay in the presence of a railroad station and a telegraph office. These were quickly and quietly occupied by Lt. Feldmann's troops, who had arrived in Ulflingen in a fleet of commandeered motorcars. About half an hour later, a messenger arrived with the Kaiser's recall orders, and Lt. Feldmann promptly withdrew his troops, informing the villagers, who were as astonished to see the soldiers go as they had been to see them arrive, that "a mistake has been made." However, it would prove to be only a temporary reprieve: the German soldiers returned the following day. They would remain in Luxembourg for more than four years.

Von Moltke, meanwhile, was living up—or down—to his nickname "Sad Julius." He would write in his memoirs that "At that moment [when the Kaiser recalled the 16th Infantry Division] I thought my heart would break." Believing he had already won in his battle of wills with the Kaiser, he once again saw the intricate structure of the Schlieffen Plan collapsing in ruin, for the Luxembourg railway exchanges were vital to the initial troop movements made into France and Belgium. Once more he began pleading with the Kaiser, but this time Wilhelm was unmoved; the new orders stood.

Despairing, von Moltke left the New Palace and returned to his offices in the General Staff building, where he "burst into bitter tears of abject despair." A few moments after his arrival an aide brought the written order canceling the 16th Division's movement, but von Moltke refused to sign it, instead throwing his pen on his desk in disgust. "Do what you want with this telegram," he muttered to the astonished officer, "I will not sign it." He then slumped in his chair, brooding, immobile.

He was still there when his aide came looking for him around 11:00 p.m.—an urgent summons back to the *Neue Palas* had just arrived. Hurrying back to the Kaiser's presence, von Moltke found Wilhelm waiting for him dressed in a nightshirt over which he had thrown one of his uniform greatcoats, a telegram form in his hand. It was from Lichnowsky, who since his earlier report had spoken at length with Foreign Secretary Grey, and had learned of his mistake. After a brief explanation, Lichnowsky concluded simply, "A positive proposal by England is, on the whole, not in prospect." Wordlessly handing the telegram to von Moltke, the Kaiser waited until he had read it, then said tonelessly, "Now you can do what you like," turned and walked into his bedchamber.

This latest turn of events would prove to be too much for the Field Marshal, and something inside of him broke in that moment. As he made his way back to the General Staff headquarters, all of the self-doubt which he had harbored for so long, the by-product of living with a famous name while working, sometimes literally, in the shadow of his uncle—or at least, of statues of him—overwhelmed him. "That was my first experience of the war," he would write a few months later. "I was never the same thereafter." Before six more weeks would pass von Moltke would be relieved of his duties after he bungled critical movement orders for the German armies in France: he had lost all capacity for decisive leadership.

Five o'clock in the evening in Berlin was 7:00 p.m. in St. Petersburg, and it was at this hour that Ambassador von Pourtalés was shown into the office of Foreign Minister Sazonov. There was no hiding what was coming, and both men knew it: the next few moments would be among the most painful of their lives. Despite the sometimes acrimonious exchanges that had passed between them in the previous weeks, none of the animosity was personal. In fact, a genuine friendship had developed between them during von Pourtalés' seven-year tenure, and both knew it was about to end, likely forever.

Drawing himself up to his full six foot height, von Pourtalés carefully followed the formal protocol, and three times asked Sazonov if Russia had undertaken to halt the mobilization of her army; three times Sazonov replied in the negative. At this point, the German Ambassador, his pale blue eyes red-rimmed, his hands trembling with suppressed emotion, presented Germany's declaration of war.

Presented by the German Ambassador to St. Petersburg

The Imperial German Government have used every effort since the beginning of the crisis to bring about a peaceful settlement. In compliance with a wish expressed to him by His Majesty the Tsar of Russia, the German Emperor had undertaken, in concert with Great Britain, the part of mediator between the Cabinets of Vienna and St. Petersburg; but Russia, without waiting for any result, proceeded to a general mobilization of her forces both on land and sea.

In consequence of this threatening step, which was not justified by any military proceedings on the part of Germany, the German Empire was faced by a grave and imminent danger. If the German Government had failed to guard against this peril, they would have compromised the safety and the very existence of Germany.

The German Government were, therefore, obliged to make representations to the Government of His Majesty the Tsar of All the Russias and to insist upon a cessation of the aforesaid military acts. Russia having refused to comply with this demand, and having shown by this refusal that her action was directed against Germany, I have the honor, on the instructions of my Government, to inform your Excellency as follows:

His Majesty the Emperor, my august Sovereign, in the

name of the German Empire, accepts the challenge,
and considers himself at war with Russia.

Sazonov's emotions momentarily got the better of him as he finished
reading the note and he blurted out in a mixture of anger and despair,
   "The curses of the nations will be upon you!"
   "We are defending our honor," von Pourtalés replied.
   "Your honor was not involved. But there is a divine justice."
   "That's true," von Pourtalés agreed, turning to a window, hoping
that Sazonov would not see the tears beginning to course down his
cheeks. "So this is the end of my mission."
   The Foreign Minister came and stood by his friend for a moment,
laying a reassuring hand on the ambassador's shoulder. A few more
minutes passed in silence, then von Pourtalés turned to the door,
murmured, "Goodbye, goodbye," and never saw Sazonov again. It
was official: Germany and Russia were at war.
   At least one man in Berlin understood the enormity of what had
just transpired. Admiral Alfred von Tirpitz, the Naval Secretary, had
point-blank asked von Bethmann-Hollweg and von Jagow why was a
declaration of war on Russia necessary if, as the diplomats
maintained, there were no plans in hand to attack Russia. To do so
was strategic foolishness, for once Germany became an active
belligerent, she was vulnerable to attack. Of course, von Tirpitz was
thinking of his navy, and in particular the possibility of a surprise
attack by the Royal Navy against the High Seas Fleet anchorages at
Kiel and Wilhelmshaven, should Great Britain decide to stand
alongside France and Russia. It was a question which had vexed the
Chancellor as well, although his concern was naturally more political
than strategic. Part of the twisted logic von Bethmann-Hollweg had
invoked in his decision to back Austria-Hungary and risk war with
Russia was his certainty that Russia would be the first to declare war,
allowing him to justify the conflict to the German people with the
argument that they were fighting in self-defense. Despairing over this
latest turn of events, von Tirpitz remarked that by declaring war first
"it will scarcely be possible to place the guilt of a European conflagration on Russia" and would "place us, in the eyes of our own
people, in an untenable position."

It was a futile protest. Experts on international law at the Foreign Ministry argued that because the structure of the German mobilization plan required that the German Army go over to the offensive even before the mobilization was complete, a declaration of war was the "correct" thing to do. Besides, once the war was over and Germany was victorious, what would it matter who had declared war first?

Von Bethmann-Hollweg had little time to dwell on such details now, for new complications had arisen. The iron bindings of the Schlieffen Plan were now at work, turning the focus of the Chancellor—along with the rest of the German government and military hierarchy—to the west and the question of Belgian neutrality. In the afternoon of July 31, a telegram from the Foreign Office in London arrived at the Foreign Ministry in Berlin; in it the British Foreign Secretary had asked Germany for an affirmation of Belgium's neutrality. Von Bethmann-Hollweg immediately saw the trap being laid by Sir Edward Grey: should Germany reaffirm Belgium's neutrality, then later invade, regardless of whether or not the Belgians chose to resist, Germany would be saddled with a reputation for duplicity which might require decades to overcome. On the other hand, should the German government in any way indicate that a violation of Belgian neutrality was being contemplated, however minor, it would strengthen the hand of the interventionist faction in the British Cabinet: Belgium would automatically become one of those small nations struggling for its freedom which so endeared themselves to Gladstone Liberals.

One border violation had already occurred—the incursion into Luxembourg—but that could be easily and convincingly explained as an accident. As there had been no loss of life or destruction of property in the incident, such an explanation would seem plausible and almost certainly be accepted by France and Great Britain. What the Schlieffen Plan intended for Belgium, however, was no mere incursion but rather an all-out invasion. Here the terms of the 1839 Treaty came into play, and the German government hoped that the Belgians might choose to grant permission to the German Army for free passage across the Flanders plain. To accomplish this, von Jagow's office drew up what seemed to the Kaiser, von Bethmann-

Hollweg, von Jagow and von Moltke to be a reasonable and friendly request for just such permission.

However, this latest diplomatic overture was every bit as heavy-handed and inept as German diplomacy had been in the previous decade. The document showed little respect for Belgium's status as a sovereign nation, and its condescension toward the little kingdom bordered on the contemptuous. Worse, its tone indicated that Germany regarded permission to march her armies across Belgium as a right, while any expectation by the Belgians that their sovereignty should be acknowledged and respected would be regarded as undue interference with Germany's natural prerogatives. Absent was any attempt at persuasion, neither was there any hint of an offer to negotiate: the "request" was phrased as a straightforward, "either-or" demand.

> Reliable information has been received by the German Government to the effect that French forces intend to march on the line of the Meuse by Givet and Namur. This information leaves no doubt as to the intention of France to march through Belgian territory against Germany.
>
> The German Government cannot but fear that Belgium, in spite of the utmost goodwill, will be unable, without assistance, to repel so considerable a French invasion with sufficient prospect of success to afford an adequate guarantee against danger to Germany. It is essential for the self-defense of Germany that she should anticipate any such hostile attack. The German Government would, however, feel the deepest regret if Belgium regarded as an act of hostility against herself the fact that the measures of Germany's opponents force Germany, for her own protection, to enter Belgian territory.
>
> In order to exclude any possibility of misunder-standing, the German Government make the following declaration:
>
> 1. Germany has in view no act of hostility against

Belgium. In the event of Belgium being prepared in the coming war to maintain an attitude of friendly neutrality towards Germany, the German Government bind them selves, at the conclusion of peace, to guarantee the possessions and independence of the Belgian Kingdom in full.

2. Germany undertakes, under the above-mentioned condition, to evacuate Belgian territory on the conclusion of peace.

3. If Belgium adopts a friendly attitude, Germany is prepared, in cooperation with the Belgian authorities, to purchase all necessaries for her troops against a cash payment, and to pay an indemnity for any damage that may have been caused by German troops.

4. Should Belgium oppose the German troops, and in particular should she throw difficulties in the way of their march by a resistance of the fortresses on the Meuse, or by destroying railways, roads, tunnels, or other similar works, Germany will, to her regret, be compelled to consider Belgium as an enemy.

In this event, Germany can undertake no obligations towards Belgium, but the eventual adjustment of the relations between the two States must be left to the decision of arms.

The German Government, however, entertain the distinct hope that this eventuality will not occur, and that the Belgian Government will know how to take the necessary measures to prevent the occurrence of incidents such as those mentioned. In this case the friendly ties which bind the two neighboring States will grow stronger and more enduring.

Of particular significance, at least for posterity, were the circumstances in which this ultimatum—for that is in truth what it was—had been drawn up and communicated to the German ambassador in Brussels. It is utterly revealing—and utterly damning—about German intentions from the outset of the crisis.

The ultimatum was created by, of all people, Field Marshal von Moltke, who submitted the original draft to the Foreign Office on July 26—two days before Austria-Hungary declared war on Serbia. The implications of this are little short of staggering, for it means that von Moltke began working on his draft on July 25, or possibly even July 24; the request for such a draft, in turn, would have been made no later than July 24, more likely July 23. The request could have come only from the Foreign Ministry or the Chancellery—that is, from von Jagow or von Bethmann-Hollweg—meaning that they had been contemplating the need for such a note well in advance of the Austro-Hungarian ultimatum being delivered in Belgrade. In other words, even before a crisis which might eventually grow to the point where such a note would be required had come into being, even before there actually was any crisis, Germany was actively making preparations to go to war with Russia and France. It could be argued that because Vienna had kept Berlin fully informed of the contents of the ultimatum to be sent to Serbia, as well as the Austrian's determination that no Serbian reply short of total capitulation would be accepted, some sort of crisis was anticipated if not openly expected. There is, however, another side to the argument: if, as they would later claim, the Germans never expected the Russians to give more than moral support to the Serbs, the request for a draft ultimatum to Belgium can only mean that Germany had already decided to act as *agent provocateur*. The crisis would be sustained and aggravated until an open confrontation finally erupted between Russia and Austria-Hungary, giving Germany a pretext for the preemptive war which the Kaiser, his generals, his chancellor, and all of his senior statesmen believed was inevitable and utterly necessary.

Upon its receipt at the Foreign Ministry, von Moltke's draft was then honed and revised over the course of the following week, until it was delivered via diplomatic courier to the German Ambassador to Brussels, Baron Klaus von Below-Saleske, on July 29. The envelope containing the note was sent heavily sealed, accompanied by instruction that it was to be opened only on explicit instructions from the Foreign Ministry. Just how much von Below-Saleske knew of Germany's plans regarding Belgium is open to debate, although it is entirely possible that he knew little or nothing: the *Wilhelmstrasse* lied to its own ambassadors with the same ease and frequency as it lied to foreign governments.

What is known is that on August 1, the French ambassador in Brussels presented an official declaration to the Belgian Minister of Foreign Affairs that France would respect the neutrality of Belgium. When queried as to whether a similar declaration would be forthcoming from Germany, von Below-Saleske replied that he had received no instructions to make such a declaration, but in his personal opinion "the security. . . [of] Belgium was justified in regarding her Eastern neighbors." Nonetheless, fearing the worst, the Belgian government issued orders to mobilize the army on August 1.

It was mid-morning on August 2 when the news broke in Brussels that war has been declared between Germany and Russia. At first just an unconfirmed rumor, still it alarmed officials at the Ministry of Foreign Affairs sufficiently that a call was placed to the German Embassy requesting details. The German Military Attaché was emphatic in declaring that "there is no war, that Germany is not at war, that the report of war is false, issued by interested persons who wish to embroil Germany with her neighbors." (Germany and Russia had officially been at war for more than twelve hours at this point.) The callers then pressed for details about a report, from "a most reliable source," that German troops had invaded the Grand Duchy of Luxembourg and seized its railways. The attaché was equally insistent in this case, saying, ". . . As for Luxembourg, nothing is known about that here; but everything leads us to believe that there is no more truth in that news than in the other. . . ." Bewildered and only partly reassured, the Foreign Affairs officers waited throughout the day for further developments.

They had to wait until 7:00 p.m. That was the hour at which Ambassador Below-Saleske, having finally received instructions from Berlin to open the sealed envelope, appeared before the Belgian Minister for Foreign Affairs and handed him, in the name of the Imperial German Government, the ultimatum demanding free passage across Belgium. The time limit for Belgium's answer was set at twelve hours from the moment the note was delivered. A Royal Council was hastily convened by the King, with all of his Ministers of

State present.

Rarely in modern history has a government met under such morally trying circumstances. What was at stake for Albert and his ministers—as well as his people—was something that transcended national honor and encroached on the issue of national existence. There was little evidence to give credence to Germany's assertion that with the restoration of peace Belgium's independence and integrity would be restored, whole and unrestricted. The choices facing the King and his counselors were simple and stark: one, to grant passage to the German armies marching against France, and trust the Germans to fulfill their promises to pay indemnities and withdraw at war's end; the other solution was to risk war and invasion by defying the greatest military power in the world. The latter, while it would save Belgian honor, would mean the devastation of the country.

Albert, at the age of thirty-nine, was relatively young as European monarchs went, and in appearance he looked more the schoolteacher than the king, but in his breast beat the heart of a lion, the Lion of Brabant. Adored by his people, he knew them well, and understood that to them a Belgium dishonored would cease to be the Belgium they loved. His decision, though agonizing, was simple: if the German Army crossed the Belgian border, Belgium would fight.

While Albert and his Council deliberated, one of the most ridiculous incidents of the entire crisis took place, the capstone of German duplicity, one last exercise of heavy-handed German diplomacy, and a final demonstration that Germany regarded her opponents, real and potential, as little more than credulous fools. Ambassador von Below-Saleske, looking and acting greatly agitated, appeared at the Ministry of Foreign Affairs around 1:30 a.m. on August 3, in order to present to the Belgian government a report from Berlin that French airships had dropped bombs on certain unnamed cities, and that French cavalry patrols had violated the border, all before war had been declared. When asked where these incidents had occurred, the Ambassador replied, "In Germany."

"In that case," replied the Belgian official who received him, "I do not understand the object of your communication." Rather lamely, von Below-Saleske replied that these actions, contravening as they did accepted international conventions, were a demonstration of French intentions, and showed France's willingness to ignore international law, which in turn could only lead to the conclusion that France would not hesitate to violate the Belgian border just as alleged in the German ultimatum. The ambassador was quickly shown to the door.

At 7:00 a.m. the Belgian reply to the German ultimatum was handed to Ambassador von Below-Saleske. Even more than ninety years later it is a stirring document, firm and unambiguous, the declaration of a small, proud nation asserting its right to exist, the final three paragraphs as moving as anything written in Colonial Philadelphia or medieval Arbroath.

> In its note of the 2nd of August, 1914, the German Government has stated that, according to reliable information, the French forces are said to intend marching upon the Meuse by way of Givet and Namur, and that Belgium, despite her best intentions, would not be in a position to repulse an advance of the French troops without assistance.
>
> The German Government would hold itself obliged to forestall this attack, and to violate Belgian territory. Under these conditions Germany proposes to assume a friendly attitude toward the Government of the King, and engages itself, upon the conclusion of peace, to guarantee the integrity of the kingdom and of the whole extent of its possessions. The note adds that if Belgium places obstacles in the way of the advance of the German troops, Germany will be forced to regard her as an enemy and to leave the eventual settlement between the two States to the decision of arms.
>
> This note has profoundly and painfully astonished the King's Government.
>
> The intentions which it attributes to France are contrary to the precise declarations which were made to us on the 1st of August in the name of the Government of the Republic.
>
> Moreover, if, contrary to our expectation, a violation of Belgian neutrality should be committed by

France, Belgium would fulfil all her international obligations, and her army would oppose the invader by the most vigorous resistance.

The Treaties of 1839, confirmed by the Treaties of 1870, ratify the independence of Belgium under the guarantee of the Powers, and notably of the Government of His Majesty the King of Prussia.

Belgium has always been faithful to her international obligations; she has neglected no effort to maintain her neutrality or to cause it to be respected.

The attack upon her independence with which the German Government threatens her would constitute a flagrant violation of the law of nations. No strategic interest justifies the violation of justice. The Belgian Government, by accepting the proposals which have been put before it, would sacrifice the honor of the nation, while at the same time it would betray its obligations to Europe.

Conscious of the part which Belgium has played for more than eighty years in the civilization of the world, it refuses to believe that the independence of Belgium can be preserved only at the cost of a violation of her neutrality.

If this hope should be betrayed, the Belgian Government is firmly determined to repulse by all means in its power every attack upon its authority.

It was not the answer for which the Kaiser and his government had hoped, but it was one which they anticipated. Even if it chose to offer more than token resistance, the Belgian Army, all six divisions of it, would hardly be an obstacle: aside from their rifles, the Belgian forces lacked much in the way of modern equipment, particularly machine-guns and heavy artillery. Belgian resistance, however valiant, would be little or no impediment to the advancing German armies. More dangerous to the inflexible and unforgiving schedule of the Schlieffen Plan were the cities of Liege and Namur, each of which was ringed by defenses which were among the strongest and most modern fortifications in Europe. However, even here German thoroughness had provided a solution, for monstrous howitzers, far larger than any yet produced, had been designed and constructed for the sole purpose of demolishing the Belgian forts. Even as the German ultimatum was being considered by Albert and his ministers, these enormous guns were on railway flatcars headed for the Belgian border.

A more critical concern for Wilhelm and his ministers was whether or not Albert would choose to invoke the terms of the 1839 treaty and request French or British assistance in repelling the German invasion. The General Staff was quick to reassure the Kaiser that even if this became the case, the French Army would be unable to alter its deployment and shift troops to the north in time to prevent the German Army from sweeping across Flanders and falling on the exposed French left flank. As for the British, their "contemptible little army," hardly bigger than Belgium's, would simply be overwhelmed by the advancing tide of *feldgrau*. The Schlieffen Plan was irresistible, invincible. What mattered now was coming to grips with the French, the rout of the French Army, and the defeat of France.

Chapter X

RESOLUTION IN PARIS

As the July passed into August, the comprehension slowly began dawning on the people of the French Republic that *la patrie* was closer to war than it had been at any time since 1870. As long as the crisis in Central Europe remained confined to Austria-Hungary and Serbia, and possibly Russia—and at first it gave every indication of that being the case—there was no real cause for concern or alarm. That changed in the days after the Austro-Hungarian ultimatum was delivered and tensions began increasing between Russia and Germany: the French government saw the possibility of war with Germany growing more and more likely with each passing hour. By the time Germany declared the *Kriegesgefahr Zustand*, it was clear that war was inevitable—not as a consequence of any French provocation but simply because Berlin wanted it so. France's leaders and people alike began mentally and spiritually bracing themselves for the trials ahead. Churchill, writing after the war, summed up the grandeur, the glory, and the tragedy of the coming hours:

> There was never any chance of France being allowed to escape her ordeal. Even cowardice and dishonour would not have saved her. The Germans had resolved that if war came from any cause, they would take and break France forthwith as its first operation. The German military chiefs burned to give the signal, and were sure of the result. She would have begged for mercy in vain. She did not beg.

It was fortunate for France that in the days of the July crisis the French government would have to make no great decisions, for the nation found itself in the hands of two men who were barely equal to the task before them. It was a testimony to the character and courage of the French people that they could and did rally so solidly at the cry "*La patrie en danger!*" for neither of those men possessed the charisma to stir the nation. They were the President of the French Republic, Raymond Poincaré, and the Premier (Prime Minister), Rene Viviani. Of Raymond Poincaré it can truly be said that he was a man who had greatness thrust at him, but never upon him. Poincaré was the son of an engineer, born in 1860 in the village of Bar-le-duc in Lorraine. When he was ten years old war broke out between France and Prussia, and Poincaré would remember for the rest of his life the German Army of occupation marching through his little town, of having Prussian troops billeted in his family's house, then later being told that his home province was being forcibly separated from France and incorporated into the new German Reich. He studied law at the University of Paris, later setting up practice in the French capital. Wearing his Lorrainer birth like a martyr's mantle, he won election to the Chamber of Deputies in 1887, and was given his first cabinet post in 1893—at age thirty-three he was the youngest person to hold a ministry in the history of the republic. For the next thirteen years he held a variety of cabinet positions, including the ministries of education and finance. In 1912 he became premier of a coalition government, simultaneously carrying the portfolio of foreign minister. The following year he defeated Georges Clemenceau in a bid for the French presidency.

A conservative and an arch-nationalist, Poincaré believed his greatest responsibility as president was to strengthen France's army. To this end he became the champion of an armed forces bill introduced into the Chamber of Deputies which increased the duration of a conscript soldier's national service from two years with the colors to three years, which would increase the strength of France's standing army so that it achieved numerical parity with that of Germany's. He also worked tirelessly to strengthen the Franco-Russian alliance and increase the ties that bound France and Great Britain in the Entente Cordiale. The cornerstone of French foreign policy, as Poincaré conceived it, was that France should never again face Germany alone.

If Poincaré had possessed a moral grandeur and vision equal to the depth of his patriotism, he would have been a sublime wartime leader. Instead, he was saddled with a cold demeanor, a bland personality, a stubborn nature and an obsessively legalistic mind. He lacked charisma and the ability to inspire by example; more than one historian has referred to him as little more than a narrow-minded, self-righteous, pettifogging lawyer. He wanted the Three-Year Service Law to be the crowning achievement of his Presidency, but the measure was hugely unpopular with the Socialist Deputies, who feared the possibility of a stronger army becoming the tool of reactionary politicians and ambitious generals even more than they feared Germany. As a result, the legislative and political battle to have the measure passed into law was prolonged and ugly.

The popular image abroad of the French was that of a nation of rather lazy, decadent trouble makers possessed of questionable morals, slightly too fond of food, wine, and sex, and ready to riot at the drop of a hat over some imagined infringement of their "rights." The truth was that most French men and women were hard working, devoutly religious, and far more dedicated to home and hearth than to rabble-rousing politics. The French deserved better political leaders than those with whom they all too often were saddled—a problem not confined merely to France or the first decades of the 20th century. The most intelligent, talented men usually sought careers in business or the professions; it was mostly the mediocrities who made their careers in politics. Too few Frenchmen regarded government service in the same light as did the majority of their British counterparts of the day—as a "duty" or a "privilege."

Rene Viviani was a typical French politician, one of those individuals of whom it could be fairly stated that his outstanding political asset was the mediocrity of his character as a man. Born in Algeria in 1863, Viviani's early career was spent working as a lawyer in Algiers before coming to France. Moving to Paris in 1873, he focused his practice on the defense of trade union workers and socialists. Elected to the Chamber of Deputies in 1893, there, together with two other left-leaning politicians, Jean Jaures and Aristide

Briand, he established the French Socialist Party. Viviani was also co-founder of *L'Humanite*, a Paris-based, socialist-leaning newspaper, which first appeared in 1904; he used it as a forum for giving voice to his moderate-socialist political views. He left the Socialist Party in 1906 in order to accept a post in Georges Clemenceau's moderate government, where he was named Minister of Labor, remaining in office until November 1910. He came back to office in December 1913 as Minister of Education; six months later he was asked by President Poincaré to form a government, which he succeeded in doing at the second attempt.

A passionate, eloquent orator in the Chamber of Deputies, Viviani was a sort of "accidental" Premier. He was not Poincaré's first choice, indeed he was the fifth candidate selected: he became Premier simply because he was able to form a government. The Three-Year Service bill had created a remarkably deep, sharp division within the Chamber of Deputies, and passions ran high on both sides of the issue, with compromise an attribute almost forgotten by everyone. Poincaré let it be known that only a candidate who supported the Three-Year Service bill would be acceptable to him as Premier, and the first four men he asked to take the post either were unable to give the bill their whole-hearted support, or if they did, were unable to form a stable, working government. When Viviani indicated that as Premier, while he had voted against the bill and still had personal reservations about it, he would actively work to prevent its repeal, Poincaré gave him the nod, and to everyone's amazement, within a few days Viviani had selected a Cabinet. However, Poincaré never really trusted Viviani, because of his earlier opposition to the Three-Year Service bill.

The Cabinet was far from flawless, of course: it was more remarkable for who was not in it than for who was. France's ablest politicians, including three former premiers, Georges Clemenceau, Aristide Briand, and Joseph Caillaux, were in opposition. The Minister of Marine, Jean Augagneur, was a medical doctor who took the post when his predecessor was forced to resign as a result of a political scandal and Viviani had to serve as his own Foreign Minister, having been unable to find a qualified candidate who would accept the post. Viviani had other problems as well: volatile and emotional, he was given to extreme mood swings, while he was rarely able to directly face opposition. His usual tactic when he encountered someone who disagreed with him was to throw up his hands and begin shouting, then turn and walk away, muttering oaths and insults at his opponent. It was not a manner particularly conducive to getting much accomplished.

He had been in office less than two weeks when the news broke of Archduke Franz Ferdinand's assassination in Sarajevo on June 23. At the time Viviani and Poincaré were aboard the battleship *La France*, somewhere in the Baltic Sea, en route for the long-planned state visit to Russia, the cause of Austria-Hungary deliberately staying her hand in issuing the ultimatum to Serbia. When word of the ultimatum, along with some of its details, finally reached Viviani and Poincaré by wireless, they quickly cancelled a scheduled visit to Copenhagen and hurried directly back to France.

While they were in St. Petersburg, the French President and Premier had discussed at some length with the Tsar and his ministers the terms and conditions of the Franco-Russian alliance, and also the possible course the confrontation between Austria-Hungary and Serbia might take. Although at that point Vienna's ultimatum had yet to be sent to Belgrade, everyone knew that some sort of showdown between the two nations was inevitable, and given Russia's role as the protector of the Slavs, the possibility of Russian involvement had to be considered. If, in turn, Austria-Hungary's ally Germany was drawn into the fracas, then the French government had to face the very real possibility that war was on the horizon.

At some point in the visit, the strain of office and the looming crisis became too much for Viviani, and he suffered what he later admitted as being a mild nervous breakdown. He suddenly began talking to himself, at times bursting into loud bouts of swearing, or wandering off in the middle of meetings and receptions, and generally becoming so unpredictable that Ambassador Paléologue summoned a doctor and had the Premier hospitalized and isolated for much of the visit. Their Russian hosts tactfully made no comment, but the incident was particularly galling for Poincaré, since Viviani had been his appointee.

A foreign crisis, particularly one which might involve Germany, was the last thing Poincaré wanted to face, particularly with Viviani apparently being given over to the vapors by the strain. There were enough problems within France at that time. Labor troubles were wide-spread, and farmers were staging protests over wages and prices. It appeared more likely with each passing day that the Three-Year Service Law would be repealed, as the government was already in trouble, with the Socialists gaining strength in each by-election. At a sensational murder trial in Paris, embarrassing revelations about the inner workings of the French government were being made almost daily, the story dominating the headlines of every paper in France.

In March, a Madame Henriette Caillaux, wife of the former premier Joseph Caillaux, had walked into the office of the editor of the Paris daily *Le Figaro*, Gaston Calmette, and shot him dead. Calmette had, for political reasons, been publishing intimate details of an adulterous affair Caillaux and his wife had carried on before they were married. The resultant trial of Madame Caillaux became a national sensation and scandal: politicized from the start, it grew even more dramatic, as both prosecution and defense each day revealed new and unpleasant irregularities in finance, the press, the courts, and the government as part of their arguments. For more than four months the trial swept every other story from the front pages of French newspapers, and in the cafés and *estaminets*, people talked of nothing else.

What seemed amazing, even surreal, to European diplomats at the time—and has baffled some historians since—was that the French people seemed vastly more interested by the murder trial in Paris than in an evolving crisis in the heart of Europe which would ultimately bring the Teutonic enemy almost to the very gates of that city. Yet to believe that the French people were genuinely more concerned with the legal fate of Madame Caillaux than with the looming war with Germany underestimates them and does them a grave injustice. The ever-present menace of the German Army on France's eastern frontier, the psychological and spiritual scars created by the dismemberment of Alsace and Lorraine, the humiliation of 1871, and the repeated abnegation at the hands of Germany to which France had to submit in the decades to follow all created a national consciousness among French men and women which was particularly sensitive to shifts in

Europe's political landscape. The trial of Madame Caillaux was not the focus of French attention in the summer of 1914—it was merely a diversion.

It was not, as one historian has asserted, a case where "One day the French woke up to find Mme. Caillaux on page two—and the sudden, awful knowledge that France faced war." If anything, it was Poincaré and Viviani, isolated as they had been aboard *La France*, who were more out of touch with events than the French populace. On July 29, at Dunkerque, when the steamer bringing Poincaré and Viviani ashore from *La France* drew closer to the shore, the two politicians were stunned to see the docks, the quay, and the waterfront itself lined with people, waving hats, handkerchiefs, and *tricoleurs*, shouting themselves hoarse with repeated cries of "*Vive la France!*" and "*Vive la Republique!*" The French people indeed knew that the menace of war was at hand. It was the same on the train ride from Dunkerque to Paris: at every whistle-stop, every crossing, every town, stood hundreds, thousands of Frenchmen and Frenchwomen, offering the same outpouring of love and loyalty for *la patrie*.

Once in Paris, Poincaré, Viviani, and the rest of the government spent the remainder of that day and most of the next, July 30, learning just what all had happened while the President and Premier had been out of touch. One of the first things they discovered was that at this point there was little if any chance of Great Britain declaring that she would stand by France in the event of a German attack. The second was that the French ambassador to St. Petersburg, Maurice Paléologue, had been methodically lying to the French government as well as to the Russian, and was probably lying to himself as well.

The news that Great Britain still refused to make any official declaration as to her intentions was vexing, though hardly surprising. Ambassador Cambon had dutifully reported that the Warning Telegram had gone out to Britain's army and navy, but had done so on the same afternoon that he had held his uncomfortable conversation with Sir Edward Grey. That was when Grey informed Cambon that France should look to protecting her own interests without reference to Great Britain, the same interview which had concluded with Cambon's exasperated exclamation of "*Et l'honneur? Est-ce-que l'Angleterre comprend ce que c'est honneur?*"

As for Paléologue, as early as July 25, despite specific instructions from Paris, he had done nothing to inform the French government that the Russians were considering a partial mobilization in the south. It was no small oversight, since the terms of the Franco-Russian alliance required that Russia first consult with France in the event of any mobilization, and when Sazonov had raised the subject with Paléologue, he believed he was fulfilling that requirement. Consequently, when it was learned on the afternoon of July 29 that Russia would begin a partial mobilization the next day, the government in Paris was stunned. There had been no opportunity for any coordinated diplomatic action, no chance for Russia to explain to her ally that her preparations were meant to merely intimidate, rather than threaten, the Dual Monarchy—a small but not insignificant distinction. Paris had not been allowed to express to St. Petersburg French fears of an early Russian attack on Austria-Hungary provoking intervention by Germany, which automatically meant war with France. Pouring fuel on the fire, Paléologue sent a telegram that same afternoon to the *Quai d'Orsay*, where the French Foreign Ministry was located, stating that "the Russian General Staff confirms that Austria is accelerating its military preparations against Russia." Neither was true—no such confirmation had been offered by anyone in the Russian military, and Austria-Hungary was actually accelerating her mobilization against Serbia, hoping, in a small-scale version of the Schlieffen Plan, to knock Serbia out of the war before the Russian mobilization had been completed.

Viviani, acting in the role of Foreign Minister, immediately cabled Paléologue with instructions to urge Russia's Foreign Minister, Sazonov, "to take no immediate action that would offer Germany a pretext for a partial or total mobilization of her forces." Paléologue never bothered to communicate any of this to Sazonov; what was worse, he never informed Paris that Russia's partial mobilization had been canceled and a total mobilization ordered in its place for the following day. In Paris, no decision about a mobilization of the French Army had yet been made, although the orders were being drawn up for such an eventuality.

On one issue Poincaré and Viviani were in unhesitating agreement: France needed Great Britain as an ally. While Ambassador

Cambon's report was that unconditional neutrality was still Britain's official position, neither the President nor the Premier regarded the situation as yet to be hopeless. One consideration stood above all in their efforts to persuade the British to stand by France: it was imperative that France be seen as unquestionably the victim of aggression. There must be no question in London as to who was attacked and by whom: the moral and physical opprobrium of aggression must be laid in its totality upon Germany. To avoid the possibility of some "overanxious" French cavalry patrol or the troops of some frontier post accidentally crossing the border, Viviani, "haunted by a fear that war might burst from a clump of trees, from a meeting of two patrols, from a threatening gesture. . . a black look, a brutal word, a shot," at Poincaré's suggestion implemented a daring and extraordinary measure. On July 30 an order went out to all units of the French Army stationed along the frontier with Germany from Switzerland to Luxembourg: they would immediately withdraw ten kilometers from the border. Let Germany provide the inevitable "border incidents."

At the same time the order was telegraphed to the French corps commanders, a cable was sent to the French embassy in London, instructing Ambassador Cambon to inform the Foreign Office of the measure. It was hoped that the withdrawal would be seen as incontrovertible proof that, if war actually came to the west, France had done nothing to provoke it: any political benefits which might be gained would outweigh any military disadvantages that might result from the withdrawal.

It was a chance "never before taken in history," to borrow the phrase from Viviani, although its strategic significance was nowhere near as great as its possible implications for French morale. Given the scale of the maneuvers planned by both the French and the Germans should war actually break out, the loss of ten kilometers was negligible—three hours' marching at worst—it gave up no significant advantage in time or distance. It was, however, a bitter pill to ask any officer to swallow, particularly French officers who had been trained to believe that every square meter of French soil was sacred. Nevertheless, with the same monolithic calm that would greet the news of every reverse and success in the weeks and months to come, the Commander-in-Chief of the French Army, General Joseph Joffre, accepted this new set of orders and made certain that the appropriate instructions had gone out to the units posted along the French frontier.

The same age as the sixty-two year-old von Moltke, Joffre was as tall and powerfully built as his German counterpart, but there any similarity ended. He would never be described as "cerebral" or possessed of any exceptional intelligence, though he was possessed of a great deal of peasant cunning; at the same time he was burdened with none of von Moltke's insecurities or neuroses. Joffre was impressive and imposing in a way that the German general could never hope to be. While von Moltke perpetually projected an air of gloom and anxiety, Joffre radiated an imperturbable calm. He was known as "Papa Joffre" both for his concern for the welfare of his soldiers and the stern, paternalistic manner with which he imposed his discipline upon them. Joffre first saw service during the siege of Paris during the Franco-Prussian War of 1870–71, afterwards serving in the French colonies. Upon the recommendation of his mentor, General Joseph Gallieni, he was appointed Chief of the French General Staff in 1911.

It was during his tenure as Chief of Staff that the hapless Plan XVII was first drawn up, although how much Joffre directly contributed to its conception is debatable. More critical was his devotion to the plan once it had been adopted as the official strategic doctrine of the French Army. He was unquestionably a disciple of the offensive. He has been criticized by some historians with only a superficial knowledge of military affairs for his wholesale sacking—sometimes described as a "purge"—of officers who were "defensively minded" once he assumed the post of Commander-in-Chief. The harsh fact is that Joffre understood that an army that lacks offensive spirit often finds itself lacking the will to fight at all—a bitter lesson that France and the French Army would learn to their disgrace a generation later. Joffre knew that an army keen to attack will if need be defend tenaciously, if only to seek opportunities to go over to the assault.

The day after the President and Premier returned to France, July 30, Joffre, rightly sensing that war was unavoidable, began demanding that the government issue the order to mobilize the whole of the reserves—or at least cancel the furloughs issued to the active duty forces, many of whom had been allowed to return home for the autumn harvest. At the same time, he ordered the deployment of a screen of cavalry and light infantry, hoping to detect any German incursions as soon as possible. By his own admission Joffre had little more than contempt for politicians in general, and there was little reason to have much faith in Viviani's new cabinet—the tenth government to be formed in the past five years. He was not above using his authority and presence to intimidate recalcitrant ministers, and did his best to marginalize civilian authority as far as its influence on the army's affairs were concerned. He had some basis for his lack of confidence: Viviani was, in his own words, in a state of "frightful nervous tension" and on military questions almost automatically deferred to Poincaré, who had little constitutional power but whose moral authority was growing with each passing day. Events so overwhelmed the Minister of Marine that he "forgot" to order the French fleet to put to sea from Marseilles and Toulon so that it could cover the transfer of French colonial troops from North Africa to Metropolitan France; he was instantly dismissed.

Joffre was not above using a bit of hyperbole to make his point with the government. At one point, when demanding that the mobilization orders be issued, he declared that the German Army would "enter France without firing a shot" unless he was given the five corps of infantry and cavalry he felt necessary to screen the frontier. Viviani, knowing that a flurry of diplomatic overtures and offers of arbitration were humming across Europe's telegraph lines, still held out hope of a diplomatic solution and not wanting to give the appearance of escalating the tension, agreed to cancel all outstanding furloughs in order to constitute the five corps Joffre required, but still refused to call out the reservists.

From London, Ambassador Cambon was still reporting that the British attitude toward intervention was, at best, "tepid." He did not know that the previous day Foreign Secretary Grey had informed Ambassador Lichnowsky that Britain's neutrality could not be assured. Nor could he know that in Berlin the German Foreign Minister had informed the British Ambassador that if Germany mobilized her army, France would be attacked, regardless of whether or not she posed an actual threat to Germany. Nor did he know of von Bethmann-Hollweg's early morning offer to Grey, attempting to buy British neutrality by guaranteeing that Germany would make no territorial demands on France or Belgium once the war had ended, an offer Grey had dismissed as "a disgrace." Events were rapidly overtaking those in Britain who opposed intervention, but Cambon was naturally unaware of the turmoil in the British Cabinet, so that all the ambassador could say was that thus far the threat to France was of "no interest to Great Britain."

Events accelerated rapidly the following day, July 31. Just before noon word reached the Cabinet that Germany had ordered the *Kriegesgefahr*; shortly afterwards, a formal diplomatic request arrived from London: Sir Edward Grey was asking both Paris and Berlin to give unequivocal assurances of their intention to respect Belgium's neutrality. Within an hour Viviani had cabled the French reply: France was prepared to honor Belgian neutrality in all respects, and would only enter that country in the event that another nation violated her neutrality first, and then only at the request of the Belgian government. By late afternoon, rumors were spreading on the streets of Paris that Germany had sent an ultimatum to Russia, demanding that the Russians begin demobilization or face war with Germany. Deep within the *Quai d'Orsay*, French cryptographers were busily deciphering the latest set of instructions sent from Berlin to Ambassador von Schoen.

It was at 7:00 p.m. that Baron von Schoen appeared at the Foreign Office. A diplomat of the old school, when ambassadors were not just mouthpieces for their nations' capitals, but bore real authority to make critical decisions concerning foreign relations, he felt that the terms of the ultimatum he had been asked to deliver were nothing short of "brutal." In its own way, the German ultimatum—for that is what it was in substance—was as humiliating as the Ems dispatch, which had precipitated the Franco-Prussian war forty-four years earlier. It demanded to know if the French intended to remain neutral in the coming Russo-German war. If so, then the French would be required, as a pledge of their good will, to turn over the fortresses of Toul and Verdun to the Germans for the duration of the war. The French were not fools: they needed no crystal ball to foresee that once those fortresses, the anchors of the French defenses along their eastern frontiers, were in German hands it was highly unlikely that they would ever leave them. To von Schoen this was insulting to France and dishonorable of Germany, so he refused to present such an affronting demand. Instead, on his own initiative, he modified Berlin's cable, and handed Viviani a straightforward request for a declaration of neutrality, saying that he would return at 1:00 p.m. the following day to receive France's answer. The French, though, had compromised von Schoen's diplomatic cipher some years before, and so Viviani knew all about the offensive passage the Baron had omitted. For his part, he said nothing of it; he also knew that Germany was delivering an ultimatum to Russia at that same moment.

Although there could be no doubt that France would refuse the German demand, the French government perversely sat and dithered for the next two hours. It was while they were debating what steps to take once the refusal was given that a messenger rushed into the meeting room, and breathlessly announced that Jean Jaures had just been assassinated in a Paris café. Jaures, a dedicated pacifist, was one of the leaders of international socialism and had been the most vocal opponent of the Three-Year Service law. He was hugely popular among the workers, and his murder might well fracture French society along class lines at the very moment when national solidarity was desperately needed. Visions of riots, barricades in the streets, the red banner flying over Paris, even another Commune, all ran through the minds of the assembled ministers. The more conservative immediately demanded that "Carnet B," a plan for arresting and detaining known agitators, anarchists, pacifists, and suspected spies, be put into effect. The Minister of the Interior, whose office held authority over the metropolitan police forces, favored doing so, as did the Paris Prefect of Police. However, Viviani and his more liberal colleagues were opposed to the idea, believing that it would only be a detriment to national unity. Troops garrisoned in Paris were placed on alert should any rioting break out, and the arrest of certain, specific foreigners who were suspected of being spies was ordered, but Carnet B was never put into action, and another crisis was averted.

Once the formal vote to reject the German ultimatum was taken, the ministers adjourned sometime before midnight. Exhausted, President Poincaré went straight to bed, but was awakened at 2:00

a.m. when the Russian ambassador, Alexander Isvolsky, appeared at his door. Neurotic and high-strung, something of a gadfly, Isvolsky never felt secure about the alliance with Paris, and was always trying to reassure himself and St. Petersburg of France's loyalty. Appearing unannounced at Poincaré's residence, looking, in the French president's recollection, "very distressed and very agitated," he demanded to know what France was going to do. At almost that same moment, the Russian military attaché was presented to the Minister of War, Adolphe Messimy. Standing in Messimy's bedroom in full diplomatic dress, he posed the same question as Isvolsky: "What is France going to do?"

Poincaré, who as President of the Republic had no constitutional authority to make any declaration one way or the other, a not insignificant detail apparently lost on Isvolsky, responded with admirable tact, assuring the Russian ambassador that a Cabinet meeting was scheduled within a few hours which would supply the answer to his query. Messimy for his part simply dismissed the Russian attaché, then telephoned Viviani and told him what had just happened. Amazed at the Russians' temerity, he exclaimed, "Good God! These Russians are worse insomniacs than they are drinkers!" Then, ironically, given his own recent history of agitation, he suggested to Messimy, *"Du calme, du calme et encore du calme!"*

The necessity for calm was self-evident—the ability to maintain it was another matter, and understandably so. Unsure of Great Britain's support, with the Russians demanding to know France's intentions, and Joffre clamoring for mobilization, the French ministers found calm was not easy to come by. Joffre had appeared at the War Office at 8:00 a.m. to once again press his case with Messimy. Together they went to that morning's Cabinet meeting, where Joffre made the strategic situation explicitly clear. Now that the French Army had withdrawn the specified ten kilometers from the frontier, calculations of time and space were coming into play which were working against France. If the mobilization were to begin by midnight, he said, it was imperative that the order be issued by 4:00 p.m.—that was the latest that the General Post Office would be able to telegraph the order throughout France in time. At this point, every day's delay in the mobilization would be tantamount to a twenty-kilometer loss of territory; Germany already had what amounted to a twenty-four hour head start, since the *Kriegesgefahr* had been announced the previous day. If the government chose to surrender so much of the sacred soil of France, on their own heads be it. With that, Joffre left.

Poincaré, acting decisively for perhaps the first time in his life, was prepared to issue the mobilization order. But it was Viviani who had the authority to do so, and Viviani was still hopeful that a diplomatic solution would present itself. In the meantime, there was still the question of exactly how the German demand for neutrality was to be answered. Once more figuratively donning the hat of the Foreign Minister, Viviani made his way to the Foreign Office at 11:00 a.m., where Baron von Schoen was already waiting. Observing the formalities, the ambassador asked Viviani if France was prepared to stay neutral in a Russo-German war. "My question is rather naive," he admitted, "for we know you have a treaty of alliance."

"That is true," Viviani replied, then he gave the answer he and Poincaré had worked out only moments earlier: "France will act in accordance with her interests." Von Schoen retired to the German Embassy, deflated and defeated; he knew what was coming, and ordered the embassy staff to begin packing. While a rather ambiguous statement of French intentions, Viviani's reply was not the clear and explicit declaration of neutrality which Berlin demanded. Whether or not von Schoen was aware that the German mobilization would begin that day is unknown; he certainly understood that it was only a matter of hours, days at most, before it was ordered, and with it would follow a declaration of war on France.

Moments after von Schoen departed, a breathless Isvolsky rushed into Viviani's office, announcing the German ultimatum to Russia. For once Isvolsky had performed a useful function, for when Viviani returned to the Cabinet, he was able to announce that he had official confirmation of what the French intelligence service had already suspected: Germany was about to declare war on Russia. This news galvanized the Cabinet, which immediately authorized the French mobilization. With the signed order in hand, Messimy set out for the Ministry of War offices in the *Rue St. Dominique*; Viviani, still clinging to the fading hopes of diplomacy, asked the War Minister to delay releasing the order until 3:30 p.m. Messimy agreed, for while the delay would leave the mobilization schedule unaffected, it still allowed time for a diplomatic miracle to happen.

No miracle materialized, however, and at 3:30 p.m. an officer from Joffre's staff, General Ebener, was presented to Messimy, along with two aides-de-camp. It was a solemn, silent meeting, pregnant with possibilities, almost all of them unhappy, as Messimy handed over the order. "Conscious of the gigantic and infinite results to spread from that little piece of paper, all four of us felt our hearts tighten," was how he would later remember the moment. He shook hands with each of the three officers, who in turn saluted him, then wordlessly left. Within minutes the telegraph keys of the General Post Office began clicking, spreading the word across France that mobilization would begin at midnight.

The effect was electric. Almost immediately reservists began assembling, marching off to the *Gare de l'Est*, as civilians pressed bouquets of flowers into their hands. One group stopped in the *Place de la Concorde* before the black-draped statue representing Strasbourg, and silently placed those flowers at the base of the plinth. Across the way another group shouted *"Vive l'Alsace"* and ripped away the shroud that had covered the statue since 1870. Motorcars and lorries of every description, to be used to transport troops to the front, were quickly commandeered in the streets by officials of the War Ministry; crowds poured out onto the streets as they did so, waving and cheering. In the fashionable *Bois de Boulogne*, the manager stepped forward and silenced the orchestra with a wave of his hand. Dancers froze in mid-step as he announced "Mobilization has been ordered. It begins at midnight. Play the 'Marseillaise.'" The French anthem was then quickly followed by the national anthems of Russia and Great Britain.

Dawn came bright and early on August 1, the first full day of the French mobilization. There was little for the government to do now that the decision to mobilize had been made. In Berlin, von Bethmann-Hollweg was pleased, for both Russia and France had mobilized before Germany, which would allow him to go to the German people and present the *Vaterland* as a victim of combined Gallic and Slavic aggression, ensuring that the German Socialists would support the German war effort. However, it would prove to be a hollow victory, for even as he was winning in the court of public approval at home, the Chancellor and his Foreign Minister were about to lose that same battle abroad.

The invasion of Luxembourg had startled and affronted Europe, both for its brazen nature and for the utter lack of necessity. When the German Chancellor offered by way of explanation that the tiny Grand Duchy had been occupied "for the protection of the Luxembourg railways under our management there, against attack by the French. . . ." Luxembourg's prime minister made certain to point out to every capital in Europe that the French had already torn up the rail lines running into France at the border, and that since Luxembourg's railways and railroad facilities within the Grand Duchy were run by the Prussian State Railway, the Germans already had control of them, obviating any need for intervening "protection."

On August 2, at 7:00 p.m., when the German ambassador to Brussels delivered Germany's ultimatum to Belgium, Fortune again smiled on the French. Here was the cause that could unify British interests and British honor, a challenge to Great Britain's moral integrity which it could not refuse to answer—or so it seemed at first. However, under the terms of the 1839 treaty, Belgium could allow Germany the rite of passage and offer either no resistance at all, or merely symbolic resistance which would be a salve to Belgian honor. Only if the Belgians chose to actively resist the Germans and requested help from the other signatory powers could Britain intervene—an eventuality that German military and political leadership, ignoring Ambassador Lichnowsky's warnings from London, had already discounted as highly unlikely. The ultimatum gave the Belgians twelve hours to decide whether or not they would resist: after that, no matter what the answer, the German Army would cross the Belgian border *en masse*.

That night's events proved that Belgium's King Albert I was made of far sterner stuff than the Germans ever suspected. A remarkably calm Council of State meeting was held immediately after the delivery of the German ultimatum though in reality there was little to discuss as submitting to Germany's demands was tantamount to surrendering Belgium's sovereignty. This was something Albert could never condone, a stand in which the whole of the Council of State joined him. The Belgian Foreign Minister was instructed to inform the

German ambassador, when he called for the formal reply to the ultimatum, that Belgium "would sacrifice the honor of the nation and betray its duty to Europe" if she were to submit to the German demands. Belgium was "firmly resolved to repel by all means in its power every attack upon its rights."

German troops began flooding across the Belgian border the following morning, August 3. Albert and his officers had few illusions about the ability of the Belgian Army, which amounted to barely six divisions, to delay the German flood for long, but they had tremendous confidence that the massive fortifications built around the cities of Liege and Namur would slow the German advance, perhaps long enough for France or Great Britain to come to Belgium's aid. It was believed by some that the fortresses could hold out indefinitely, but whatever their fate, it was clear that Germany had blundered, and badly. No matter how eloquently they might plead the constraints of military necessity or that they were merely acting in self-defense to pre-empt the attacks of the Russians and the French (which the Germans knew existed only in their own imaginations), Germany had presented herself to the world as an aggressor, trampling international law and small nations underfoot with equal disdain.

That same day, Baron von Schoen received instructions from Berlin that he should be prepared to deliver Germany's declaration of war on France that evening. Due to errors by German telegraphists, most of the text was indecipherable, leaving von Schoen to improvise as best he could from the bits and pieces he did receive. The completed document was a conglomeration of alleged aerial attacks on German cities by French aircraft and flagrant border violations by French troops, none of which were true. Von Schoen, an honorable man under any circumstances, would be presenting a declaration of war based purely on fabrication. By that time, of course, the Germans were past caring: what mattered was that the declaration was presented before any clash of armies had taken place, satisfying all of the required legalities. When presented with the German declaration, Viviani displayed, according to von Schoen, an "icy composure" that was "without any sign of emotion." Viviani can hardly be blamed for his distant attitude: France was about to be forced into a war she neither wanted nor was fully prepared to fight, that had begun because Germany had provoked a confrontation with France's ally, Russia. The French Premier, who almost certainly knew that the German embassy staff had already packed up and were ready to depart Paris, made arrangements to return von Schoen's passports and arrange for safe passage out of France for the embassy personnel.

Up to this moment, aside from some skirmishing between Austro-Hungarian patrols and their Serbian opposites, and the bombardment of Belgrade, none of the Great Powers were actually engaged in combat with one another; but almost all of them were at war. There was one faint glimmer of hope, fast fading, that the war might be contained in the east after all, but this last chance for peace would be decided by only two of the Great Powers, one of whom was already at war, while the other was still hoping to avoid being drawn into the conflict. In the end, whether what might have been simply the Third Balkan War would become the Great War would be decided by Germany and Great Britain.

Chapter XI

THE LAST CHANCE

On the morning of August 1, Prime Minister Asquith and Foreign Secretary Grey decided that the issue must be put before the Cabinet: would Great Britain stand beside Belgium, and by implication France as well, should the Germans do as they were giving every indication they intended—invade Belgium? Options were steadily diminishing in number—any hope of arbitration had already been abandoned, and even direct communications between monarchs were proving fruitless. Very late on July 31, Asquith learned that the Kaiser had let it be known his efforts to keep Vienna and St. Petersburg talking had been frustrated when the Tsar had issued his decree to mobilize the Russian Army. Believing that if Britain's monarch joined his voice with that of Germany's in asking Russia to demobilize, Tsar Nicholas might relent, Asquith had gone to Buckingham Palace just after midnight. The King was roused from his bed, and reviewed the draft proposal to that effect which the Prime Minister brought him.

Agreeing that any effort was worth making if it could salvage the peace, George V signed the proposal, making only two changes: the salutation was altered to read "My dear Nicky" and he closed it by signing himself "Georgie." Asquith then rushed over to the Foreign Office, where the message was promptly cabled to St. Petersburg. It was nearly twelve hours later when a reply finally came; the Tsar would have "gladly accepted your proposals had not the German ambassador this afternoon presented a note to my government declaring war." The

Germans were acting: decisions made in Berlin were becoming deeds; Asquith was in danger of being overtaken by events.

When the Cabinet convened at 11:00 a.m. that morning and the question of what Great Britain would do was mooted, no clear answer was immediately apparent. One argument which was quickly raised was whether the extent of the invasion would actually warrant British intervention, even if the Belgians formally requested it. Opening up a map of France and the Low Countries, David Lloyd George drew his finger down the shortest route from Germany to Paris, which he believed would be the path any German invasion would take. It crossed only a small corner of Belgium; such an invasion would, he said, be a "little violation," and he thought it insufficient grounds for declaring war on Germany. The Welshman was not indulging in mere pettifogging: if the German Army did follow this route, though undeniably a violation of Belgian neutrality, it was hardly a threat to Belgian sovereignty, which was what the 1839 Treaty had been drawn up to protect. It was a conclusion which brought nods of approval from a number of members seated around the table.

At that moment, any action which smacked of intervention was still unacceptable to a majority of the Cabinet. When Churchill, who had not yet informed his colleagues that he had never authorized the Fleet to disperse after its practice mobilization, disingenuously asked for permission to recall the naval reservists, he provoked a "sharp discussion," and then was summarily refused. When Grey asked for authority to implement the promises made to the French Navy, Lord Morley, John Burns, Sir John Simon, and Lewis Harcourt proposed to resign. Individually, none of the four carried sufficient political weight to threaten Asquith's government, but together their resignations might have encouraged others, so the issue was not pressed.

What still is not clear, more than ninety years later, is exactly what was Asquith's attitude: just how firm was his commitment to intervention, and at what point—if any—would he believe the case for intervention to be compelling enough to draw the line, and accept resignations, convinced the House and the nation would still support him. What is beyond doubt is that if Sir Edward Grey resigned, as he vowed he would do should Britain choose unconditional neutrality, the government would fall, such was Grey's stature within the House of Commons. A Liberal government without Grey in it could never survive a call for a vote of "no confidence." Asquith knew this, and it is quite possible that his support for Grey was more a question of political expedience than actual conviction. True, Asquith was one of the original "Liberal Imperialists," to whom the balance of power on the Continent was an article of faith, but more than that, Asquith was one of the first "professional" politicians to sit in the House of Commons, the first such to hold the office of Prime Minister—that is, he had no living outside of the salary of his office. For personal reasons, to Asquith, holding onto office could be of a higher priority than upholding political convictions.

A similar question could also have been raised about some of those ministers who were posturing over the question of intervention and threatening resignation if Britain did not remain neutral in the coming war. The division within the Cabinet was bitter, but no one was yet prepared to make decisions they might later regret and be unable to withdraw; resignations were hinted but not yet offered. Eleven members were opposed to joining in a war for the sake of Russia and France, two nations which until only a few years previous had been Great Britain's long-standing antagonists. Of that eleven, the most prominent were Lord John Morley, John Burns (the first Labour Member of Parliament to ever hold a Cabinet post), Walter Runciman, and David Lloyd George. Morley and Burns were determined that they would resign should Britain go to war, no matter for what reason or apparent obligation: while they were prestigious members of Parliament, they did not carry sufficient political strength to bring down the government by themselves. Runciman, the President of the Board of Trade, was widely respected for being an able administrator, and might be persuaded to favor intervention under the right circumstances, while Lloyd George, who was displaying an increasing penchant for demagoguery and a hunger for power, could be counted on to go whichever way the prevailing political wind was blowing at the moment a decision became necessary. The balance of the eleven would almost certainly do as they were doing at the moment: carrying out what they believed were the wishes of British people.

In contrast, eight Cabinet members were publicly and whole-heartedly in support of intervention, among them Richard Haldane, Reginald McKenna, Winston Churchill, Sir Edward Grey and—nominally at least—Asquith. There was also strong support for intervention in the House among the ranks of the opposition, although at this point there was no assurance that if a vote were taken in the House enough Conservative members would vote with the government to ensure its survival. The question of intervention was not yet one which could transcend party politics.

Still, those members who supported intervention were mustering powerful arguments. An analysis by Eyre Crowe, acknowledged to be the Foreign Office's leading expert on Germany as well as a keen analyst of foreign policy, concluded that should Great Britain make an unconditional declaration of neutrality,

> the whole policy of the *Entente* can have no meaning if it does not signify that in a just quarrel England would stand by her friends. This honourable expectation has been raised. We cannot repudiate it without exposing our good name to grave criticism.

It would be tantamount, said Crowe, "to political suicide." With that conclusion Crowe, whose situation in the Foreign Office was not dependent upon which party was in power and so could afford to be dispassionate, began moving the issue away from being decided merely by party doctrine and into the realm of a question of British honor.

Here Churchill's observations are once more particularly useful, as he summarized how the arguments of those Cabinet members who wanted to keep Britain out of the war at all costs had systematically fallen apart.

> The Cabinet was overwhelmingly pacifistic. At least three-quarters of its members were determined not to be drawn into a European quarrel, unless Great Britain were herself to be attacked, which was not likely. Those who were in this mood were inclined to believe first of all Austria and Serbia would not

come to blows; secondly, that if they did, Russia would not intervene; thirdly, if Russia intervened, that Germany would not strike; fourthly, they hoped that if Germany struck at Russia, it ought to be possible for France and Germany to neutralize each other without fighting. They did not believe that if Germany attacked France, she would attack through Belgium or that if she did the Belgians would forcibly resist. . . .

For decades the dogma of the Liberal Party had been Free Trade, Retrenchment, and Reform. Wars fought in the name of guaranteeing free trade were grudgingly accepted as necessary evils; wars fought for the Gladstonian ideal of "oppressed peoples struggling for their freedom" were wholeheartedly embraced. A war fought for the sake of a "balance of power" in Europe was not something that the majority of the men sitting in Asquith's Cabinet were prepared to defend to their constituents. And yet, what if the direst predictions of Grey and Churchill came true, and Germany did overrun Belgium and France, then turned on Russia? How could these men then justify having stood aside and done nothing?

History was on the side of Grey, Churchill, and those who supported them, and few nations have ever been as conscious of history as was Great Britain in the last years of the Edwardian Era. The foundation, growth and success of the British Empire had come about because of Britain's devotion to the idea of a Continental balance of power. Britain had always prospered when that balance was maintained, and suffered to greater or lesser degrees when it was altered. The reason was trade—a balanced Europe was a peaceful Europe, where business could be sensibly and peaceably conducted. Consequently, the Cabinet members who opposed intervention were hoist on their own petard, for the Free Trade which they held so dearly was dependent on the balance of power which they allegedly abhorred.

Meanwhile, as the Cabinet meeting progressed, Asquith sat tight, while his opponents writhed in their dilemma. Outside, on the streets of every major city in Great Britain, news of the "Willy-Nicky" telegrams competed for attention with breaking stories of German ultimata to Russia and France. Because Britain at the time possessed the highest literacy rate in history, the British public were remarkably well-informed: no one, from the Crown to the lowliest factory worker, had the slightest doubt that war was about to sweep across the whole Continent, a prospect which dismayed everyone. However, even at this late date most Britons regarded the approaching war as just one more chapter in the endless conflict between France and Germany. Belgium was not yet an urgent subject among the people, though it would soon become one.

Back in the Cabinet room, Grey excused himself and placed a telephone call to Ambassador Lichnowsky. Their conversation—and Lichnowsky's misunderstanding of it—would be the gist of the Ambassador's urgent report to Berlin that afternoon, which would prompt the Kaiser to attempt to turn the whole of the German Army to the east, only to be overridden by von Moltke. Grey also took time to speak with Ambassador Cambon, and being completely frank with him, said that because there could be no assurance of British intervention, "France must take her own decision at this moment without reckoning on an assistance we are not now in a position to give." It was this declaration which would later allow Grey to say with utter conviction and in clear conscience that the British government's freedom of action had never been restricted by any firm and fast commitments to France. Later, Cambon confided that all he could think at that moment was *Ils vont nous ideher!*" ("They are going to desert us!").

When dinnertime approached, the Cabinet adjourned, once again having reached no definite decision as to what direction British policy would take. Sir Edward Grey shared his dinner with Ambassador Cambon, while Churchill returned to the Admiralty buildings in Whitehall, where F. E. Smith (the future Lord Birkenhead) and Max Aitken (the future Lord Beaverbrook), friends from the Opposition, joined him for dinner. Afterwards they played bridge. It was during one of the rubbers that a messenger brought in a red dispatch box for the First Lord. Opening it, Churchill extracted a single sheet of paper which contained a single line of text: "Germany has declared war on Russia." Any lingering doubts that Germany meant to fall upon France, and to do so would go through Belgium, were rapidly fading.

The Admiralty Building was just across the Horse Guards Parade from No. 10 Downing Street, and Churchill immediately went there, making a major decision as he traversed the hundred or so yards that separated the two. He found Grey, Haldane, and Lord Crewe, the Secretary for India, already gathered with the Prime Minister. "Notwithstanding the Cabinet decision," he said, he was going to "instantly mobilize the fleet." Asquith said nothing, but a few moments later Grey took the First Lord aside and informed him that, almost as if he had anticipated Churchill's decision, "I have just done a very important thing. I have told Cambon that we shall not allow the German fleet to come into the Channel." Churchill promptly returned to the Admiralty and "gave forthwith the order to mobilize."

Within the hour, wireless receivers and telegraph sets in Royal Navy ships, dockyards, and stations all over the world began sparking and clacking with the dots and dashes of a fateful message:

Admiralty to all HM Ships
and Naval Establishments

Signal
1 August 1914
11 pm Admiralty
COMMENCE MOBILIZATION IMMEDIATELY

Through these two acts—Churchill's mobilization order and Grey's promise to France—the two men were essentially forcing the Cabinet's hand, for both decisions would have to be approved at the next day's Cabinet meeting. If either one, or both, were repudiated, their resignations would be inevitable.

August 2 would prove to be the pivotal day for Asquith and the Cabinet. The Prime Minister's official day began with a breakfast with Prince Lichnowsky. The German ambassador was very emotional—according to Asquith he was on the verge of tears more than once during their conversation—and he begged the Prime Minister to keep Britain neutral. Caught between France and Russia, he said, it was more likely Germany who would be crushed in the coming war, not France. Asquith was explicit with Lichnowsky, telling him that the surest way Germany could guarantee Great Britain's neutrality was to not invade Belgium and to keep the German Navy from attacking France's Channel coast.

The Cabinet was scheduled to meet at 11:00 a.m. on August 2, yet even before it convened, wholesale changes were taking place in the moods and attitudes of some of the members. News of Germany's invasion of Luxembourg broke that morning, and cut away a great deal of ground from beneath those Cabinet members opposed to Britain becoming involved in a Continental war. It underlined the reality of Great Britain's treaty obligations, and began moving the issue away from the realm of politics and into that of a moral obligation. It was this dilemma which compelled six of the eleven opponents of intervention—including Runciman and Lloyd George— to draw up a statement which declared that "we are not prepared to go to war now, but. . . in certain events we might reconsider [the] position such as the invasion wholesale of Belgium." For Lloyd George in particular it was a masterful effort at hedging his bets, but the underlying truth was that it was becoming clearer almost by the hour that there were circumstances in which Britain's honor and her interests would become inextricably intertwined, where the "balance of power" had a meaning beyond being a catchphrase for politicians with imperialistic ambitions.

Because so many of the members' opinions were now in a state of flux, the first Cabinet meeting essentially decided not to decide anything, although one member, John Burns, felt he'd had enough and submitted his resignation. Asquith was certain that others would follow, but his concern for the viability of his government had been largely relieved by a meeting held earlier in the day with Lord Landsdowne and Bonar Law, the leaders of the Conservative Party for the House of Lords and the House of Commons respectively. Together the two men assured Asquith that the Opposition would support the government over the issue of intervention, although it was never made clear if that pledge was made only if Belgium were invaded or if it applied to support for France under any circumstances. A second meeting was called for 6:30 p.m. that same day, when the vote to approve or disapprove Churchill's mobilization of the fleet and Grey's promise of protection for France's Channel coast, would be taken.

The evening of August 2 would prove to be filled with drama, as the Germans dropped two more diplomatic bombshells in the Cabinet's collective lap. At 7:00 p.m. (local time), the German ambassador to Brussels delivered Berlin's ultimatum to Belgium. Depending on the Belgian response, here was the cause that could unify British interests and British honor. However, only if the Belgians chose to actively resist the Germans and requested help from the other signatory powers could Britain intervene—an eventuality that German military and political leadership discounted as highly unlikely. When asked about the possibility of Britain entering the war to honor her treaty obligations to Belgium, the German Chancellor dismissed the idea out of hand.

In his arrogance, von Bethmann-Hollweg had underestimated the Belgians, who joined their king in being firmly resolved that their little country would "repel by all means in its power every attack upon its rights." Belgian defiance of German might electrified the world, and in particular Great Britain. What had been perceived by most Britons as just the latest chapter in the ongoing quarrel between Germany and France now acquired an unexpected dimension. Lord Baden Powell remarked that, "There are two things above all others which Britons, down to the very lowest among them, inherently appreciate: Pluck and Fair Play." The plight of Belgium embraced both, and the Belgians were universally admired by the British people. The choices for those in the government who opposed intervention were narrowing still further.

The second bombshell came within moments of the first, the revelation that Germany had declared war on France. With all uncertainty about German intentions removed, the choices for Great Britain were at last sharply defined now that the element of "what if?" was no longer a factor. Thus there was little meaningful debate at the second Cabinet meeting. Churchill and Grey were both affirmed in their decisions, while the general policy was agreed upon: if Belgian neutrality was violated and the Belgians resisted, asking the British for help, Great Britain would go to war.

The change in the mood of the Cabinet had coincided—or in some ways caught up—with a dramatic shift in the mood of the British people. On August 1, if asked, and a great many of them were, the majority of Britons would have flatly stated that they believed there was no reason to become involved in a war on the Continent. A huge antiwar demonstration was set to take place on August 2, in Trafalgar Square in the heart of London: tens of thousands of Londoners were expected to show and express their opposition to any British participation in the war. Then in quick succession the news broke of Germany's declarations of war on Russia and France, her occupation of Luxembourg, and then the ultimatum to Belgium, with its alternatives of either invasion or occupation. A wave of anger swept across Britain, anger at what was perceived as Germany's arrogance and aggression. Instead of a peace rally at Trafalgar Square, an equally large crowd gathered in Whitehall and Downing Street, loudly chanting for war with Germany.

When the Cabinet met on the morning of August 3, three more ministers who opposed any British involvement in the war resigned, but by then theirs was a useless gesture. Those ministers who had yet to firmly make up their minds had seen (and heard) the crowds the previous day, and, on their way once again to No. 10 Downing Street, now could see from the newspapers that the attitude of the British people across the country had begun resolving itself in favor of standing by Belgium and standing up to Germany. Like all good politicians everywhere, they promptly resolved to follow where the people led.

The issue was ultimately decided by a speech given that afternoon by Sir Edward Grey, usually an unemotional, almost pedestrian, speaker. At 3:00 p.m. Grey rose in the House of Commons, which was "crowded to the roof and tense with doubt and dreadful expectation," to present His Majesty's Government's first official and public statement about the crisis on the Continent. That day circumstances gave the Foreign Minister's words a ring and resonance that they never had before; conviction lent him an eloquence that transcended mere rational argument and stirred the hearts and souls of the House of Commons and the British people.

He began simply enough by reminding the House that the Government was "working for peace not only for this country, but to preserve the peace of Europe," though because of the events of the previous week, "it is clear that the peace of Europe cannot be preserved." Here he was emphatic:

[We] have consistently worked with a single mind, with all the earnestness in our power, to preserve peace. The House may be satisfied on that point. We have always done it. . . . Throughout the Balkan crisis [of 1912], by general admission, we worked for peace. The cooperation of the great powers of Europe was successful in working for peace in the Balkan crisis. . . . It took much time and labour and discussion before they could settle their differences, but peace was secured, because peace was their main object, and they were willing to give time and trouble rather than accentuate differences rapidly. . . .

Now, however, the situation had changed dramatically for the worse,

. . . because there has been little time, and there has been a disposition—at any rate in some quarters on which I will not dwell—to force things rapidly to an issue, at any rate to the great risk of peace, and, as we now know, the result of that is that the policy of peace as far as the great powers generally are concerned is in danger.

Then, refusing for the moment to name names among the Powers "which were most disposed to risk war or endanger peace," he took the first step toward establishing a link between Great Britain's treaty obligations to Belgium and what he believed were her moral obligations toward France:

I can say this with the most absolute confidence—no government and no country has less desire to be involved in war. . . than the country of France. They are involved in it because of their obligation of honour under a definite alliance with Russia.

He asked the House:

to approach this crisis in which we are now from the point of view of British interests, British honour, and British obligations, free from all passion as to why peace has not yet been preserved. . . .

Now Grey undertook a careful demonstration of how all three were inextricably tied together by the German threat to Belgium, and by implication, the German threat to France. He began by reminding the House of Great Britain's "long-standing friendship with France"— and here one member shouted out "And with Germany!", proof that Grey was not preaching to the converted—that "these two nations, who had had perpetual differences in the past, had cleared these differences away," and suggesting that "some benign influence had been at work to produce the cordial atmosphere that had made that possible." Now Grey began to subtly shift the question of standing by France away from party politics and into the realm of personal honor:

> But how far that friendship entails obligation—it has been a friendship between the nations and ratified by the nations— how far that entails an obligation, let every man look into his own heart, and his own feelings, and construe the extent of the obligation for himself. . . . The House, individually and collectively, may judge for itself.

He reminded the gathered Members that the French battlefleet had moved to the Mediterranean, specifically because of strategic talks and informal agreements between the staffs of the Royal Navy and the French fleet, a move which left the French coast denuded of French naval protection. Here, if nowhere else, was something Grey saw as a clear-cut moral obligation:

> My own feeling is that if a foreign fleet, engaged in a war which France had not sought, and in which she had not been the aggressor, came down the English Channel and bombarded and battered the undefended coasts of France, we could not stand aside and see this going on practically within sight of our eyes, with our arms folded, looking on dispassionately. . .

Here the normally unemotional Grey brought a fist crashing down on the red dispatch box before him:

> . . . doing nothing. I believe that would be the feeling of this

country. There are times when one feels that if these circumstances actually did arise, it would be a feeling which would spread with irresistible force throughout the land!

Then, for the first time, the House reacted as cheers broke out from both benches. Not from all of the Members, to be sure, but enough to give Grey confidence that he would not be repudiated for the announcement he was about to make.

He explained that there were reciprocal risks to French security and British interests created by the movement of the French Navy to the Mediterranean at the same time that the bulk of the British fleet in the inland sea had been withdrawn to home waters. Without formal commitment, France was willingly undertaking to protect Britain's trade route through the Mediterranean, at the same time that "she leaves her northern and western coasts absolutely undefended, at the mercy of a German fleet coming down the Channel to do as it pleases in a war which is a war of life and death between them." Accordingly, France had a right to know if those coastlines would, in turn, be protected by the Royal Navy. As Grey saw it, it was quite simply a matter of protecting British interests, and to that end:

> yesterday afternoon I gave to the French Ambassador the following statement:
>
>> I am authorised to give an assurance that if the German fleet comes into the Channel or through the North Sea to undertake hostile operations against the French coasts or shipping, the British fleet will give all the protection in its power. This assurance is, of course, subject to the policy of his Majesty's Government receiving the support of Parliament, and must not be taken as binding his Majesty's Government to take any action until the above contingency of action by the German fleet takes place.

The House sat silent. It was a pivotal moment, for had there been any significant demonstration against Grey's announcement from within the ranks of the Liberals, it would have compelled his resignation on the spot, which would have brought down the Government. Instead the House listened with rapt attention, perhaps sensing that they were watching a great event unfold in their presence. They were and it was.

Grey was careful to emphasize that the actions taken had not in any way bound Britain to France, arguing persuasively that they had left His Majesty's Government with complete freedom of action in any circumstance. Then he moved inexorably forward, declaring that "Things move very hurriedly from hour to hour. . . becoming more serious every hour. . . ." The most serious consideration, he said, was the issue of Belgian neutrality.

For this he had saved his most eloquent and passionate arguments. Quickly reviewing the events of the previous week, he then described how he had simultaneously requested reassurances from both Paris and Berlin that they were prepared to respect the neutrality of Belgium. The French government quickly responded, saying it was:

> resolved to respect the neutrality of Belgium, and it would only be in the event of some other power violating that neutrality that France might find herself under the necessity, in order to assure the defence of her security, to act otherwise.

Then, almost drily, Grey said "From the German Government the reply was: 'The Secretary of State for Foreign Affairs could not possibly give an answer before consulting the Emperor and the Imperial Chancellor.'" After that, from Berlin came only silence. Now, Grey said, news had arrived only that morning—and still awaited confirmation—that Germany had given an ultimatum to Belgium, "the object of which was to offer Belgium friendly relations with Germany on condition that she would facilitate the passage of German troops through Belgium." Here the House rocked with laughter, much of it ironic, for the Commons had as little doubt about the nature of German "friendly relations" as did the Belgians themselves. At this point Grey probably began to sense that the House had begun to shift its sympathies, and so hammered home the next point.

We were sounded in the course of last week as to whether, if a guarantee were given that, after the war, Belgian integrity would be preserved, that would content us. We replied that we could not bargain away whatever interests or obligations we had in Belgian neutrality.

With these words the House broke into cheering, for whatever questions might linger over British interests, it was clear that Grey was not about to compromise Britain's honor.

Then Grey revealed that shortly before he had entered the House of Commons, he was told that King Albert of Belgium had sent a personal telegram to King George V, which the British monarch had passed on to the Foreign Secretary. It read:

Remembering the numerous proofs of your Majesty's friendship and that of your predecessors, and the friendly attitude of England in 1870, and the proof of friendship she has just given us again, I make a supreme appeal to the diplomatic intervention of your Majesty's Government to safeguard the integrity of Belgium.

The silence in the chamber was total: the appeal to the Crown had made the transcendence of party politics complete. Now the Members would be responsible to the most demanding courts of all—the courts of their own consciences. "Diplomatic intervention took place last week on our part," Grey told them. "What can diplomatic intervention do now? We have great and vital interests in the independence—and integrity is the least part—of Belgium." Once again both benches erupted in cheers.

Quoting Gladstone, Grey made those Liberals who opposed intervention squirm when he pointedly asked, "'Could this country stand by and witness the direst crime that ever stained the pages of history and thus become participators in the sin?'" Now Grey inextricably linked British interests and British honor:

If it be the case that there has been anything in the nature of an ultimatum to Belgium, asking her to compromise or violate her neutrality, whatever may have been offered to her in return, her independence is gone if that holds. If her independence goes, the independence of Holland will follow. I ask the House from the point of view of British interests to consider what may be at stake. If France is beaten in a struggle of life and death, beaten to her knees, loses her position as a great power, becomes subordinate to the will and power of one greater than herself. . . and if Belgium fell under the same dominating influence, and then Holland, and then Denmark, then would not Mr. Gladstone's words come true, that just opposite to us there would be a common interest against the unmeasured aggrandisement of any power?

Neutrality, however tempting, was not a choice British honor or interests could endure:

It may be said, I suppose, that we might stand aside, husband our strength, and that whatever happened in the course of the war, at the end of it, intervene with the effect to put things right and to adjust them to our point of view.

The cost of doing so, however, would be ruinous:

. . . if in a crisis like this, we ran away from those obligations of honour and interest as regards the Belgian Treaty, I doubt whether whatever material force we might have at the end of the war would be of very much value in the face of the respect we should have lost. . . . I do not believe for a moment that, at the end of this war, even if we stood aside, we should be able to undo what had happened in the course of the war, to prevent the whole of the west of Europe opposite to us—if that had been the result of the war—falling under the domination of a single power, and I am quite sure that our moral position would be such as—

Here the rest of Grey's sentence—"to have lost us all respect"—was cut off as the Members, anticipating where he was leading, rose in a chorus of cheers for the courage Grey's blunt words had laid bare.

Grey then stepped into a short but vital aside. Addressing the question of Ireland, which only a few days earlier had dominated all conversation in Great Britain, he declared,

> The one bright spot in the whole of this terrible situation is Ireland. The general feeling throughout Ireland, and I would like this to be clearly understood abroad, does not make that a consideration that we feel we have to take into account.

In other words, the loyalty of Ireland, north and south, was assured, and would not be a distraction to Britain upon which foreign powers could play.

Grey was approaching his summation, and with it the pinnacle of his political career. While it may be the goal of every government official charged with the responsibility of formulating and implementing a nation's foreign policy, Foreign Secretary, Foreign Minister, Secretary of State, or however the title is styled, of keeping that nation at peace, there will inevitably come moments when the best interests of the nation can only be upheld through war when war is thrust upon them. So it was with Grey.

> I have told the House how far we have at present gone in commitments, and the conditions which influence our policy; and I have put and dealt at length to the House upon how vital the condition of the neutrality of Belgium is. What other policy is there before the House? There is but one way in which the Government could make certain at the present moment of keeping outside this war, and that would be that it should immediately issue a proclamation of unconditional neutrality. We cannot do that. We have made the commitment to France. . . . We have got the consideration of Belgium which prevents us also from any unconditional neutrality. . . . If we did take that line by saying, 'We will have nothing whatever to do with this matter'. . . if we were to say that all those things matter nothing, were as nothing, and to say we would stand aside, we should, I believe, sacrifice our respect and good

name and reputation before the world, and should not escape the most serious and grave economic consequences.

Here a lone voice from one of the back benches shouted out "No!" and the House shook again with cheering.

Finally, Grey placed "the issue and the choice" squarely before the House, acknowledging that "The most awful responsibility is resting upon the Government in deciding what to advise the House of Commons to do." In any case, his mind and conscience were clear:

> We have disclosed the issue, the information which we have, and made clear to the House, I trust, that we are prepared to face that situation, and that . . . we will face it. We worked for peace up to the last moment, and beyond the last moment. How hard, how persistently, and how earnestly we strove for peace last week the House will see. . . . But that is over, as far as the peace of Europe is concerned. . . .

He closed with a solemn declaration:

> I believe, when the country realises what is at stake, what the real issues are, the magnitude of the impending dangers in the west of Europe, which I have endeavored to describe to the House, we shall be supported throughout, not only by the House of Commons, but by the determination, the resolution, the courage, and the endurance of the whole country.

With that Grey sat down, and suddenly overcome by the emotional tide which had surged within him and swept over the whole of the House of Commons, he quietly wept. He was a diplomat who had spent his entire career devoted to the pursuit of peace, and yet he had almost certainly led Great Britain into a war.

In barely more than an hour, Grey had prepared Parliament and the British people for the conflict to come. Though there would be dissenting voices heard among the Labour and Liberal parties, for most of the men sitting in Parliament, Grey's arguments had been sufficient: he had given them a cause, a just cause as they perceived it, for intervention, for standing beside Belgium and France. It was a belief which came to be shared by most of the nation. Grey's eloquence and passion had shown that the war which had begun as merely a dynastic squabble in Central Europe had now legitimately escalated into a threat to Britain's interests, and even more important to most Britons, to her honor. What had been a divided nation was now united in its determination to stand against what had been utterly exposed as naked German aggression.

Given the mood of the House after Grey's speech, it came as no surprise to anyone in any party that an overwhelming majority approved of Grey's assurances to France regarding the protection of the French coasts. Another resolution was quickly passed which authorized Grey to warn the German government that Great Britain was prepared to take action on Belgium's behalf should Germany violate that kingdom's neutrality. Everyone knew that the next day's Cabinet meeting would draft an ultimatum to Germany, demanding a complete and immediate withdrawal of all German troops from Belgian territory, the alternative being war with Great Britain. Already Lord Haldane, who had been Secretary of State for War from 1905 to 1912 and who still carried enormous personal influence within the Army, had gone to the War Office and summoned the War Council, instructing them to begin mobilizing the B.E.F. and the Territorial Force. When asked if they should prepare for a movement overseas, he replied:

> the question of whether the Expeditionary Force would actually be dispatched . . . would not be decided until the issue of peace or war had been disposed of by the Cabinet, the Sovereign, and Parliament, but they must be ready.

After the debate, Grey left the House accompanied by Churchill, who asked simply, "What happens now?"

"Now we shall send them an ultimatum to stop the invasion of Belgium within twenty-four hours." With that Grey returned to his office and later met there with the United States' ambassador, Walter Hines Page. The American had followed the European crisis very closely and had kept the American president, Woodrow Wilson, carefully informed on the course of events; like Wilson, Page believed there was little if any reason for the United States to be anything more than a passive observer in the coming war. At the same time, Page agreed with Grey as to the extent of Great Britain's moral responsibilities, both to France and Belgium. Did Grey believe, Page asked, that Germany would submit to the terms of the British ultimatum in order to avoid war with the Empire? Grey shook his head and said simply, "No, of course everybody knows there will be a war." The Foreign Secretary paused, struggling with his emotions, and turned to a window, looking out on the streets of London. "Thus, the efforts of a lifetime go for nothing," he continued softly. "I feel like a man who has wasted his life." Night was falling, and outside a lamplighter was making his rounds, moving from lantern to lantern. Grey watched the man for a few seconds, then quietly murmured the eulogy for a generation and for a world: "The lamps are going out all over Europe. We shall not see them lit again in our time."

When the Cabinet met on Tuesday morning, it was for what Asquith would later sardonically describe as an "interesting" session. As the ministers were meeting official confirmation arrived that the German invasion of Belgium had already begun. That led to the only real piece of business at hand, the ultimatum to Germany. There was no real complexity, just a single issue demanding a single answer: Germany would be given until 12:00 midnight Berlin time to make an open declaration that the withdrawal of all German troops from Belgium had begun or else consider the German Empire to be in a state of war with the British Empire. As the message was being sent to Ambassador Goschen in Berlin, Asquith was informing the House of Commons that it was on its way; the House took the news "very calmly and with a good deal of dignity." Outside, the streets of Whitehall were once again jammed with cheering crowds, but Asquith took no comfort in them. He would write later that day, "This whole thing fills me with sadness. We are on the eve of terrible things."

Asquith went out for a solitary drive. Members of the Cabinet drifted in and out of the Cabinet Room all afternoon, while they awaited the expiration of Great Britain's ultimatum, or—hoping against hope—word that Germany had backed down and, rather than face a war with Britain, had agreed to withdraw from Belgium. When

Asquith returned, he joined Haldane, Churchill, and Grey in the Cabinet Room; Lloyd George came in later that evening. By 9:00 p.m. most of the Cabinet was assembled, sitting together in almost total silence. They could hear the crowds outside singing "Rule Britannia" and "God Save the King." Midnight in Berlin was 11:00 p.m. in London, and as the strokes of Big Ben began to fall at that hour, all eyes went to the telephone sitting on a small sideboard in a corner of the Cabinet Room, willing it to ring. The moment passed with no last-minute reprieve, and with it expired the ultimatum. Great Britain and Germany were now at war.

Earlier that day, across the North Sea, in Berlin, the Imperial German Chancellor, Theobald von Bethmann-Hollweg, had stood in the Speaker's podium of the Reichstag. The question before the assembled deputies was a vote to approve war credits, in effect bonds which would finance the coming struggle. The Chancellor was determined to give the assembled body a full accounting of how Germany had come to war with Russia and France. It is not known if he had knowledge of the speech Sir Edward Grey had made before the House of Commons the previous day, but whether by coincidence or design, von Bethmann-Hollweg opened his address at the same hour Grey had begun his, 3:00 p.m. Replete with all the excess and bombast which was so characteristic of so much of the Second Reich, it lacked the restrained eloquence which had marked the Foreign Secretary's delivery; in this respect von Bethmann-Hollweg's speech more closely resembled Viviani's. As an exercise in deceit, hypocrisy, and self-justification, however, it had no equals.

"A momentous fate is breaking over Europe. In the forty-four years since we created the German Empire and gained the respect of Europe in war, we have lived in peace and guarded the peace of Europe." But now, he said, "Russia has put the torch to our house. We have been forced into war with Russia and France." At this the Reichstag burst into thunderous applause.

A recapitulation of the events following the June 28 assassinations in Sarajevo followed, the Chancellor declaring that all of the Great Powers had worked to localize the crisis between Serbia and Austria-Hungary; only Russia claimed the right to interfere. At the same time that the Tsar had personally requested the Kaiser's mediation with

Vienna, St. Petersburg began mobilization. Here von Bethmann-Hollweg was at his duplicitous best, adroitly sidestepping the fact that Russia had begun a partial mobilization against Austria-Hungary only, while trying to avoid any provocation along the German frontier. Nevertheless, as the Chancellor told the tale, the Russians were warned that Germany would be forced to respond, but continued with their preparations, while at the same time their ally, France, ". . . to be sure, had not yet mobilized, but was taking preparatory military measures, as it admits. And we?—We had at that point, for the sake of European peace, deliberately not called up a single recruit!" An unarmed Germany would find herself trapped between the two armies, "and it would have been treason to expose Germany to such a danger." The Russians were told that only by demobilizing could the peace be preserved—anything else meant war.

France, meanwhile, was asked to remain neutral and refused. Again von Bethmann-Hollweg was judicious in his choice of which facts to present: he did not tell the Reichstag that the German demand for French neutrality had been framed to guarantee its rejection. Still, the Kaiser gave strict orders to respect the French border. What came next was a short excursion into fantasyland, as the Chancellor described how, in return, France launched air raids on German towns, French infantry and cavalry repeatedly violated the Franco-German border, and eighty French officers wearing Prussian uniforms had tried to cross the frontier in twelve motorcars. "With those actions, though war had not been declared, France broke the peace by attacking us." The only incident where a similar violation might have been committed by a German unit was unconfirmed, as the troops in question had been "shot to pieces. Only one man returned." He then turned to the question of Belgium and Luxembourg, and his next words would be remembered as one of the worst blunders von Bethmann-Hollweg ever made.

> Gentlemen, we are at present in a state war, a war of necessity, and *necessity knows no law*! Our troops have occupied Luxembourg and have perhaps already entered Belgium. This is contrary to the dictates of international law. France has, it is true, declared to Brussels that she was prepared to respect

the neutrality of Belgium so long as it was respected by her adversary. But we knew that France was ready to invade Belgium. France could wait; we could not. A French attack upon our flank in the region of the Lower Rhine might have been fatal. We were, therefore, compelled to ride roughshod over the legitimate protests of the Governments of Luxembourg and Belgium. The wrong—-I speak openly—-the wrong which thereby we commit, we shall try to make good as soon as our military aim is attained. Anyone in such grave danger as ourselves is not allowed to have any other consideration beyond that how he will hack his way through!

Next came a rather lame assurance that as long as Great Britain remained neutral—the Chancellor had no idea at that moment the British ultimatum was on its way—the German Navy would leave the coasts of France untouched, then von Bethmann-Hollweg launched into his peroration:

> I repeat the words of the Kaiser: "Germany goes into battle with a clear conscience!". . . The great hour of testing for our people has struck. But we meet it with complete confidence. Our army is in the field, our fleet is battle-ready—and behind them stands the entire German nation! The entire German nation down to the last man!

Just as had happened when Viviani finished his speech to the French Parliament, the assembled Reichstag went wild, cheering, whistling, applauding. Left-wing radicals joined with right-wing reactionaries in voting unanimously for war credits. The Kaiser, so moved by this display of national unity, would declare with a sweep of his arm, "Today I see no political parties! Today I see only Germans!"

Yet even as von Bethmann-Hollweg was speaking, the British Ambassador, Sir Edward Goschen, was meeting with the German Foreign Minister, von Jagow. As precisely as his instructions from London directed, he inquired, in the name of His Majesty's Government, whether the Imperial German Government would refrain from violating Belgian neutrality. Von Jagow replied that he was sorry to say that the answer was "No." German troops, he explained, had already crossed the Belgian border that morning, consequently Belgian neutrality had been already violated.

Von Jagow went on to explain, as if that bit of semantic sophistry might not be sufficient explanation, that Germany had been "obliged" to invade Belgium in order to take "the quickest and easiest way" into France, in order to strike a decisive blow as early as possible. It was, von Jagow said, "a matter of life and death" for Germany; the southern route into France was so heavily defended that there was no chance for a German breakthrough there. Germany had no choice but to go through Belgium.

Adhering to the sort of verbal fencing at which diplomats of the day excelled, Goschen pointed out to von Jagow that the violation of the Belgian frontier rendered the situation "exceedingly grave," and asked if there was still time in which the German troops could be withdrawn "and avoid possible consequences, which both he and I would deplore." Goschen was being deliberately vague, as von Jagow knew, indicating that the German invasion of Belgium would be the *casus belli* for Great Britain without directly stating as much and so requiring a formal response from Germany. Von Jagow had no choice, however; he replied that things had gone so far that it was now impossible to draw the troops back. With that Goschen left the Foreign Ministry and returned to the embassy.

Waiting for him there was a second communication from London, this one containing the terms of Great Britain's ultimatum to Germany, along with instructions that it be delivered immediately, as it would expire at midnight. Unless "the Imperial Government could give the assurance. . . that they would proceed no further with their violation of the Belgian frontier and stop their advance," Goschen was to ask for his passports, and inform the Imperial German government "that His Majesty's Government would have to take all steps in their power to uphold the neutrality of Belgium and the observance of a treaty to which Germany was as much a party as themselves."

Goschen promptly returned to the Foreign Ministry and at 7:00 p.m. was again shown into von Jagow's office, where he immediately presented the British ultimatum, emphasizing that it expired at midnight. Von Jagow could only repeat his earlier answer, that "the safety of the Empire rendered it absolutely necessary that the Imperial troops should advance through Belgium." Pressing the issue, for there could be no turning back now, Goschen asked von Jagow if, "in view of the terrible consequences which would necessarily ensue," the German government could possibly reconsider that answer.

Von Jagow, who was utterly dismayed at this turn of events, responded by saying that no matter when the ultimatum expired, the answer would still be the same. At that the British ambassador asked for his passports; von Jagow lamented that his entire time in office had been devoted to strengthening Germany's ties to Great Britain, and hopefully through Britain eventually drawing closer to France. This had been the Chancellor's policy as well, and now it was all "crumbling" before his eyes.

Goschen was sympathetic, for his tenure in Berlin was being terminated in a way no diplomat ever wanted to see his work end. At the same time, despite his "deep regret and disappointment," Goschen was firm in insisting that "under the circumstances and in view of our engagements, His Majesty's Government could not possibly have acted otherwise than they had done." At the mention of the Chancellor, Goschen saw one last glimmer of hope: if von Jagow lacked the authority—or the courage—to override the German Army, perhaps von Bethmann-Hollweg would possess the necessary resolve. He was encouraged in this belief when von Jagow "begged" him to speak with the Chancellor.

In von Bethmann-Hollweg's office, Goschen found the Chancellor "very agitated." The Chancellor began a long monologue, which Goschen later described as "a harangue," lasting for almost twenty minutes, repeating all the same tired arguments that von Jagow had trotted out earlier. What came next stunned Goschen. Von Bethmann-Hollweg had seemed at times to be his own and Germany's worst enemy, and his next blunder would seal for all time the absolute nature of Germany's burden of guilt for the war which was about to consume Europe. The step taken by the British government was "terrible to a degree;" it was scarcely credible, the Chancellor fumed, that Great Britain would make war with a "kindred people who desired nothing better than to be friends with the British," all for just a word—"neutrality,"—written on "a scrap of paper."

He went on, ranting about how all of his efforts to prevent and contain the war had been rendered useless by Britain's decision; about how Goschen knew that the Chancellor had devoted himself to keeping the peace since he had taken office. What Great Britain had done was "unthinkable—it was like striking a man from behind while he was fighting for his life against two assailants." As far as von Bethmann-Hollweg was concerned, his hands were clean—Great Britain alone was responsible for all the terrible events that might happen.

Goschen, deeply offended, fired back. It was Germany, he knew, not Great Britain, who had been the first of the Great Powers to declare war on another—Russia. It was Germany who had adopted a strategy—the Schlieffen Plan—which demanded an attack on a nation with whom Germany had no immediate quarrel—France. It was Germany, represented by the Chancellor, who had declared that "necessity knows no law." And now it was Germany who dismissed her own treaty with Belgium as "a scrap of paper." For none of this was Great Britain responsible, yet it was precisely those acts which had carried Europe into Armageddon.

If Germany felt compelled as "a matter of life and death" to invade Belgium in order to attack France, said Goschen, then it was equally a matter of life and death for Great Britain to honor her treaty obligations to Belgium. "That solemn compact simply had to be kept," Goschen declared, "or what confidence could any one have in engagements given by Great Britain in the future?" Cynically, von Bethmann-Hollweg retorted, "But at what price will that compact have been kept? Has the British Government thought of that?" The Ambassador, abandoning any semblance of diplomatic tact, told the Chancellor straight out that "the fear of consequences could hardly be regarded as an excuse for breaking solemn engagements." Von Bethmann-Hollweg, too caught up in his own ranting to pay any attention to Goschen, said nothing in reply, and in his turn Goschen realized that any further words would simply be wasted, and prepared to leave.

As Goschen was departing, von Bethmann-Hollweg offered one last observation. He said that "the blow of Great Britain joining Germany's enemies was all the greater" as he and the German

government had worked so hard to effect a peaceful settlement
between Austria and Russia. It is impossible to know if Goschen
allowed himself the luxury of sarcasm in his reply to such blatant
hypocrisy; in any event he told the Chancellor that the situation
which was now at hand was the inevitable outcome when one nation
asked another to abandon the solemn obligations it had taken on. The
Chancellor would understand, Goschen was sure, that no one
regretted that more than he.

One last scene remained to be played out in Berlin. At about 9.30
p.m. Arthur Zimmermann, the Under-Secretary of State, came to the
British Embassy and asked to see Goschen. When he was brought in
to the Ambassador, Zimmermann regretted that both official and
personal relations were coming to an end, for the Under-Secretary and
Goschen had become friends. Then, almost casually, Zimmermann
asked if the British ambassador's demand for his passports was to be
taken as a declaration of war. To Goschen this seemed a curious
question, as the Under-Secretary was a recognized authority on international law; apparently Zimmermann, in the finest tradition of
German legalism, was making absolutely certain of the status between
Germany and Great Britain.

Goschen remarked that history was replete with situations where
two nations had broken off diplomatic relations and nevertheless not
gone to war. But in this case, Goschen's instructions were explicit: His
Majesty's Government had required a specific answer to a definite
question by midnight, and in the absence of what was considered a
"satisfactory answer"—that German troops would begin
withdrawing from Belgium—Great Britain would be forced "to take
such steps" as the situation required.

That, according to Zimmermann, was tantamount to a
declaration of war, as there was no possibility of the Imperial
Government acceding to such a demand that night or any other night.
Without further discussion or ceremony, Goschen was presented with
his passports, and with that, diplomatic relations between Germany
and Great Britain were formally severed. Goschen would depart for
Hamburg in the morning, where a British steamship given a guarantee
of safe conduct would take him and the Embassy staff home to the
British Isles. The two Empires were at war.

So the deeds were done; the whole Continent had gone to war with itself. Bound by treaty or sentiment, propelled by ambition or fear, filled with righteous indignation or base self-interest, each of the Great Powers of Europe had by its actions triggered the reactions of friends and foes, until all were at war. Europe had avoided such a war for nearly a century, yet in a matter of a few weeks, a relatively minor diplomatic crisis had erupted into what would soon become known as the World War. Chained together as surely as any band of prisoners, one by one the Great Powers slipped over the precipice into the nightmare abyss which they had all so desperately feared, and on the edge of which they had stood for so long. What none of them had ever contemplated, though, was that they would fall into it not by accident or because they chose to, but because they would be pushed by one of their own: Imperial Germany.

Chapter XII

THE BURDEN OF GUILT

Eleven p.m. passed on the fourth of August without word of any intention of a German withdrawal from Belgium, and so Great Britain and Germany found themselves at war. Accordingly, the orders went out to dispatch the British Expeditionary Force, the B.E.F., to Belgium. There it would take up positions on the left of the French Seventh Army, and prepare to meet the German juggernaut, which was bound by the strategic dogma of the Schlieffen Plan. The main body of the B.E.F. began crossing the Channel on August 12. Every day for the next week an average of thirteen troopships sailed each day from Southampton to Le Havre or Boulogne. One hundred and forty thousand men were safely transported, the single largest movement of troops in history up to that time.

To the German General Staff, the B.E.F. was so small as to be almost not worth consideration—indeed Kaiser Wilhelm II had referred to it as a "contemptible little army," giving rise to the nickname which the officers and rankers of the B.E.F. adopted as a badge of honor, "The Old Contemptibles." German derision notwithstanding, those six divisions were, man for man, the finest troops Europe had ever seen or would ever see again. When they finally met the oncoming waves of *feldgrau* on August 22, they handed the advancing Germans setback after bloody setback for the next month, retreating only when their exposed flanks were threatened, their numbers slowly but irrevocably dwindling, as the supporting French armies, bleeding and demoralized, reeled from the shock, surprise, and sheer weight of the German assault.

While the French armies desperately sidestepped to the west in the hope of forming a line which would finally stop and then throw back the German invaders, the courage and tenacity of the B.E.F. inflicted fatal delays and diversions on the Germans' unforgiving schedule for advance. Despite the dire predictions of von Schlieffen himself, the Plan appeared to be about to hand Germany the crushing victory she was seeking, for the French had been overextended to the east in their thrust into Lorraine. Had the B.E.F. not taken up its position on the extreme French left, the Germans would have swept in behind the French Army, encircling it, exactly as von Schlieffen had hoped it might.

However, when the German Army was within sight of Paris, a hastily assembled French Army, not letting the time bought so dearly by the B.E.F. go to waste, launched a devastating counterattack, as von Schlieffen had foreseen and feared, into the German right flank, while the Tommies turned about and lunged at their *feldgrau*-clad pursuers. These blows threw the now more-than-weary Germans back some forty miles, with the exhausted armies all finally coming to a halt on September 22.

By the end of the year, after a series of sidesteps called the "Race to the Sea" had ended, two thin, snake-like lines of opposing trenches, growing more and more elaborate with each passing week, had been dug from the Swiss border to the Channel, depriving each side of the opportunity to maneuver, as the armies began looking for a way to break the enemy's lines. A slightly discordant note began to slip into the strains of *Die Wacht am Rhein,* or the *Marseillaise,* or "Tipperary" being sung as the *soldaten, poilus,* and Tommies left for the front, as it slowly dawned on the generals and politicians alike, and even more slowly on the general public, that something had gone terribly wrong in the calculations that had been made and the assurances given before the troops marched off to war.

It would all be over in six weeks, eight at the most, they had believed; the troops would be "home before the leaves fall." But when the leaves fell, they only covered the fresh graves of the dead, or swirled into the newly dug graves of those still dying. Then the cry was that the war would be over before Christmas, but Christmas came and went and there was no end in sight, either of the war or the casualty lists. Soon entire military traditions were being overthrown, as realization began to dawn on the Germans and French that neither intellect nor *elán* were about to deliver a quick victory, and the British saw that their magnificent but tiny B.E.F., decimated in the first four months of combat, could never be resurrected.

What was developing, and what would become the lasting collective memories of the Great War, were methods of living and dying that could only find parallels in the darker passages of writers like Edgar Rice Burroughs, Jules Verne, or H. G. Wells. Open movement ceased as the troops literally went to ground, and the trenches, originally shallow and improvised, evolved into sophisticated systems of deep defensive positions, listening posts, dugouts, bunkers, and communication cuttings. Strategically, the Allies were faced with the task of forcibly ejecting the Germans from occupied Belgium and France. Tactically, it was a bloody and almost hopeless undertaking, as time and again the French and British armies surged forward against the waiting German defenses—and each time found some hellish new innovation that cut them down by the thousands. Machine guns proliferated behind huge entanglements of barbed wire which appeared, with barbs the size of a man's thumb, the better to catch on uniforms, accouterments, and flesh, pinning the hapless victims long enough for the stuttering Spandau machine-guns to find them. Mine-throwers and mortars made their debut, as did flame-throwers and poison gas.

Soldiers learned that sounds were dangerous—the steady mechanical rattle of the Spandau or the Vickers; the "whoosh" and roar of the *flammenwerfer*; the unforgettable "click-clack, clack-click" of a round being chambered in a Lee-Enfield rifle; the short, sharp scraping of the primer cord being drawn from the handle of a potato-masher hand grenade. And always, always, always the shells—howling, whistling, warbling, chugging like freight locomotives, whizzing like hornets, or whining like banshees. And there was always the sound you never heard—the one that got you.

Even colors were perilous. There were red Very lights at night signaling corrections to artillery bombardments; green or yellow mists, the terrible tendrils of phosgene or mustard gas, snaking along the ground. White on a man's gums or blue on his feet announced the presence of trench mouth or trench foot; black on a wounded soldier's body declared that gangrene had already set in.

Mud, blood, gore, long days or weeks of boredom punctuated by hours of absolute terror, were frame for the sights, sounds, and smells of men living a nightmare where they and their comrades were shot, torn, gassed, pulverized, immolated and obliterated in ways that human beings had never before suffered and endured. As gruesome as recounting such sights, sounds, and images may be, it is necessary, for it is required that there be an awareness (not an "understanding"— only those who experienced those days can ever "understand" them) of what the survivors of the Great War endured in order to comprehend what happened when peace returned to Europe.

It was an article of faith that the enemy always suffered the worst. The French in particular refined their talent for self-deception, somehow formulating the absurd idea that for every two Frenchmen who died in action, three Germans had been killed—but the truth was that the slaughter was appalling for both sides. In the First Battle of Ypres, in October 1914, wave after wave of German infantry, many of them university students advancing arm-in-arm singing patriotic songs, were cut down by the deadly, accurate British rifle fire. One German division lost over 9,300 men dead out of a strength of 12,000—in a single morning. Later, when the Allies were on the offensive, time and again the Tommies and *poilus* would clamber over the top of their trenches after artillery bombardments that had lasted for hours, sometimes days, or even weeks, waiting for the second-hands of their officers' watches to touch zero hour, when they would begin their methodical advance, the British to the sound of the officers' whistles, the more romantic French to bugles blaring the *Pas de Charge*. They stepped out with dressed ranks and at precise intervals across the shell-torn mudscape that stretched between the opposing lines of trenches known as No Man's Land. The Germans, having weathered the barrage in the relative safety of their deep dugouts, would emerge to assume their prepared positions and bring down a withering hail of rifle, machine gun, and artillery fire on the advancing troops. The results were inevitable. More often than not, there would not be enough soldiers left alive among the attackers to take the objective and hold it, or if the Allied troops did reach their goal, the cost was prohibitive—at the Somme, one attack that advanced barely 700 yards took three weeks at a cost of nearly 30,000 lives. Even on days when the public communiqués would read "all quiet on the Western Front" (the German read *"in dem West ist nicht neuen"*), nearly 5,000 men were becoming casualties, victims of sniper fire and random shelling. It was as if a small town was being methodically wiped off the face of the earth each day. The British, who in some ways were becoming even more methodical than the Germans, referred to such losses as "normal wastage."

In the post-war years, the commanding generals on both sides would be pilloried as mindless brutes who could conceive of no alternative but to feed endless masses of men into a vast killing machine, in the hope that the enemy would run out of troops first. In fact the generals, much maligned as incompetents as they are, and some of them deservedly, really did not intend to slaughter the finest generation of young men their nations would ever produce. Certainly, none of them ever enjoyed it, no matter what the slanderers might say in later years. The hard, painful truth was that they were unprepared—there was no way they could have been prepared—for the war they found themselves given the responsibility of fighting. For years it had been a tenet of military faith, and correctly so, that the day of the frontal assault was over—the American Civil War and the Franco-Prussian War had first demonstrated that, and the Russo-Japanese War of 1905 and the Balkan War of 1912 had only reinforced the lesson. Modern firepower made frontal assaults too costly, for infantry in even a hastily prepared defensive position could hold off several times their number of attacking troops, inflicting unacceptable losses in the process. So for decades the emphasis had been placed on conducting wars of maneuver, which gave an army the opportunity to turn a foe's flank, and achieve a decisive result in battle without having to resort to the terrible waste of lives of frontal attacks. What the generals never anticipated was a war where maneuver would be impossible, where there would be no flanks to turn, and the dreadful frontal assaults the only option remaining to them. The result was a slaughter the like of which had never been seen before or since.

And yet, somehow, there is still a rose-tinged nimbus of romance that surrounds the Great War. It was the songs—"Keep the Home Fires Burning," "Lili Marlene," "Pack Up Your Troubles," "Till We Meet Again," and everyone's favorite, "Tipperary." It was the magnificently anachronistic traditions—French cuirassier regiments and squadrons of German *uhlans* looked as if they had just stepped out of a Phillipoteaux painting of the Napoleonic Wars; the Germans wearing faintly absurd spiked *Pickelhauben* helmets; in England, a tradition harking back to the Hundred Years' War found newly commissioned subalterns visiting an armorer to have their swords sharpened before leaving for the front.

It was the grandeur of an age that was in fact its shroud. France and Germany had armies of conscripts, it is true, but conscription had been a national institution for generations—what made these conscripts conspicuous was how few tried to evade their responsibility. In Great Britain the situation was even more astonishing: not until 1916, when Britain would be compelled to field the largest army the Empire had ever mustered to carry out the Somme Offensive, would the British Army have to resort to a draft to fill its ranks. These young men, rightly called the flower of European youth, were the most idealistic the world would ever see, untainted by the cynicism and affected, postured disdain of later generations. Instead they steadfastly believed in *Ein Volk, ein Kaiser, ein Reich*, or *Liberté, Egalité, Fraternité!* and *Vive le Republique!*, or fighting for King and Country.

What Europe was killing, no matter how willing the victims, was the vitality that would leave later generations listless and disillusioned: the fire that had driven the Continent for a thousand years was being quenched forever. By the end of May 1916 nearly two million soldiers once clad in khaki, *feldgrau* or *horizon bleu* were dead or missing on the Western Front, while another four million had been wounded. And the bloodiest years were yet to come. . . .

It has been said that one death is a tragedy, one thousand dead is a disaster, and one hundred thousand dead is a statistic. The numbers that would be forever associated with the Western Front would be statistics which bordered on the incomprehensible. Yet each one was, individually, a tragedy. Eric Bogle captured the essence of both these truths in his song *No Man's Land*, the ballad of a visitor to a British military cemetery who happens upon the grave of "Private Willie McBride:"

> And did you leave a wife or a sweetheart behind?
> And in that faithful heart does your memory still shine?
> And although you died back in nineteen-sixteen
> In that loyal heart are you always nineteen?
>
> Or are you a stranger without even a name,
> Forever enshrined behind a glass pane
> In an old photograph torn and tattered and stained
> And fading to yellow in a brown leather frame?

July 1, 1916, the first day of the Somme Offensive, would forever be remembered as the Black Day of the British Army. At 6:00 a.m. one hundred twenty thousand Tommies went "over the top" to attack the Hindenburg Line. By nightfall, barely more than twelve hours later, half of them had become casualties, twenty thousand of them dead. The Somme attack had been launched in order to take pressure off the French Army, which was locked in a death struggle with the German Army around the fortress city of Verdun. In the ten months of that battle, each army would lose more than 350,000 dead in an area little more than ten miles square.

The Somme did not end on the first day; the battle continued with a fury that ebbed and flowed until November, with the British eventually gaining a seven-mile advance, at a cost of 420,000 British soldiers killed, wounded, or missing; the Germans losses totaled nearly a quarter of a million men. But while the British Army's hopes for a breakthrough had perished in mud and barbed wire, the strategic horizons for the German Army seemed bright with promise. While no one was winning the war on the Western Front, by all appearances Germany and her allies were winning it everywhere else.

The Central Powers (as Germany and Austria-Hungary now styled themselves) began their string of strategic victories in the autumn of 1915, when Bulgaria joined the alliance and helped the

Austrian armies overrun Serbia. Even before the Serbs collapsed, an attempt by the Allies to knock the Ottoman Empire out of the war by a *coup-de-main* had failed at the Dardanelles: over the next two years the Turks would fight the British Empire to a strategic draw. The Kingdom of Rumania, sensing an opportunity to aggrandize itself at the expense of Austria-Hungary, declared war on the Central Powers in August of 1916; by December the Rumanians were suing for peace.

Italy, who had not earned and did not deserve the Great Power status she accorded herself, had ignored her alliance with Germany and Austria-Hungary in the crisis of the summer of 1914. The theme of the Italian Prime Minister, Antonio Salandra, during those crucial weeks was endless repetitions of "Compensation! Compensation!" letting it be known that Italy was available to the highest bidder; there had been no takers. However, by the spring of 1915 the Italian government perceived an opportunity to exploit the Dual Monarchy's preoccupation with the Serbs to the south and the Russians to the north, and declared war, hoping to annex Trentino and the Tyrol, and seize the Adriatic port of Trieste. Instead her attacks were stopped cold by the Austro-Hungarian forces, and a bitter stalemate had imposed itself along the Isonzo River, where the Italians attacked and the Austrians repulsed them with bloody regularity.

To be sure, there were moments of alarm for the Central Powers. When a German U-boat sank the British passenger liner *Lusitania* in May 1915, the ensuing diplomatic confrontation with Washington DC left Berlin with the realization that sooner or later the United States would be added to the list of Germany's foes. And the Brusilov Offensive, launched by the Russian Army in the summer of 1916, was perhaps the most skillfully executed operation of the war, and came perilously close to routing the Austro-Hungarian Army. Only swift German reinforcement stiffened the sagging morale of Franz Josef's troops, and the Dual Monarchy fought on.

The Allies took the offensive again in 1917, and it would prove to be an *annus horribilis*. The overture came in April, along a sector of the Western Front known as the *Chemin des Dames*, where the French, who believed that they had discovered a tactical "formula" which would break the stalemate, opened their great attack. The abortive "Nivelle Offensive," named after the French commanding officer who conceived and executed the plan, lasted three weeks, cost 187,000 casualties, and gained less than a mile. The French Army, already morally and physically debilitated by the charnel house of Verdun, had been pushed at last to the limits of human endurance. The ranks of the *poilus* erupted in mutiny. French soldiers would continue to defend *la patrie* but they would never again be asked to carry out great offensives.

Thus the burden fell once more on Great Britain. A carefully developed plan, strategically sound but betrayed by weather, geology, and—worst of all—politicians, resulted in the British Army's collective Golgotha. Officially known as the Third Battle of Ypres, it would be forever immortalized as Passchendaele, after a village which stood squarely in the center of the British line of advance. Five months of fighting gave a gain of five miles and a casualty list 315,000 names long. It had been the Tommies' supreme effort: they had no more to give. If France was morally and spiritually exhausted, Britain had become physically so: there were, quite literally, no more fit men to replenish the ranks of His Majesty's regiments. Scraping the bottom of the barrel accomplished nothing, for there was nothing there: it is a matter of record that draft notices were sent to men who were maimed, or mentally ill, or even, in a few instances, already dead.

On the other side of the trenches, the human cost for Germany in each of these battles was equally horrible as that of the Allies. Ultimately, German losses at Verdun, the Somme, and Passchendaele exceeded those of France and Great Britain, and for Germany, with a much smaller population relative to the Allies, replacements were harder to muster. Nor were the losses merely numerical: by the end of 1916 whatever qualitative superiority over the Allies' soldiers the German *soldaten* once possessed had dissipated, and only the German Army's technical superiority kept it ascendant. By the end of 1917, even that was being eroded.

And there was another force, its results less readily visible or immediately obvious, insidiously eroding German and Austrian strength. Neither nation was self-sufficient in food production, and before the war close to a third of Germany's foodstuffs were imported from overseas. Now the Royal Navy's blockade of Germany cut off altogether those sources of supply, and by the summer of 1916 shortages became increasingly frequent, while as 1916 turned into 1917, starvation began to loom over the civilian populations of the Central Powers. One way or another, 1918 would be the decisive year of the war.

In the east, battles equally costly in lives but even greater in scope than those of the Western Front would be fought between the Central Powers and Imperial Russia, bearing names like Tannenburg, the Masaurian Lakes, Tagenrog, Gorlicc-Tarnow, Lake Naroch, and the Brusilov Offensive. Only the immense distances of the Eastern Front prevented these battles from being individually decisive—it would be their cumulative effect which would play into the hands of the Bolsheviks and other revolutionaries who eventually brought down the Romanov dynasty and then toppled the Provisional Government. Eight decades of Soviet meddling and "revision" have left the reliability of the records of those years suspect, but at the very least it can be stated with certainty that close to four million soldiers, Russian, Austro-Hungarian, and German, died in battle between August 1914 and November 1917. How many more, mostly Russian, died of disease and malnutrition is impossible to calculate, although the total could easily be double the number of combat deaths.

However, if 1918 was to be the decisive year of the war, 1917 was the pivotal one, and in it the wheel of fate turned against the Central Powers. The moral affront of the resumption of unrestricted submarine warfare and the blundering attempt at "diplomacy" which became known as "the Zimmermann telegram" had pushed the forbearance of the American people and their government past the breaking point, and on April 6, the United States declared war on Germany. Almost a year would pass, however, before the weight of American manpower and industry would begin to make itself felt; when it did so, the Allies would be invincible. Germany's only hope of victory now lay in forcing the French and British to come to terms before the American juggernaut materialized. The collapse of Imperial Russia released sixty German divisions to be redeployed in the West, where for the first time since the opening weeks of the war the Kaiser's army would enjoy a numerical superiority over the Allies. It was an opportunity that the German General Staff did not intend to waste.

As 1918 dawned, it was clear to the political and military leadership on both sides that the armies of all the warring nations were approaching exhaustion—the question was who would falter first. Russia had already given up in December 1917: wracked by revolutions at home that lurched successive governments further and further to the left, and dissent, defeatism, and disillusion within the army, she finally made a separate peace with Germany at Brest-Litovsk. The French Army had stood on the brink of self-destruction in 1917, and even now replacements marching to the front were heard counting the cadence "*Une, deux, trois, merde!*" and *baaaa*-ing like sheep being led to the slaughterhouse. Great Britain had already reached the limits of her manpower, now the German U-boats were taking a dreadful toll of the merchant shipping that was Britain's lifeline: in April 1917 there was less than three weeks' supply of food left in the country. The introduction of convoys by the Royal Navy that same month, long resisted by civilian shipping interests, narrowly averted a catastrophe.

Germany's position was, on the whole, even worse, for the British blockade had been slowly starving the German Empire to death for more than three years. Meat and milk were all but non-existent; turnips had replaced potatoes as a dietary staple; flour for making bread often contained as much sawdust and chalk as wheat. With its new-found numerical superiority on the Western Front, the German Army High Command believed that it had the strength for one last great offensive, but after that there would be no hope of victory: Germany was as exhausted as her foes.

The result was a succession of hammer-blows thrown against the Allied lines, collectively known as the "*Kaiserschlacht*"—the Kaiser's Battle—beginning in late March 1918, with a new offensive opening with each passing month until the July. The first, landing on the British Army, was the most successful, for it had the advantages of superiority in manpower and materiel as well as strategic surprise; yet in the end it failed, for while the British Army fell back, the Tommies held their line, and dreadful losses were inflicted on the attacking German divisions. It would prove to be a decisive development, for each of the four German offensives which followed were launched with diminishing numbers and declining morale, while the Allies were marshaling their strength and regaining a measure of confidence as each following German offensive was contained and then repulsed.

By the end of July the Germans had lost more than 600,000 killed, wounded, and missing—irreplaceable losses—in this succession of offensives with little to show for them: some territory had been gained, but no strategic breakthrough had been achieved, no decisive result attained, and the German Army was finally exhausted. At the same time, the Allies, infuscd with new strength in manpower, materiel, and morale as the American Army began to arrive in France in significant numbers, went over to the offensive. In August and September, their numerical superiority regained, the Allies attacked the German line relentlessly; moreover, by this time they were also gaining a tactical and technological ascendency as well. One by one, through the month of October and into November, Germany's allies fell away, and finally, in the first week of November, revolution swept over the Reich, the monarchy was dissolved, and the German government, now a republic, asked the Allies for an armistice. At 11:00 a.m. on November 11, 1918, the fighting ceased.

In January 1919, representatives from the Allied powers began assembling in Paris to begin drafting the peace treaties with the Central Powers. There would be five such documents, each to become known to history by the name of the *environ* of Paris in which it was signed: the Treaty of Versailles, the settlement with Germany; the Treaty of St. Germain-en-Laye, with Austria; the Treaty of Trianon, with Hungary; the Treaty of Neuilly, with Bulgaria; and the Treaty of Sèvres, with Turkey. The first of the five, at Versailles, was signed on June 28, 1919, exactly five years to the day after the assassination of Franz Ferdinand and Sophie; the last, Sèvres, was not signed until August 10, 1920.

Each of the treaties would be a source of discontent for victor and vanquished alike: in each of them the victors felt that they were deprived in some manner of some portion of their war aims; the defeated powers unanimously believed that the terms imposed were needlessly punitive and overly harsh. The Treaty of Versailles would become the best known of these treaties and synonymous with them collectively. It methodically stripped Germany of nearly a quarter of her territory, all but abolished her navy, reduced her army to barely more than a glorified police force, and imposed a crushing indemnity intended to repay the Allies for the costs of four years of carnage. The Allies were determined to ensure that Germany would never again wage an aggressive war.

For the German people, however, the most deplorable, most humiliating, of the Treaty's provisions was Article 231, which read:

> The Allied and Associated Governments affirm and Germany accepts the responsibility of Germany and her allies for causing all the loss and damage to which the Allied and Associated Governments and their nationals have been subjected as a consequence of the war imposed upon them by the aggression of Germany and her allies.

In other words, Germany was to bear the sole blame for the war.

It was no small point: Germany's "guilt" provided the legal underpinnings, the legitimacy, for dismembering the German Reich—Silesia, sections of East Prussia and the Rhineland were all taken away from Germany and either demilitarized or given to one of the newly formed nations in Central Europe—as well as the imposition of what was meant to be crippling reparations and the dissolution of Germany's armed forces. More than any other of the Allies' punitive provisions in the treaty, this would be deeply resented by the German people, an open wound for which there was no healing. Eventually it became a grudge which the German people bore against the Allies, and which demagogues and agitators would use as a weapon to hack away at the limitations and provisions of the Versailles Treaty, claiming that it was unfair to saddle the German nation and people with the total guilt for a conflict in which all the warring nations, victors and vanquished, bore some degree of responsibility.

In the hands—and voices—of the best rabble-rousers it soon became a persuasive argument, especially when the sheer scale of the carnage and destruction wrought between 1914 and 1918—carnage and destruction never before imagined let alone seen—became more and more apparent, particularly to the Allies. As the years passed and the tale was endlessly repeated, it became easier to believe that the Great War was not the product of one nation's design or ambition.

The Great War was what has become known among historians as a "world-historical event": it fundamentally altered how humanity viewed itself, its societies and institutions, its values and morals. The world which emerged from the war in 1918 was far, far different from that which entered it in 1914. The Great War was (and remains) the greatest cataclysm in Western history since the fall of Rome.

Materially, the cost of the war was staggering. It has been estimated that the monetary expenditure of the war exceeded $186,000,000,000 (at 1918 values). But the human cost was almost beyond measure, for it embraced not only casualty lists, which become almost mind-numbing in their length, but also the toll extracted on Western civilization, one which could never be repaid or replaced. The total dead and missing for uniformed soldiers of all services of all the combatant nations surpassed ten million; the number of wounded was twice that. France for one never recovered from her losses—to this day the growth rate for the French population lags behind that of all of her European neighbors, including Germany: the young men who should have been proud, happy fathers lay moldering in military cemeteries scattered along the length of the Western Front.

More than lives were lost, though. The four years of the Great War swept away fifteen hundred years of Europe's social and economic progress. Before 1914, though it is a fact little grasped or understood today, Europe was essentially a feudal society. Institutions which had endured for centuries were adapting—or being forced to adapt—to social and economic changes the like of which had never before been experienced. Yet they were adapting, and save for a relative handful of reactionaries and diehards, most Europeans were willing to embrace the changes, provided they were not too radical and too rapid. However, in the wake of the Great War, the Romanov, Hohenzollern, and Hapsburg dynasties were swept away, taking with them the institutions and social mechanisms which had spelled security and continuity for so many generations. In their place were revolution and dissolution, as Russia was taken over by the Bolsheviks, Germany struggled to construct a republic to take the place of the Reich, and Austria-Hungary was hacked to pieces. In France, faith in the Republic remained, but confidence in the men who led it plummeted, never to be fully restored. In Britain the demagoguery of Lloyd George and his following reached new heights as the old, conservative social order was blamed for everything that had gone wrong in the war. Europe's *ancien regime* was not allowed to peacefully die a natural death and fade away—instead, it was massacred.

Inevitably, then, the question arose: how could just one nation be responsible for such a devastating event? It soon became fashionable for the political, economic, and academic leaders of the Allies to hold that such a belief was the height of arrogance: mistaking cause for responsibility, they began to ask how Germany alone could have brought about such a cataclysm. Only a shared, collective responsibility, they argued, had the power to so fundamentally alter the course and nature of Western civilization. The war was not just Germany's fault, it was everyone's fault. Within a handful of years of the signing of the Treaty of Versailles, doubt had crept into the hearts and minds of the Allies. The question began to be asked if the Versailles settlement had been needlessly harsh, in particular Article 231, which had become popularly known as the "war guilt clause." It was the British who most frequently gave voice to this question, in the early throes of the self-doubt which, save for a few years in the early 1940s, would become the foundation of all of Britain's foreign and domestic policies for the remainder of the 20th century.

And yet, somewhere the process had to have begun by which a relatively simple quarrel between Austria-Hungary and Serbia escalated into a Continent-wide conflagration. The diplomatic crises of 1908, 1911, or 1912 were far more dangerous than that of July 1914, for the issues at hand involved questions of national integrity and national honor—neither a minor consideration in those years— and yet they had not ended in war. So why did a pair of murders in the Balkans in June 1914 explode into the Great War? There was no significant difference between 1914 and the previous crises save for one thing: in the earlier years Germany, by her own admission, was not yet ready to go to war. By July 1914, the German Army was not only prepared for war, the government and military authorities believed that it must come: to delay it any further would only see Germany's strength decline relative to that of her enemies. This was a conclusion those leaders had reached years earlier: the 1912 conference at Potsdam was nothing more than an articulation of that belief. The Schlieffen Plan itself was the quintessential embodiment of aggression, and it was adopted as Germany's grand strategy a decade before the Great War began. For Germany, war was not simply an extension of national policy by non-political means, it was not the last resort when all other options had failed, it had become the first choice as a means of resolving Germany's problems, internal and external, and maintaining German prestige, power, and influence.

The foundation of Germany's guilt, then, was laid almost ten years before the Sarajevo assassinations, when Field Marshal von Schlieffen first prepared the offensive plan of operations which would subsequently bear his name. When it was adopted as the Reich's official war plan in 1905, Germany took the first steps down the slippery slope toward the Great War. All of the Great Powers had concocted war plans that were aggressive: what set the Schlieffen Plan apart from the strategies of all of the other Great Powers, including Austria-Hungary, was that it made no distinction between mobilization, deployment, and attack, first on France, then on Russia. Each automatically followed the other in a rapid succession, with no allowance for changes in circumstances which might make such attacks unnecessary or even counter-productive—which was precisely what happened. All of the other Great Powers, save for Great Britain, which had no definitive war plan at all, had formulated strategic plans which required their governments to make a conscious decision, once mobilization was complete, to go to war; mobilization was not an irrevocable step. Only Germany possessed a strategy in which mobilization was, for all practical purposes, part of the offensive operations, a plan which automatically committed Germany to war with two other Great Powers, whether or not the actual political or military circumstances required it.

Likewise each of the Great Powers, again with the exception of Great Britain, was willing to accept a war with one or more of the other Great Powers, should one be *forced* upon them, as a means of resolving their particular problems. However, none of them, save for Germany, was prepared to *provoke* that war. In July of 1914, that is precisely what happened. The Kaiser, his ministers, and his generals seized on every opportunity to aggravate the crisis of July 1914 and propel it farther down the road to war, all the while knowing that they also possessed the power to halt that progress. That the German leaders knowingly chose to make decisions which would drag all of Europe into open conflict makes the unanswerable argument that Germany did, indeed, bear the burden of guilt for the Great War.

Three distinct opportunities presented themselves between June 28 and August 3, 1914, when Germany, in some combination of the persons of the Kaiser, the Chancellor, or the Chief of the Army General Staff could have prevented the crisis from escalating into open conflict. The first came at the very beginning of the chain of events which led to the crisis in the last week of July. When given the news of Archduke Franz Ferdinand's assassination, Kaiser Wilhelm had initially been cautious, even circumspect, reminding the Austro-Hungarian ambassador to Berlin that the issue was primarily a problem between Serbia and Austria-Hungary, and hesitating to make any commitments to the Dual Monarchy on the part of the Reich. Had the situation been left at that, the entire crisis of July 1914 would have never have come about. However, Wilhelm blundered badly when, a few hours later, he suddenly declared that Germany would without reservation support Austria-Hungary in whatever course of action Vienna chose to take. This has come down to posterity as "the blank check."

It was not an irrecoverable mistake, however: always something of a political naif, Wilhelm clearly believed that his declaration would be taken as a simple statement of moral support for a fellow monarch, the Emperor Franz Josef. However, naivety, political or otherwise, was not one of Chancellor von Bethmann-Hollweg's faults. Wilhelm's promise of unconditional support would have been meaningless in practical terms had it not been in effect "counter-signed" by the Chancellor. Under the Imperial German constitution, von Bethmann-Hollweg was responsible for formulating and executing the Empire's foreign policy and more than once during his tenure in office he would remind the Kaiser of precisely that fact. As the Kaiser's first minister, he was expected to act as a moderating influence when Wilhelm's impulsive nature led him to make one of his embarrassing statements or ill-considered decisions. In this case, because the Kaiser's promise of unqualified support for Austria-Hungary suited von Bethmann-Hollweg's own political agenda, he allowed it to stand, and indeed gave it added legitimacy by publicly endorsing it.

The "blank check" had the effect, as von Bethmann-Hollweg knew it would, of effectively removing any restraints on Austria-Hungary's retaliation against Serbia (for that is really what it was) for the Sarajevo murders. All through July, as he was working frantically to keep Wilhelm uninformed about the growing crisis in Central Europe, the Chancellor was urging, sometimes demanding, swift action by Vienna, pressing Count Tisza and Count Berchtold into an armed confrontation with Serbia. The Chancellor was certain that this would bring war with Russia, a war which he believed would solve the worst of his domestic political problems, and one which, he was convinced, Germany could win, offering resolution to a host of challenges to German foreign policy as well.

It follows then that had the German government genuinely desired a peaceful solution to the July crisis, the entire charade acted out over Russia's mobilization would have never been staged. From the moment Tsar Nicholas II began considering a partial mobilization of the Russian Army, in those military districts which shared a common border with Austria-Hungary, he made it clear, through his Foreign Minister, Sazonov, as well as his ambassadors abroad, that his purpose was to intimidate, not threaten, the Dual Monarchy. It was no small distinction: intimidation is akin to rattling the saber, an implicit reminder from one nation to another that it possesses the power to impose its will; drawing the saber, however, is a threat, an explicit statement of intent to use that power, to resort to force.

The Tsar also made certain that Germany and Austria-Hungary were aware that he had no hostile intentions; the Russian Army, once mobilized, was not automatically committed to an attack on either nation, something already known in Berlin and Vienna. In plain fact, the partial mobilization achieved exactly what Nicholas hoped it would—it forced Austria-Hungary to redeploy her armies, and in so doing, left her with insufficient strength to mount a successful attack on Serbia, thus fulfilling Russia's mission as the protector of the Slavs without the necessity of firing a single shot. It had been an exercise in old-fashioned, dynastic, power diplomacy, one which was understood with perfect clarity in Vienna. There the situation could have remained, indefinitely, while Austria-Hungary, Serbia, and Russia groped toward a negotiated settlement.

However, in Berlin, the dual confrontation between Vienna and Belgrade on one hand and Vienna and St. Petersburg on the other, could not be permitted to end in a stalemate. Germany needed a *casus belli* so that the mobilization of her army could be ordered and the clockwork-like operations of the Schlieffen Plan be put into motion. The condescending tone adopted by the Kaiser throughout the whole of the "Willy-Nicky" exchange was hardly that of a head of state seeking to maintain the peace. Even allowing for his megalomania, Wilhelm's telegrams fairly drip with hypocrisy, particularly those passages where he reassured Nicholas that he was personally intervening with Vienna in order to begin mediation; he was making no such effort, while von Bethmann-Hollweg was urging Tisza and Berchtold to disregard any Russian overtures in that direction. At the same time, the repeated threats of German mobilization eventually produced the result for which Berlin had been hoping: a total Russian mobilization. Russia had no choice, for it was no secret that a German mobilization was the precursor to an immediate attack. In this case, German "diplomacy" was not meant to be intimidating, but explicitly threatening.

However, it need not have happened. Without German agitation, Vienna and St. Petersburg could have settled their differences: Sazonov had readily admitted that the Serbs deserved to be punished in some way, not just for Sarajevo, where a *prima facie* case had never been fully established for Serbian complicity, but for the prolonged and frequently bloody agitation Serbia had encouraged and sponsored for decades within the Dual Monarchy. Russia was willing to countenance Serbia's chastisement: what Russia would not tolerate was seeing Serbia dismembered or extinguished. The opportunity for compromise was there—it was Germany that swept that opportunity away.

Instead the Kaiser and the Chancellor provoked the Tsar into ordering a full mobilization, which in turn led to the German ultimatum to Russia requiring that her army demobilize and the demand for France to declare her neutrality, both issued in the almost-absolute certainty that they would be rejected—which they were.

Germany now had her *casus belli*, and so the German Army was mobilized. War was now inevitable, the only question remaining would be how broad its scope. Here the Germans had one last chance to confine the war to Eastern Europe, and give neither France nor Great Britain any cause to become involved.

War was something that France most assuredly had no desire to see in the summer of 1914. Her government was chaotic, her economy mildly depressed, her Army still undergoing reforms. President Poincaré and Premier Viviani made it quite clear to von Bethmann-Hollweg and von Jagow that France would do nothing to provoke a German attack; indeed preventive measures were taken almost immediately after the two men returned from their state visit to Russia to avoid any sort of "incident" upon which the Germans could seize as a reason for hostile action against France. All the same, the French possessed the courage to stand on their honor when Germany demanded French neutrality in the event of a war in the east, requiring guarantees which would have left the country all but defenseless.

Still, if there was to be war between France and Germany, the French government was determined that it would not be France which started it. The decision would be left to Germany, and it is here that the German burden of guilt becomes the heaviest. God, Providence, Chance, or Fate had given Wilhelm, his ministers, and his generals one last chance to avoid a continent-wide war. In the early evening of August 1, misunderstanding the meaning of a telegram from Lichnowsky in London, the Kaiser told Field Marshal von Moltke to turn the whole of the German Army eastward to face Russia. Though the offer that Wilhelm believed the British were making—that they would guarantee the neutrality of France as well as their own if Germany would give her assurance that France would not be attacked—was mistaken, had von Moltke carried out the Kaiser's orders, the same result would have been accomplished. The French were not prepared to attack the Germans, and the British had no cause to enter what was clearly a central European quarrel. It was Helmuth von Moltke who made complete the case for Germany's guilt in forcing the Great War upon Europe: he knew that the planning and staffwork existed which could have made the Kaiser's command a reality, but instead, in a combination of his blind devotion to the Schlieffen Plan and his own lack of moral conviction, he lied to his monarch, and so committed the German Army to an attack which need not ever have taken place. But because it did, the Germany, Europe, and world that von Moltke knew would be swept away in the four years of war that followed.

Arguably, there was even possibly a fourth opportunity: the British ultimatum to Germany delivered on August 4 was one last chance for peace. The Kaiser, the Chancellor, the Foreign Minister, and the Army Chief of Staff all knew that Germany was risking war with Great Britain by invading Belgium: once King Albert's appeal for Britain's aid in repelling the invader was made, that risk became a certainty unless the German Army withdrew. This could have provided Wilhelm with the ultimate justification for insisting that the Army be redeployed to the east, regardless of what von Moltke decreed was and was not feasible. Without the invasion of Belgium, war with France would have become not only strategically impossible, it would have been unnecessary. By that time, however, rationalization and self-justification had utterly supplanted morality and integrity. Despite whatever political and military advantages such a decision might have offered, the German government never considered the option of simply stopping the offensive into Belgium.

It was too far along the road of moral dissolution. Von Bethmann-Hollweg's strident declaration to the Reichstag on August 4 that "Necessity knows no law!" became a statement of national policy, and set a dreadful precedent for Germany's future. That the German civilian and military authorities had reached a point of moral bankruptcy would only be further established by the tactics of terror which were being applied in the occupied portions of France and Belgium. German records captured after the war showed that systematic execution of civilian hostages in Belgium began as early as August 4, and in one of the most horrific examples of *Schrecklichkeit* ("frightfulness"—terror tactics), on August 21 and 23, 1914, the Prussian 101st Grenadiers, one of the "elite" units of the German Army, carried out a series of systematic executions in the city of Dinant; a total of 639 civilians were killed in cold blood—seven of the victims were less than two years old, the youngest of them three-week-old Mariette Fivet, who died in her father's arms. The "offense" against the Germans that had provoked the massacre was never revealed. A year later, on September 22, 1915, four French civilians were shot for assisting French prisoners of war to escape. Two weeks later, in an act that outraged the whole of the Western world, a 49-year-old British nurse, Edith Cavell, was executed by firing squad for helping captured British soldiers escape.

Documents discovered after the armistice made clear the fact that even before the war began it had been decided that *Schrecklichkeit* would be the official German policy, reprisals the standard response, to any show of defiance or resistance. For the rest of the war, occupied Belgium and France lived in fear, as every town and village had its spies and informers, whose suspicions resulted in arrests, disappearances and executions.

The rot had begun at the very top, among the Kaiser and his ministers. First, legality replaced morality, and then necessity replaced legality. When Chancellor von Bethmann-Hollweg announced to the Reichstag that "Necessity knows no law!" he was declaring German policy for the next four years, as even cruelest acts became acceptable as long as they could be wrapped in the mantle of a legal justification or a demonstration of necessity—and of course "necessity" was defined by those committing the acts. It appears that it never occurred to the Kaiser, his Ministers, or his generals and admirals, that while such actions might be acceptable to the German people, with their passion for adhering to legal niceties and correctness, it was only serving to harden the hearts of the British and French, with whom they might someday have to negotiate a peace settlement, and alienating the Americans, who eventually provided the Allies with the manpower and industrial capacity to overwhelm Germany.

The implications this moral expediency would hold for Germany's future were disturbing. While in so many ways the spirit and nature of Wilhelmine Germany was unquestionably a far cry from that of the regime of the National Socialists, it is possible to see the framework of the Third Reich being erected within the edifice of the Second. Chancellor von Bethmann-Hollweg's speech to the Reichstag on August 4 is readily discernable as the prototype of *der Grosse Lüge* ("the Big Lie") which would be perfected by Adolf Hitler and Josef Göbbels. As a display of rhetorical skill, it was perhaps von Bethmann-Hollweg's finest performance; as an accounting of how and why Germany had gone to war, it was as much fantasy as fact. However, because no one within Germany could gainsay him—or if they could were not prepared to do so—the Chancellor's version of the "facts" was accepted as gospel by the German people. Thus they were stunned when, five years later, the Treaty of Versailles required that Germany accept full responsibility for the war. Having been deceived for so long, the German people had embraced the deception, and the truth was regarded as a lie.

Within Germany and across Europe, the old order was discredited and discarded in the decade following the Great War, sometimes as much a victim of its own arrogance as of any machinations by those who stood in opposition to it. For the most part, however, it was undone by one of the most enduring tragedies of the war, scarcely comprehended at the time and still often overlooked today. Save for a relative handful, the men who should have been leading their nations in the 1920s and 1930s were instead lying beneath the soil of France, Belgium, Gallipoli, or Poland. In their absence, a moral vacuum came into being as their places were taken by a collection of second-raters, men who, as they strove for power, regarded truth as something to be manipulated to an end, and integrity a matter of expedience rather than a character trait to be cultivated. Depending on their purpose they would shamelessly exploit their countrymen's sorrow, horror, fear, anger, or hatred. There were Liberals, Conservatives, Communists, Socialists, Fascists, by varying degrees all bent on harnessing national energies to rebuild engines of destruction, men who sought power without responsibility, pacifists for whom pacifism was synonymous with "peace at any price," and appeasers who would trade away preparedness for hollow promises. Their names would be remembered, though with no pride, by their countrymen—names like Albert Sarraut, Leon Blum, Camille Chautemps, Stanley Baldwin, Neville Chamberlain—as well as Benito Mussolini and Adolf Hitler. They were truly the spawn of the Great War, for without the empty spaces it created among the ranks of those who should have been leading their nations, they would have never risen to positions of power and prominence.

The process began in the months following the signing of the Treaty of Versailles. The German people would come to regard the treaty as a *Diktat*, an ultimatum, because it was imposed upon Germany by the Allies rather than being the product of a negotiated settlement. Yet in practical terms it was no more harsh than the settlement the new-minted German Empire had imposed on France in 1871, while the treaty of Brest-Litovsk was far more punitive. However, the popular perception would prove critical, for it fostered a receptive audience to the lie, put about by the defeated German generals, that the German Army, fighting valiantly at the front, had been stabbed in the back by pacifists and revolutionaries at home. The Versailles treaty reduced the German Army to a strength of 100,000 men, stripped the High Seas Fleet of all of its ships but an obsolescent handful, and banned the existence of a German air force. Additionally, the Weimar Republic, the political successor to the Hohenzollern dynasty, was prohibited from possessing modern heavy weapons while forbidden the capacity to produce them. All of this was humiliating to a people which had bestowed an inordinate degree of national pride in their armed forces.

Hardly was the ink dry on the treaty than the Chancellor of the new Republic, Karl Wirth, was meeting with General Hans von Seekt, commander of the *Reichswehr*, as Weimar's truncated army was styled, exploring ways to evade the despised document's disarmament clauses. For more than seven years they worked in deepest secrecy, for an Allied Control Commission had been imposed on the Ruhr, Germany's industrial heartland, to ensure that the provisions of Versailles were strictly enforced. Accordingly, each year the German government would carefully announce that "the Treaty of Versailles is also a law of Germany, and by reason of this it is binding on all German citizens. This commitment outranks even the provisions of the German constitution." Thus reassured, the Allies' watch on Germany slept.

By 1927, however, such reassurances were no longer forthcoming from Berlin. The Allied Control Commission had been dissolved, and while rearmament was still being carried out in secret, Germany's political leaders began to speak more and more openly about revising the terms of Versailles, or abandoning them altogether. By the time another five years had passed, Germany was openly rebuilding her army and navy, and establishing an air force. By the end of the next five years, she was the dominant military and political power in Europe, and once more threatening the Continent with war. What had happened?

The answer lies in the moral exhaustion which finally overtook the Allies in the late 1920s. In imposing the terms of the Versailles treaty on Germany went the implied responsibility for the Allies of enforcing them. But as the 1920s ebbed, the wartime generation of fiery Allied leaders passed away or faded into retirement, their places taken by men who had no stomach for such responsibility. However, representative governments are only symptomatic of the mood of their peoples, and as the 1920s passed into the 1930s, that mood in France and Great Britain became increasingly ostrich-like. The French and the British had, understandably and inevitably, sharply recoiled in horror from the national experiences of the Great War. An entire generation had been maimed, emotionally as well as physically, by Verdun, the *Chemin des Dames*, the Somme and Passchendaele.

The Great War had been called "the war to end all wars," and French and British people passionately wanted to believe that it was so. International peace conferences and disarmament treaties, protest marches and rallies denouncing war, were all the rage. In 1928, the Kellogg-Briand Pact was drawn up in Paris, "providing for the renunciation of war as an instrument of national policy." It was eventually signed by sixty-one nations, representing every continent. No one in France or Britain, and apparently no one else either, ever wanted to go to war again, and it was inconceivable on either side of the Channel that there might be those who did.

However, that is exactly what happened. In January 1933, what had once been an obscure splinter party in Bavaria became the single most powerful political force in Germany. Styled the National Socialist German Workers' Party *(Nationalsozialistische Deutsche Arbeiterpartie*—the NSDAP, soon known world-wide by their abbreviated title, Nazis), exploiting the economic crisis of the Great Depression and taking advantage of loopholes in the Weimar Constitution, the Nazis formed a coalition in the Reichstag which allowed their leader, Adolf Hitler, to assume the Chancellorship. Within days of taking office, Hitler was confirmed as absolute dictator of Germany by a clutch of enabling acts passed by a Nazi-dominated Reichstag.

Austrian by birth, a former corporal in the German Army, Hitler was an extreme right-wing demagogue, gifted with a cunning intelligence and a remarkable charisma. The doctrines of Hitler's NSDAP were built on racism, paranoia, and revenge. Skillfully manipulating the wounded pride of the German people, he vowed to tear up the Treaty of Versailles and avenge the wrongs done to Germany—and reverse the decision of November 11, 1918. Having blustered and bullied his way to power, he now turned those same tactics on Germany's neighbors, holding forth the threat of the war which they wished to avoid and refused to believe he would actually launch to achieve his objectives.

Unbelieving that anyone would want another war, and not realizing how weak Hitler's initial position truly was, the former allies allowed themselves to be cowed by the German *Führer*. The first test came on March 7, 1936, when three battalions of German *soldaten* goose-stepped across the Rhine bridges and occupied the Rhineland, which had been demilitarized under the terms of Versailles. It was the greatest gamble of Hitler's career, for had the French unsheathed so much as a single bayonet, the *feldgrau*-clad troops would have abruptly done an about face and stomped right back across those same bridges. They represented the total of Germany's ready reserves of troops. Hitler and his minions held their collective breath: by Hitler's own admission, had he been forced to back down before determined French opposition, it would have spelled the end of the Nazi regime then and there.

However, in London the Prime Minister, Stanley Baldwin, announced to the House of Commons that Britain would take no action against this flagrant breach of the terms of Versailles: the nation lacked the resources necessary to enforce the treaty. In Paris, the government of Albert Sarraut, which was prepared to take its cue from the British, then dithered and ultimately did nothing. Winston Churchill, banished at the time to the political wilderness because his repeated warnings of the threat posed by a rearming Germany were unpopular, was prompted to rise in the House of Commons and condemn the Baldwin Government as being "decided only to be undecided, resolved to be irresolute, adamant for drift, solid for fluidity, all-powerful to be impotent."

Encouraged by what he rightly took to be a total absence of Allied resolve, Hitler followed up this coup over the next three years with the Anschluss with Austria, the annexation of the Sudetenland, and finally the forcible occupation of the rump of Czechoslovakia. Each time the leaders of France and Great Britain would respond with negotiation, compromise and appeasement, always avoiding the open clash that they so desperately dreaded, but always in doing so sacrificing another people, another nation.

To be sure, there were lonely voices in the wilderness, most notably that of Churchill, crying out warnings that sooner or later Hitler must be stopped, and that the longer the French and British waited to take action, the more costly it would be. But they were ignored: their opinions were unpopular and unwelcome. The men who now led France and Great Britain were not men who had fought in the trenches of the Western Front, who understood why the Tommies and *poilus* had endured what they did in order to bring an end to the aggression of Imperial Germany. They were not the men of 1914, who while they never sought war, would not flinch if it were forced upon them, or who would choose to stand in defiance of an aggressor rather than temporize with him. They were not men to whom solemn agreements between nations were a people's bonded word. Instead, they were men who understood only that they did not want a war, but did not understand why they did not want it, and could not comprehend the price they were paying to avoid one.

They would eventually force Europe into a Second World War, the outcome of which merely reaffirmed the conclusions reached in the First. The burden of guilt which Germany would bear out of that second war would be so great that it has yet to be expunged, but it was simply a compounding, though a vast one, of the guilt Germany bore from the first. For the Allies, though, that could be no consolation, for they had to bear a burden of guilt of their own, knowing that having won the war, they ultimately lost the peace.

POSTSCRIPT

Now the sun's shining down on the green fields of France,
The warm breezes blow and the red poppies dance.
The trenches have long vanished under the plow,
There's no gas and no barbed wire, no guns firing now.

But here in this graveyard which is still No Man's Land,
The countless white crosses in mute witness stand
To Man's own indifference to his fellow man,
And a whole generation that was slaughtered and damned. . . .

—From No Man's Land
by Eric Bogle
used with permission

Appendix I

THE AUSTRO-HUNGARIAN NOTE TO SERBIA AND THE SERBIAN REPLY

Vienna, July 22, 1914

Your Excellency will present the following note to the Royal Government on the afternoon of Thursday, July 23: On the 31st of March, 1909, the Royal Serbian Minister at the Court of Vienna made, in the name of his Government, the following declaration to the Imperial and Royal Government:

Serbia recognizes that her rights were not affected by the state of affairs created in Bosnia, and states that she will accordingly accommodate herself to the decisions to be reached by the Powers in connection with Article 25 of the Treaty of Berlin. Serbia, in accepting the advice of the Great Powers, binds herself to desist from the attitude of protest and opposition which she has assumed with regard to the annexation since October last, and she furthermore binds herself to alter the tendency of her present policy toward Austria-Hungary, and to live on the footing of friendly and neighborly relations with the latter in the future.

Now the history of the past few years, and particularly the painful events of the 28th of June, have proved the existence of a subversive movement in Serbia, whose object it is to separate certain portions of its territory from the Austro-Hungarian Monarchy. This movement, which came into being under the very eyes of the Serbian

Government, subsequently found expression outside of the territory of the Kingdom in acts of terrorism, in a number of attempts at assassination, and in murders.

Far from fulfilling the formal obligations contained in its declaration of the 31st of March, 1909, the Royal Serbian Government has done nothing to suppress this movement. It has tolerated the criminal activities of the various unions and associations directed against the Monarchy, the unchecked utterances of the press, the glorification of the authors of assassinations, the participation of officers and officials in subversive intrigues; it has tolerated an unhealthy propaganda in its public instruction; and it has tolerated, finally, every manifestation which could betray the people of Serbia into hatred of the Monarchy and contempt for its institutions.

This toleration of which the Royal Serbian Government was guilty, was still in evidence at that moment when the events of the twenty-eighth of June exhibited to the whole world the dreadful consequences of such tolerance.

It is clear from the statements and confessions of the criminal authors of the assassination of the twenty-eighth of June, that the murder at Sarajevo was conceived at Belgrade, that the murderers received the weapons and the bombs with which they were equipped from Serbian officers and officials who belonged to the Narodna Odbrana, and, finally, that the dispatch of the criminals and of their weapons to Bosnia was arranged and effected under the conduct of Serbian frontier authorities.

The results brought out by the inquiry no longer permit the Imperial and Royal Government to maintain the attitude of patient tolerance which it has observed for years toward those agitations which center at Belgrade and are spread thence into the territories of the Monarchy. Instead, these results impose upon the Imperial and Royal Government the obligation to put an end to those intrigues, which constitute a standing menace to the peace of the Monarchy.

In order to attain this end, the Imperial and Royal Government finds itself compelled to demand that the Serbian Government give official assurance that it will condemn the propaganda directed against Austria-Hungary, that is to say, the whole body of the efforts whose ultimate object it is to separate from the Monarchy territories that belong to it; and that it will obligate itself to suppress with all the means at its command this criminal and terroristic propaganda. In order to give these assurances a character of solemnity, the Royal Serbian Government will publish on the first page of its official organ of July 26/13, the following declaration:

"The Royal Serbian Government condemns the propaganda directed against Austria-Hungary, that is to say, the whole body of the efforts whose ultimate object it is to separate from the Austro-Hungarian Monarchy territories that belong to it, and it most sincerely regrets the dreadful consequences of these criminal transactions.

"The Royal Serbian Government regrets that Serbian officers and officials should have taken part in the above-mentioned propaganda and thus have endangered the friendly and neighborly relations, to the cultivation of which the Royal Government had most solemnly pledged itself by its declarations of March 31, 1909.

"The Royal Government, which disapproves and repels every idea and every attempt to interfere in the destinies of the population of whatever portion of Austria-Hungary, regards it as its duty most expressly to call attention of the officers, officials, and the whole population of the kingdom to the fact that for the future it will proceed with the utmost rigor against any persons who shall become guilty of any such activities, activities to prevent and to suppress which, the Government will bend every effort."

This declaration shall be brought to the attention of the Royal army simultaneously by an order of the day from His Majesty the King, and by publication in the official organ of the army.

The Royal Serbian Government will furthermore pledge itself:

1. to suppress every publication which shall incite to hatred and contempt of the Monarchy, and the general tendency of which shall be directed against the territorial integrity of the latter;

2. to proceed at once to the dissolution of the Narodna Odbrana to confiscate all of its means of propaganda, and in the same manner to proceed against the other unions and associations in Serbia which occupy themselves with propaganda against Austria-Hungary; the Royal Government will take such measures as are necessary to make sure that the dissolved associations may not continue their activities under other names or in other forms;

3. to eliminate without delay from public instruction in Serbia, everything, whether connected with the teaching corps or with the methods of teaching, that serves or may serve to nourish the propaganda against Austria-Hungary;

4. to remove from the military and administrative service in general all officers and officials who have been guilty of carrying on the propaganda against Austria-Hungary, whose names the Imperial and Royal Government reserves the right to make known to the Royal Government when communicating the material evidence now in its possession;

5. to agree to the cooperation in Serbia of the organs of the Imperial and Royal Government in the suppression of the subversive movement directed against the integrity of the Monarchy;

6. to institute a judicial inquiry against every participant in the conspiracy of the twenty-eighth of June who may be found in Serbian territory; the organs of the Imperial and Royal Government delegated for this purpose will take part in the proceedings held for this purpose;

7. to undertake with all haste the arrest of Major Voislav Tankosic and of one Milan Ciganovitch, a Serbian official, who have been compromised by the results of the inquiry;

8. by efficient measures to prevent the participation of Serbian authorities in the smuggling of weapons and explosives across the frontier; to dismiss from the service and to punish severely those members of the Frontier Service at Schabats and Losnitza who

assisted the authors of the crime of Sarajevo to cross the frontier;

9. to make explanations to the Imperial and Royal Government concerning the unjustifiable utterances of high Serbian functionaries in Serbia and abroad, who, without regard for their official position, have not hesitated to express themselves in a manner hostile toward Austria-Hungary since the assassination of the twenty-eighth of June;

10. to inform the Imperial and Royal Government without delay of the execution of the measures comprised in the foregoing points.

The Imperial and Royal Government awaits the reply of the Royal Government by Saturday, the twenty-fifth instant, at 6 p.m., at the latest.

A reminder of the results of the investigation about Sarajevo, to the extent they relate to the functionaries named in points 7 and 8 [above], is appended to this note.

Appendix:

The crime investigation undertaken at court in Sarajevo against Gavrilo Princip and his comrades on account of the assassination committed on the 28th of June this year, along with the guilt of accomplices, has up until now led to the following conclusions:

1. The plan of murdering Archduke Franz Ferdinand during his stay in Sarajevo was concocted in Belgrade by Gavrilo Princip, Nedeljko Cabrinovic, a certain Milan Ciganovic, and Trifko Grabesch with the assistance of Major Voija Takosic.

2. The six bombs and four Browning pistols along with ammunition—used as tools by the criminals—were procured and given to Princip, Cabrinovic and Grabesch in Belgrade by a certain Milan Ciganovic and Major Voija Takosic.

3. The bombs are hand grenades originating from the weapons depot of the Serbian army in Kragujevatz.

4. To guarantee the success of the assassination, Ciganovic instructed Princip, Cabrinovic and Grabesch in the use of the grenades and gave lessons on shooting Browning pistols to Princip and Grabesch in a forest next to the shooting range at Topschider.

5. To make possible Princip, Cabrinovic und Grabesch's passage across the Bosnia-Herzegovina border and the smuggling of their weapons, an entire secretive transportation system was organized by Ciganovic. The entry of the criminals and their weapons into Bosnia and Herzegovina was carried out by the main border officials of Shabatz (Rade Popovic) and Losnitza as well as by the customs agent Budivoj Grbic of Losnitza, with the complicity of several others.

The following instructions to Ambassador von Gieslingen were attached:

On the occasion of handing over this note, would Your Excellency please also add orally that—in the event that no unconditionally positive answer of the Royal government might be received in the meantime—after the course of the 48-hour deadline referred to in this note, as measured from the day and hour of your announcing it, you are commissioned to leave the I. and R. Embassy of Belgrade together with your personnel.

25 July, 1914:
The Serbian Response
to the Austro-Hungarian Ultimatum,
English Translation
The French original of this response is also available.

The Royal Government has received the communication of the Imperial and Royal Government of the 23rd inst. and is convinced that its reply will dissipate any misunderstanding which threatens to destroy the friendly and neighbourly relations between the Austrian monarchy and the kingdom of Serbia.
    The Royal Government is conscious that nowhere there have been

renewed protests against the great neighbourly monarchy like those which at one time were expressed in the Skuptschina, as well as in the declaration and actions of the responsible representatives of the state at that time, and which were terminated by the Serbian declaration of March 31st, 1909; furthermore that since that time neither the different corporations of the kingdom, nor the officials have made an attempt to alter the political and judicial condition created in Bosnia and the Heregovina. The Royal Government states that the I. and R. [Imperial and Royal] Government has made no protestation in this sense excepting in the case of a textbook, in regard to which the I. and R. Government has received an entirely satisfactory explanation. Serbia has given during the time of the Balkan crisis in numerous cases evidence of her pacific and moderate policy, and it is only owing to Serbia and the sacrifices which she has brought in the interest of the peace of Europe that this peace has been preserved.

The Royal Government cannot be made responsible for expressions of a private character, as for instance newspaper articles and the peaceable work of societies, expressions which are of very common appearance in other countries, and which ordinarily are not under the control of the state. This, all the less, as the Royal Government has shown great courtesy in the solution of a whole series of questions which have arisen between Serbia and Austria-Hungary, whereby it has succeeded to solve the greater number thereof, in favour of the progress of both countries.

The Royal Government was therefore painfully surprised by the assertions that citizens of Serbia had participated in the preparations of the outrage in Sarajevo. The Government expected to be invited to cooperate in the investigation of the crime, and it was ready, in order to prove its complete correctness, to proceed against all persons in regard to whom it would receive information.

According to the wishes of the I. and R. Government, the Royal Government is prepared to surrender to the court, without regard to position and rank, every Serbian citizen for whose participation in the crime of Sarajevo it should have received proof. It binds itself particularly on the first page of the official organ of the 26th of July to publish the following enunciation:

The Royal Serbian Government condemns every propaganda which should be directed against Austria-Hungary, i.e., the entirety of such activities as aim towards the separation of certain territories from the Austro-Hungarian monarchy, and it regrets sincerely the lamentable consequences of these criminal machinations. . . .

The Royal Government regrets that according to a communication of the I. and R. Government certain Serbian officers and functionaries have participated in the propaganda just referred to, and that these have there fore endangered the amicable relations for the observation of which the Royal Government had solemnly obliged itself through the declaration of March 31st, 1909. . . .

The Royal Government binds itself further:

1. During the next regular meeting of the Skuptschina to embody in the press laws a clause, to wit, that the incitement to hatred of, and contempt for, the Monarchy is to be most severely punished, as well as every publication whose general tendency is directed against the territorial integrity of Austria-Hungary.

It binds itself in view of the coming revision of the constitution to embody an amendment into Art. 22 of the constitutional law which permits the confiscation of such publications as is at present impossible according to the clear definition of Art. 12 of the constitution.

2. The Government possesses no proofs and the note of the I. and R. Government does not submit them that the society Narodna Odbrana and other similar societies have committed, up to the present, any criminal actions of this manner through any one of their members. Notwithstanding this, the Royal Government will accept the demand of the I. and R. Government and dissolve the society Narodna Odbrana, as well as every society which should set against Austria-Hungary.

3. The Royal Serbian Government binds itself without delay to eliminate from the public instruction in Serbia anything which might

further the propaganda directed against Austria-Hungary provided the I. and R. Government furnishes actual proofs of this propaganda.

4. The Royal Government is also ready to dismiss those officers and officials from the military and civil services in regard to whom it has been proved by judicial investigation that they have been guilty of actions against the territorial integrity of the Monarchy; it expects that the I. and R. Government communicate to it for the purpose of starting the investigation the names of these officers and officials, and the facts with which they have been charged.

5. The Royal Government confesses that it is not clear about the sense and the scope of that demand of the I. and R. Government which concerns the obligation on the part of the Royal Serbian Government to permit the cooperation of officials of the I. and R. Government on Serbian territory, but it declares that it is willing to accept every cooperation which does not run counter to international law and criminal law, as well as to the friendly and neighbourly relations.

6. The Royal Government considers it its duty as a matter of course to begin an investigation against all those persons who have participated in the outrage of June 28th and who are in its territory. As far as the cooperation in this investigation of specially delegated officials of the I. and R. Government is concerned, this cannot be accepted, as this is a violation of the constitution and of criminal procedure. Yet in some cases the result of the investigation might be communicated to the Austro-Hungarian officials.

7. The Royal Government has ordered on the evening of the day on which the note was received the arrest of Major Voislar Tankosic. However, as far as Milan Ciganovitch is concerned, who is a citizen of the Austro-Hungarian Monarchy and who has been employed till June 28th with the Railroad Department, it has as yet been impossible to locate him, wherefore a warrant has been issued against him.

The I. and R. Government is asked to make known, as soon as possible for the purpose of conducting the investigation, the existing grounds for suspicion and the proofs of guilt, obtained in the investigation at Sarajevo.

8. The Serbian Government will amplify and render more severe the existing measures against the suppression of smuggling of arms and explosives.

It is a matter of course that it will proceed at once against, and punish severely, those officials of the frontier service on the line Shabatz-Loznica who violated their duty and who have permitted the perpetrators of the crime to cross the frontier.

9. The Royal Government is ready to give explanations about the expressions which its officials in Serbia and abroad have made in interviews after the outrage and which, according to the assertion of the I. and R. Government, were hostile to the Monarchy. As soon as the I. and R. Government points out in detail where those expressions were made and succeeds in proving that those expressions have actually been made by the functionaries concerned, the Royal Government itself will take care that the necessary evidences and proofs are collected.

10. The Royal Government will notify the I. and R. Government, so far as this has not been already done by the present note, of the execution of the measures in question as soon as one of those measures has been ordered and put into execution.

The Royal Serbian Government believes it to be to the common interest not to rush the solution of this affair and it is therefore, in case the I. and R. Government should not consider itself satisfied with this answer, ready, as ever, to accept a peaceable solution, be it by referring the decision of this question to the International Court at The Hague or by leaving it to the decision of the Great Powers who have participated in the working out of the declaration given by the Serbian Government on March 18/31st, 1909.

Appendix II

THE "WILLY-NICKY" TELEGRAMS

(Note: These are the original, unedited texts, which include any errors in spelling or grammar. Both Tsar and Kaiser were fluent in English, the language used for this exchange.)

Tsar to Kaiser, July 29, 1:00 A.M.
Peter's Court Palais, 29 July 1914

Sa Majesté l'Empereur
Neues Palais

Am glad you are back. In this serious moment, I appeal to you to help me. An ignoble war has been declared to a weak country. The indignation in Russia shared fully by me is enormous. I foresee that very soon I shall be overwhelmed by the pressure forced upon me and be forced to take extreme measures which will lead to war. To try and avoid such a calamity as a European war I beg you in the name of our old friendship to do what you can to stop your allies from going too far.

Nicky

Kaiser to Tsar, July 29, 1:45 A.M.
(This and the previous telegraph crossed.)
28 July 1914

It is with the gravest concern that I hear of the impression which the action of Austria against Serbia is creating in your country. The unscrupulous agitation that has been going on in Serbia for years has resulted in the outrageous crime, to which Archduke Francis Ferdinand fell a victim. The spirit that led Serbians to murder their own king and his wife still dominates the country. You will doubtless agree with me that we both, you and me, have a common interest as well as all Sovereigns to insist that all the persons morally responsible for the dastardly murder should receive their deserved punishment. In this case politics plays no part at all.

On the other hand, I fully understand how difficult it is for you and your Government to face the drift of your public opinion. Therefore, with regard to the hearty and tender friendship which binds us both from long ago with firm ties, I am exerting my utmost influence to induce the Austrians to deal straightly to arrive to a satisfactory understanding with you. I confidently hope that you will help me in my efforts to smooth over difficulties that may still arise.

Your very sincere and devoted friend and cousin
Willy

Kaiser to Tsar, July 29, 6:30 P.M.
Berlin, 29. July 1914

I received your telegram and share your wish that peace should be maintained. But as I told you in my first telegram, I cannot consider Austria's action against Servia an "ignoble" war. Austria knows by experience that Servian promises on paper are wholly unreliable. I understand its action must be judged as trending to get full guarantee that the Servian promises shall become real facts. This my reasoning is borne out by the statement of the Austrian cabinet that Austria does not want to make any territorial conquests at the expense of Servia. I therefore suggest that it would be quite possible for Russia to remain a spectator of the austro-servian conflict without involving Europe in the most horrible war she ever witnessed. I think a direct understanding between your Government and Vienna possible and desirable, and as I already telegraphed to you, my Government is continuing its exercises to promote it. Of course military measures on the part of Russia would be looked upon by Austria as a calamity we both wish to avoid and jeopardize my position as mediator which I readily accepted on your appeal to my friendship and my help.

Willy

Tsar to Kaiser, July 29, 8:20 P.M.
Peter's Court Palace, 29 July 1914

Thanks for your telegram conciliatory and friendly. Whereas official message presented today by your ambassador to my minister was conveyed in a very different tone. Beg you to explain this divergency! It would be right to give over the Austro-servian problem to the Hague conference. Trust in your wisdom and friendship.

Your loving Nicky

Tsar to Kaiser, July 30, 1:20 A.M.
Peter's Court Palais, 30 July 1914

Thank you heartily for your quick answer. Am sending Tatischev this evening with instructions. The military measures which have now come into force were decided five days ago for reasons of defence on account of Austria's preparations. I hope from all my heart that these measures won't in any way interfere with your part as mediator which I greatly value. We need your strong pressure on Austria to come to an understanding with us.

Nicky

Kaiser to Tsar, July 30, 1:20 A.M.
Berlin, 30. July 1914

Best thanks for telegram. It is quite out of the question that my ambassadors language could have been in contradiction with the

tenor of my telegram. Count von Pourtalès was instructed to draw the attention of your government to the danger & grave consequences involved by a mobilisation; I said the same in my telegram to you. Austria has only mobilised against Servia & only a part of her army. If, as it is now the case, according to the communication by you & your Government, Russia mobilises against Austria, my rôle as mediator you kindly intrusted me with, & which I accepted at you[r] express prayer, will be endangered if not ruined. The whole weight of the decision lies solely on you[r] shoulders now, who have to bear the responsibility for Peace or War.
Willy

Kaiser to Tsar, July 31
Berlin, 31. July 1914

On your appeal to my friendship and your call for assistance began to mediate between your and the austro-hungarian Government. While this action was proceeding your troops were mobilised against Austro-Hungary, my ally. thereby, as I have already pointed out to you, my mediation has been made almost illusory.

I have nevertheless continued my action. I now receive authentic news of serious preparations for war on my Eastern frontier. Responsibility for the safety of my empire forces preventive measures of defence upon me. In my endeavours to maintain the peace of the world I have gone to the utmost limit possible. The responsibility for the disaster which is now threatening the whole civilized world will not be laid at my door. In this moment it still lies in your power to avert it. Nobody is threatening the honour or power of Russia who can well afford to await the result of my mediation. My friendship for you and your empire, transmitted to me by my grandfather on his deathbed has always been sacred to me and I have honestly often backed up Russia when she was in serious trouble especially in her last war.

The peace of Europe may still be maintained by you, if Russia will agree to stop the milit. measures which must threaten Germany and Austro-Hungary.
Willy

Tsar to Kaiser, July 31
(This and the previous telegram crossed.)

Petersburg, Palace, 31 July 1914
Sa Majesté l'Empereur, Neues Palais

I thank you heartily for your mediation which begins to give one hope
that all may yet end peacefully. It is technically impossible to stop our
military preparations which were obligatory owing to Austria's
mobilisation. We are far from wishing war. As long as the negocia-
tions with Austria on Servia's account are taking place my troops
shall not make any provocative action. I give you my solemn word for
this. I put all my trust in Gods mercy and hope in your successful
mediation in Vienna for the welfare of our countries and for the peace
of Europe.
     Your affectionate
Nicky

Tsar to Kaiser, August 1
Peter's Court, Palace, 1 August 1914
Sa Majesté l'Empereur
Berlin

received your telegram. Understand you are obliged to mobilise but
wish to have the same guarantee from you as I gave you, that these
measures do not mean war and that we shall continue negociating for
the benefit of our countries and universal peace deal to all our hearts.
Our long proved friendship must succeed, with God's help, in
avoiding bloodshed.
     Anxiously, full of confidence await your answer.
Nicky

Kaiser to Tsar, August 1
Berlin, 1. August 1914

Thanks for your telegram. I yesterday pointed out to your government the way by which alone war may be avoided. Although I requested an answer for noon today, no telegram from my ambassador conveying an answer from your Government has reached me as yet. I therefore have been obliged to mobilise my army.

Immediate affirmative clear and unmistakable answer from your government is the only way to avoid endless misery. Until I have received this answer alas, I am unable to discuss the subject of your telegram. As a matter of fact I must request you to immediatly [sic] order your troops on no account to commit the slightest act of trespassing over our frontiers.

Willy

Appendix III

GERMANY'S DEMAND FOR FREE PASSAGE THROUGH BELGIUM, AUGUST 2, 1914

Brussels, 2 August 1914
Imperial German Embassy in Belgium

HIGHLY CONFIDENTIAL

The Imperial Government possesses reliable information of the intended deployment of French forces on the Givet-Namur stretch of the Meuse. This information leaves no doubt about France's intention to advance against Germany through Belgian territory.

The Imperial Government cannot help but be concerned that without assistance Belgium, in spite of its good intentions, will not be able to repel a French attack with sufficient prospects of success to provide an adequate guarantee in the face of the threat to Germany. It is essential for Germany's survival to pre-empt this enemy attack.

The German Government would therefore consider it with utmost regret if Belgium saw an unfriendly act in the fact that measures taken by its enemies force Germany for defence purposes likewise to enter Belgian territory.

To exclude the possibility of misinterpretation, the Imperial Government makes the following declaration:

1. Germany has no hostile intentions towards Belgium whatsoever. If Belgium is willing to adopt a position of benevolent neutrality towards Germany in the imminent war, the German Government promises to fully guarantee the kingdom's possessions and independence at the conclusion of peace.

2. Subject to the conditions laid down above, Germany is committed to withdrawing from the kingdom's territory as soon as peace is made.

3. If Belgium co-operates, Germany is prepared, with the agreement of the Royal Belgian authorities, to pay for the requirements of its troops in cash and to compensate for any damage that might have been caused by German troops.

4. If Belgium should take a hostile stance against German troops, especially if she obstructs their advance by resistance from her forts on the Meuse or by destroying railways, roads, tunnels or other structures, Germany will regrettably be forced to consider the kingdom an enemy. In this case Germany would be unable to undertake any obligations towards the kingdom, but would have to leave the later resolution of relations between the two states to be decided by military force.

The Imperial German Government hopes that this eventuality will not occur, and that the Royal Belgian Government will take suitable measures to prevent the events mentioned from taking place. In which case, the friendly bonds between the two neighbouring states would undergo further and lasting consolidation.

Appendix IV

SIR EDWARD GREY'S SPEECH BEFORE THE HOUSE OF COMMONS, AUGUST 3, 1914

From: Great Britain, Parliamentary Debates, Commons, Fifth Series, Vol. LXV, 1914, columns 1809–1834.

Last week I stated that we were working for peace not only for this country, but to preserve the peace of Europe. To-day events move so rapidly that it is exceedingly difficult to state with technical accuracy the actual state of affairs, but it is clear that the peace of Europe cannot be preserved. Russia and Germany, at any rate, have declared war upon each other.

Before I proceed to state the position of his Majesty's Government I would like to clear the ground so that, before I come to state to the House what our attitude is with regard to the present crisis, the House may know exactly under what obligations the government is, or the House can be said to be, in coming to a decision on the matter. First of all, let me say, very shortly, that we have consistently worked with a single mind, with all the earnestness in our power, to preserve peace. The House may be satisfied on that point. We have always done it. During these last years, as far as his Majesty's Government are concerned, we would have no difficulty in proving that we have done so. Throughout the Balkan crisis, by general admission, we worked for peace. The cooperation of the great powers of Europe was successful in working for peace in the Balkan crisis. It is true that some of the powers had great difficulty in adjusting their points of view. It took much time and labour and discussion before they could settle their differences, but peace was secured, because peace was their main object, and they were willing to give time and trouble rather than accentuate differences rapidly.

In the present crisis it has not been possible to secure the peace of Europe: because there has been little time, and there has been a disposition—at any rate in some quarters on which I will not dwell—to force things rapidly to an issue, at any rate to the great risk of peace, and, as we now know, the result of that is that the policy of peace as far as the great powers generally are concerned is in danger. I do not want to dwell on that, and to comment on it, and to say where the blame seems to us lie, which powers were most in favour of peace, which were most disposed to risk war or endanger peace, because I would like the House to approach this crisis in which we are now from the point of view of British interests, British honour, and British obligations, free from all passion as to why peace has not yet been preserved. . . .

The situation in the present crisis is not precisely the same as it was in the Morocco question. . . . It has originated in a dispute between Austria and Servia. I can say this with the most absolute confidence—no government and no country has less desire to be involved in war over a dispute with Austria than the country of France. They are involved in it because of their obligation of honour under a definite alliance with Russia. Well, it is only fair to say to the House that that obligation of honour cannot apply in the same way to us. We are not parties to the Franco-Russian alliance. We do not even know the terms of the alliance. So far I have, I think, faithfully and completely cleared the ground with regard to the question of obligation.

I now come to what we think the situation requires of us. For many years we have had a long-standing friendship with France [An HON. MEMBER: "And with Germany!"]. I remember well the feeling in the House and my own feeling—for I spoke on the subject, I think, when the late Government made their agreement with France—the warm and cordial feeling resulting from the fact that these two nations, who had had perpetual differences in the past, had cleared these differences away; I remember saying, I think, that it seemed to me that some benign influence had been at work to produce the cordial atmosphere that had made that possible. But how far that friendship entails obligation—it has been a friendship between the nations and ratified by the nations—how far that entails an obligation, let every man look into his own heart, and his own feelings, and construe the extent of the obligation for himself. I construe it myself as I feel it, but I do not wish to urge upon any one else more than their feelings dictate as to what they should feel about the obligation. The House, individually and collectively, may judge for itself. I speak my personal view, and I have given the House my own feeling in the matter.

The French fleet is now in the Mediterranean, and the northern and western coasts of France are absolutely undefended. The French fleet being concentrated in the Mediterranean, the situation is very different from what it used to be, because the friendship which has grown up between the two countries has given them a sense of security that there was nothing to be feared from us. My own feeling is that if a foreign fleet, engaged in a war which France had not sought, and in which she had not been the aggressor, came down the English Channel and bombarded and battered the undefended coasts of France, we could not stand aside [Cheers] and see this going on practically within sight of our eyes, with our arms folded, looking on dispassionately, doing nothing. I believe that would be the feeling of this country. There are times when one feels that if these circum-stances actually did arise, it would be a feeling which would spread with irresistible force throughout the land.

But I also want to look at the matter without sentiment, and from the point of view of British interests, and it is on that that I am going to base and justify what I am presently going to say to the House. If we say nothing at this moment, what is France to do with her fleet in the Mediterranean? If she leaves it there, with no statement from us as to what we will do, she leaves her northern and western coasts absolutely undefended, at the mercy of a German fleet coming down the Channel to do as it pleases in a war which is a war of life and death between them. If we say nothing, it may be that the French fleet is withdrawn from the Mediterranean. We are in the presence of a European conflagration; can anybody set limits to the consequences that may arise out of it? Let us assume that to-day we stand aside in an attitude of neutrality, saying, "No, we cannot undertake and engage to help either party in this conflict." Let us suppose the French fleet is withdrawn from the Mediterranean; and let us assume that the consequences—which are already tremendous in what has happened in Europe even to countries which are at peace—in fact, equally whether countries are at peace or at war—let us assume that out of that come consequences unforeseen, which make it necessary at a sudden moment that, in defence of vital British interests, we should go to war; and let us assume which is quite possible—that Italy, who is now neutral [HON. MEMBERS: "Hear, hear!"]—because, as I understand, she considers that this war is an aggressive war, and the Triple Alliance being a defensive alliance her obligation did not arise—let us assume that consequences which are not yet foreseen and which, perfectly legitimately consulting her own interests—make Italy depart from her attitude of neutrality at a time when we are forced in defence of vital British interest ourselves to fight—what then will be the position in the Mediterranean? It might be that at some critical moment those consequences would be forced upon us because our trade routes in the Mediterranean might be vital to this country?

Nobody can say that in the course of the next few weeks there is any particular trade route the keeping open of which may not be vital to this country. What will be our position then? We have not kept a fleet in the Mediterranean which is equal to dealing alone with a combination of other fleet in the Mediterranean. It would be the very moment when we could not detach more ships to the Mediterranean, and we might have exposed this country from our negative attitude at the present moment to the most appalling risk. I say that from the point of view of British interest. We feel strongly that France was entitled to know—and to know at once!—whether or not in the event of attack upon her unprotected northern and western coast she could depend upon British support. In that emergency and in these compelling circumstances, yesterday afternoon I gave to the French Ambassador the following statement:

"I am authorised to give an assurance that if the German fleet comes into the Channel or through the North Sea to undertake hostile operations against the French coasts or shipping, the British fleet will give all the protection in its power. This assurance is, of course, subject to the policy of his Majesty's Government receiving the support of Parliament, and must not be taken as binding his Majesty's Government to take any action until the above contingency of action by the German fleet takes place."

I read that to the House, not as a declaration of war on our part, not as entailing immediate aggressive action on our part, but as binding us to take aggressive action should that contingency arise. Things move very hurriedly from hour to hour. French news comes in, and I cannot give this in any very formal way; but I understand that the German Government would be prepared, if we would pledge ourselves to neutrality, to agree that its fleet would not attack the northern coast of France. I have only heard that shortly before I came to the House, but it is far too narrow an engagement for us. And, Sir, there is the more serious consideration—becoming more serious every hour—there is the question of the neutrality of Belgium. . . .

I will read to the House what took place last week on this subject. When mobilisation was beginning, I knew that this question must be a most important element in our policy—a most important subject for the House of Commons. I telegraphed at the same time in similar terms to both Paris and Berlin to say that it was essential for us to know whether the French and German Governments, respectively, were prepared to undertake an engagement to respect the neutrality of Belgium. These are the replies. I got from the French Government this reply:

"The French Government are resolved to respect the neutrality of Belgium, and it would only be in the event of some other power violating that neutrality that France might find herself under the necessity, in order to assure the defence of her security, to act otherwise. This assurance has been given several times. The President of the Republic spoke of it to the King of the Belgians, and the French Minister at Brussels has spontaneously renewed the assurance to the Belgian Minister of Foreign Affairs to-day."

From the German Government the reply was:

"The Secretary of State for Foreign Affairs could not possibly give an answer before consulting the Emperor and the Imperial Chancellor."

Sir Edward Goschen, to whom I had said it was important to have an answer soon, said he hoped the answer would not be too long delayed. The German Minister for Foreign Affairs then gave Sir Edward Goschen to understand that he rather doubted whether they could answer at all, as any reply they might give could not fail, in the event of war, to have the undesirable effect of disclosing, to a certain extent, part of their plan of campaign. I telegraphed at the same time to Brussels to the Belgian Government, and I got the following reply from Sir Francis Villiers:

"The Minister for Foreign Affairs thanks me for the communication and replies that Belgium will, to the utomost of her power, maintain neutrality, and Belgium expects and desires other powers to observe and uphold it. He begged me to add that the relations between Belgium and the neighbouring Powers were excellent, and there was no reason to suspect their intentions, but that the Belgian Government believe, in the case of violence, they were in a position to defend the neutrality of their country."

It now appears from the news I have received to-day—which has come quite recently, and I am not yet quite sure how far it has reached me in an accurate form—that an ultimatum has been given to Belgium by Germany, the object of which was to offer Belgium friendly relations with Germany on condition that she would facilitate the passage of German troops through Belgium. [Ironical laughter] Well, Sir, until one has these things absolutely definite, up to the last moment I do not wish to say all that one would say if one were in a position to give the House full, complete and absolute information upon the point. We were sounded in the course of last week as to whether, if a guarantee were given that, after the war, Belgian integrity would be preserved, that would content us. We replied that we could not bargain away whatever interests or obligations we had in Belgian neutrality. [Cheers.]

Shortly before I reached the House I was informed that the following telegram had been received from the King of the Belgians by our King—King George:

"Remembering the numerous proofs of your Majesty's friendship and that of your predecessors, and the friendly attitude of England in 1870, and the proof of friendship she has just given us again, I make a supreme appeal to the diplomatic intervention of your Majesty's Government to safeguard the integrity of Belgium."

Diplomatic intervention took place last week on our part. What can diplomatic intervention do now? We have great and vital interests in the independence—and integrity is the least part—of Belgium. [Loud cheers.] If Belgium is compelled to submit to allow her neutrality to be violated, of course the situation is clear. Even if by agreement she admitted the violation of her neutrality, it is clear she could only do so under duress. The smaller States in that region of Europe ask but one thing. Their one desire is that they should be left alone and independent. The one thing they fear is, I think, not so much that their integrity but that their independence should be interfered with. If in this war, which is before Europe, the neutrality of those countries is violated, if the troops of one of the combatants violate its neutrality and no action be taken to resent it, at the end of war, whatever the integrity may be, the independence will be gone [Cheers.]. . . .

No, Sir, if it be the case that there has been anything in the nature of an ultimatum to Belgium, asking her to compromise or violate her neutrality, whatever may have been offered to her in return, her independence is gone if that holds. If her independence goes, the independence of Holland will follow. I ask the House from the point of view of British interests to consider what may be at stake. If France is beaten in a struggle of life and death, beaten to her knees, loses her position as a great power, becomes subordinate to the will and power of one greater than herself—consequences which I do not anticipate, because I am sure that France has the power to defend herself with all the energy and ability and patriotism which she has shown so often

[Loud cheers.]—still, if that were to happen and if Belgium fell under the same dominating influence, and then Holland, and then Denmark, then would not Mr. Gladstone's words come true, that just opposite to us there would be a common interest against the unmeasured aggrandisement of any power? [Loud cheers.]

It may be said, I suppose, that we might stand aside, husband our strength, and that, whatever happened in the course of this war, at the end of it intervene with effect to put things right, and to adjust them to our own point of view. If, in a crisis like this, we run away [Loud cheers.] from those obligations of honour and interest as regards the Belgian treaty, I doubt whether, whatever material force we might have at the end, it would be of very much value in face of the respect that we should have lost. And I do not believe, whether a great power stands outside this war or not, it is going to be in a position at the end of it to exert its superior strength. For us, with a powerful fleet, which we believe able to protect our commerce, to protect our shores, and to protect our interests, if we are engaged in war, we shall suffer but little more than we shall suffer even if we stand aside.

We are going to suffer, I am afraid, terribly in this war, whether we are in it or whether we stand aside. Foreign trade is going to stop, not because the trade routes are closed, but because there is no trade at the other end. Continental nations engaged in war all their populations, all their energies, all their wealth, engaged in a desperate struggle they cannot carry on the trade with us that they are carrying on in times of peace, whether we are parties to the war or whether we are not. I do not believe for a moment that at the end of this war, even if we stood aside and remained aside, we should be in a position, a material position, to use our force decisively to undo what had happened in the course of the war, to prevent the whole of the west of Europe opposite to us—if that had been the result of the war—falling under the domination of a single power, and I am quite sure that our moral position would be such as—[the rest of the sentence—"to have lost us all respect."—was lost in a loud outburst of cheering]. I can only say that I have put the question of Belgium somewhat hypothetically, because I am not yet sure of all the facts, but, if the facts turn out to be as they have reached us at present, it is quite clear that there is an obligation on this country to do its utmost to prevent the consequences to which those facts will lead if they are undisputed. . . .

. . . One thing I would say. The one bright spot in the whole of this terrible situation is Ireland. [Prolonged cheers.] The general feeling throughout Ireland, and I would like this to be clearly understood abroad, does not make that a consideration that we feel we have to take into account [Cheers.] I have told the House how far we have at present gone in commitments, and the conditions which influence our policy; and I have put and dealt at length to the House upon how vital the condition of the neutrality of Belgium is.

What other policy is there before the House? There is but one way in which the Government could make certain at the present moment of keeping outside this war, and that would be that it should immediately issue a proclamation of unconditional neutrality. We cannot do that. [Cheers.] We have made the commitment to France that I have read to the House which prevents us doing that. We have got the consideration of Belgium which prevents us also from any unconditional neutrality, and, without these conditions absolutely satisfied and satisfactory, we are bound not to shrink from proceeding to the use of all the forces in our power. If we did take that line by saying, "We will have nothing whatever to do with this matter" under no conditions—the Belgian treaty obligations, the possible position in the Mediterranean, with damage to British interests, and what may happen to France from our failure to support France—if we were to say that all those things matter nothing, were as nothing, and to say we would stand aside, we should, I believe, sacrifice our respect and good name and reputation before the world, and should not escape the most serious and grave economic consequences. [Cheers and a voice, "No."]

My object has been to explain the view of the government, and to place before the House the issue and the choice. I do not for a moment conceal, after what I have said, and after the information, incomplete as it is, that I have given to the House with regard to Belgium, that we must be prepared, and we are prepared, for the consequences of having to use all the strength we have at any moment—we know not how soon—to defend ourselves and to take our part. We know, if the facts all be as I have stated them, though I have announced no intending aggressive action on our part, no final decision to resort to force at a moment's notice, until we know the whole of the case, that the use of it may be forced upon us. As far as the forces of the Crown are concerned, we are ready. I believe the Prime Minister and my right hon. Friend, the First Lord of the Admiralty have no doubt whatever that the readiness and the efficiency of those forces were never at a higher mark than they are to-day, and never was there a time when confidence was more justified in the power of the Navy to protect our commerce and to protect our shores. The thought is with us always of the suffering and misery entailed, from which no country in Europe will escape, and from which no abdication or neutrality will save us. The amount of harm that can be done by an enemy ship to our trade is infinitesimal, compared with the amount of harm that must be done by the economic condition that is caused on the Continent.

The most awful responsibility is resting upon the Government in deciding what to advise the House of Commons to do. We have disclosed our minds to the House of Commons. We have disclosed the issue, the information which we have, and made clear to the House, I trust, that we are prepared to face that situation, and that should it develop, as probably it may develop, we will face it. We worked for peace up to the last moment, and beyond the last moment. How hard, how persistently, and how earnestly we strove for peace last week the House will see from the papers that will be before it.

But that is over, as far as the peace of Europe is concerned. We are now face to face with a situation and all the consequences which it may yet have to unfold. We believe we shall have the support of the House at large in proceeding to whatever the consequences may be and whatever measures may be forced upon us by the development of facts or action taken by others. I believe the country, so quickly has the situation been forced upon it, has not had time to realise the issue. It perhaps is still thinking of the quarrel between Austria and Servia, and not the complications of this matter which have grown out of the quarrel between Austria and Servia. Russia and Germany we know are at war. We do not yet know officially that Austria, the ally whom Germany is to support, is yet at war with Russia. We know that a good deal has been happening on the French frontier. We do not know that the German Ambassador has left Paris.

The situation has developed so rapidly that technically, as regards the condition of the war, it is most difficult to describe what has actually happened. I wanted to bring out the underlying issues which would affect our own conduct, and our own policy, and to put them clearly. I have now put the vital facts before the House, and if, as seems not improbable, we are forced, and rapidly forced, to take our stand upon those issues, then I believe, when the country realises what is at stake, what the real issues are, the magnitude of the impending dangers in the west of Europe, which I have endeavored to describe to the House, we shall be supported throughout, not only by the House of Commons, but by the determination, the resolution, the courage, and the endurance of the whole country.

[Later in the day Sir Edward added the following words:]

I want to give the House some information which I have received, and which was not in my possession when I made my statement this afternoon. It is information I have received from the Belgian Legation in London, and is to the following effect:

"Germany sent yesterday evening at seven o'clock a note proposing to Belgium friendly neutrality, covering free passage on Belgian territory, and promising maintenance of independence of the kingdom and possession at the conclusion of peace, and threatening, in case of refusal, to treat Belgium as an enemy. A time-limit of twelve hours was fixed for the reply. The Belgians have answered that an attack on their neutrality would be a flagrant violation of the rights of nations, and that to accept the German proposal would be to sacrifice the honour of a nation. Conscious of its duty, Belgium is finally resolved to repel aggression by all possible means."

Of course, I can only say that the Government are prepared to take into grave consideration the information which they have received. I make no further comment upon it.

SOURCES AND BIBLIOGRAPHY

Official Records

Austria-Hungary (Austro-Hungarian Red Book)
Diplomatische Aktenstüke zur Vorgeschichte des Krieges, 1914, 3 vols. Vienna, 1919.

Belgium (Belgian Grey Book)
Ministère des Affaires Étrangères: Recueil des Documents Diplomatiques, 28 Juillet/6 Aout 1914. London, 1915.

France (French Yellow Book)
Ministère des Affaires Étrangères, La Guerre Européene, 1914. Paris, 1914.

Germany (German White Book)
Vorlaufige denkschrift und aktenstucke zum Kriegsausbruch. Berlin, 1914.

Great Britain (British Blue Books I and II)
Great Britain and the European Crisis, Correspondence, and Statements in Parliament, together with an Introductory Narrative of Events. London, 1914.

Russia (Russian Orange Books I and II)
Ministère des Affaires Étrangères: Recueil des Documents Diplomatiques, Négociations, ayant précédé la Guerre, 10/23 Juillet-24 Juillet/6 Aout 1914. Petrograd, 1914.

Serbia (Serbian Blue Book)
Les Pourparlers Diplomatiques 16/29 Juin-3/16 Aout. Paris, 1914.

Carnegie Endowment for International Peace, *Diplomatic Documents Relating to the Outbreak of the European War*, 2 vols, ed. James Brown Scott. New York, Oxford 1916. (This is a collection of the various "color books" as they were published in 1914–15.)

Other Sources
Albertini, Luigi. *The Origins of the War of 1914.* 3 vols. Oxford University, Oxford, 1952–57.
Barnett, Corelli. *The Swordbearers.* London: Eyre & Spottiswood, 1963.
Berghahn, Volker. *Germany and the Approach of War in 1914.* New York: St. Martin's Press, 1973.
Bernhardi, Friedrich von. *Germany and the Next War.* London: n.p., 1914.
Bethmann-Hollweg, Theodor von. *Betrachtungen zum Weltkrieg.* Berlin: Reimer Hobbing, 1919–21.
Bucholz, Arden. *Moltke, Schlieffen, and Prussian War Planning.* New York: Berg Publishers, 1991.
Bussy, Carvel de. *Count Stephan Tisza, Prime Minister of Hungary: Letters, 1914-1916.* New York: Lang, Peter, 1991.
Churchill, Winston. *The World Crisis*, Vol. 1, 1911–1914, New York. Scribners, 1928.
Conrad von Hötzendorff, Field Marshal Franz. *Aus Meiner Dienstzeit*, 1906–1918, 5 vols. Vienna, 1921–1925.
Cornwall, Mark, ed. *The Last Years of Austria-Hungary: Essays in Political and Military History, 1908–1918.* Exeter, 1990.
Craig, Gordon A. *The Politics of the Prussian Army*, 1640–1945. Oxford: Clarendon Press, 1955.
Crankshaw, Edward. *The Fall of the House of Habsburg.* New York: Viking, 1963.

Delbruck, Hans, et al. (eds.) *Deutsches Weissbuch über der Verantwortlichkiet der Urheber des Krieges*. Berlin, 1919.

Eksteins, Modris. *Rites of Spring: The Great War and the Birth of the Modern Age*. Boston: Houghton, Mifflin, 1989.

Erenyi, Gustav. *Graf Stefan Tisza, ein Staatsmann und Märtyrer*. Vienna: E. P. Tal, 1935.

Falls, Cyril. *The First World War*. London: 1960.

Fay, Sidney Bradshaw. *The Origins of the World War*. 2 vols. New York: the MacMillan Company, 1928 and 1930.

Fischer, Fritz. *War of Illusions: German Policies from 1911 to 1914*. London: Chatto and Windus, 1975.

Geiss, Immanuel, ed. *Juli 1914: Das europäische Krise und der Ausbruch des Ersten Weltkriegs*. Munich: Deutscher Taschenbuch Verlag, 1965.

Gibson, Hugh. *A Journal from Our Legation in Belgium*. New York: Doubleday, 1917.

Gooch, G. P. and Harold Temperley, eds. *British Documents on the Origins of the War 1898-1914, Vol. XI*. London, 1930.

Gorlitz, Walter, ed. *The Kaiser and his Court: The Diaries, Notebooks and Letters of Admiral Georg Alexander von Müller Chief of the Naval Cabinet, 1914-1918*. New York: Harcourt, Brace & World, 1959.

Grey, Sir Edward. *Speeches on Foreign Affairs 1904-1914*. Paul Knaplund, ed. London: Allen & Unwin, 1931.

Grey, Viscount, of Fallodon, (Sir Edward Grey), *Twenty-five Years*, 2 vols. London: Hodder & Stoughton, 1925.

Hale, Oron J. *The Great Illusion, 1900–1914*. New York: Harper & Row, 1971.

Hantsch, Hugo. *Leopold Graf Berchtold: Grandseigneur und Staatsmann*. 2 vols. Vienna: Verlag Styria, 1963.

Horne, Charles F. ed. *The Great Events of the Great War*. Vols 1-2. n.l.: National Alumni, 1923.

Huddleston, Sisley. *Poincaré, A Biographical Portrait*. Boston: Little, Brown, 1924.

Jannen, *The Lions of July*–Prelude to War, 1914. Novato, CA: Presidio Press, 1996.

Kautsky, Karl, Graf Max Monteglas, and Prof. Walter Schücking, eds.

Die deutschen Dokumente zum Kriegsausbruch. Berlin: n.p., 1919.

Keegan, John. *1914: Opening Moves.* Ballantine, New York, 1972.

_____. *The First World War.* Alfred A. Knopf, New York, 1998.

_____. *The Mask of Command.* New York: Viking, 1987.

Keiger, John F. V. *France and the Origins of the First World War.* NewYork: St. Martin's Press, 1983.

Kennan, George F. *The Fateful Alliance.* New York: Pantheon, 1984.

Kennedy, Paul M. *The Rise of the Anglo-German Antagonism, 1860-1914.* London: Allen & Unwin, 1980.

_____, ed. *The War Plans of the Great Powers, 1880-1914.* London: Allen & Unwin, 1979.

Lederer, Ivo J. (ed.) *The Versailles Settlement, Was It Foredoomed to Failure?* Boston, 1960.

Lieven, D. C. B. *Russia and the Origins of the First World War.* New York: St. Martin's Press, 1983.

Lord, Walter. *The Good Years.* New York: Harper, 1960.

Manchester, William. *The Arms of Krupp 1557-1968.* New York: Little, Brown, 1968.

_____. *The Last Lion, vol. 1: Visions of Glory.* Boston: Little, Brown and Co., 1983.

Margutti, Albert von. *Kaiser Franz Josef: Persönalische Einnerungen.* Vienna: Rhombus, 1924.

Massie, Robert K. *Dreadnought: Britain, Germany, and the Coming of the Great War.* New York: Random House, 1991.

_____. *Nicholas and Alexandra.* New York: Atheneum, 1967.

Mee, Charles L., Jr. *The End of Order–Versailles 1919.* New York: E.P. Dutton, 1980.

Menning, Bruce. *Bayonets before Bullets: The Imperial Russian Army, 1861-1914.* Bloomington: Indiana University Press, 1992.

Moltke, Graf Helmuth von. *Erinnerungen. Breife. Dokumente 1877-1916.* Eliza von Moltke, ed. Stuttgart: Der Kommendetag, 1922.

Paléologue, Maurice. *An Ambassador's Memoirs,* trans. F. A. Holt, Vol. 1. London: Hutchinson, 1923.

Poincaré, Raymond. *A Service de la France* 5 vols., trans. Sir George Arthur. New York: Doubleday, 1926–29.

Ritter, Gerhard. *The Schlieffen Plan, Critique of a Myth.* London:

Oswald Wolff, 1958.

_____. *The Sword and the Scepter*. 2 vols. Coral Gables, FL: University of Miami Press, 1965.

Rothenberg, Gunther E. *The Army of Francis Joseph*. West Lafayette, IN: Purdue University Press, 1976.

Sazonov, Sergei, *Fateful Years, 1909-16*. New York: Stokes, 1928.

Steiner, Zara. *Britain and the Origins of the First World War*. New York: St. Martin's Press, 1977.

Tuchman, Barbara, *The Guns of August*. New York: MacMillan, 1962.

_____. *The Proud Tower: A Portrait of the World Before the War, 1890-1914*. New York: Scribner, 1966.

Tunstall, Graydon A., Jr. *Planning for War Against Russia and Serbia: Austro-Hungarian and German Military Strategies, 1871-1914*. New York: Columbia University Press, 1993.

Vermes, Gabor. *Istvan Tisza*. New York: Columbia University Press, 1985.

Viviani, René. *As We See It*. New York: Harpers, 1923.

Whitlock, Brand. *Belgium: A Personal Narrative, Vol. 1*. New York: Appleton, 1920

Williamson, Samuel R., Jr. *Austria-Hungary and the Origins of the First World War*. New York: St. Martin's Press, 1991.

Wohl, R. *The Generation of 1914*. Cambridge, MA: 1979.

INDEX